My Life as an M.P.

My Life as an M.P.

A hilarious look at life as a
US Army M.P. in the 1960s

Thomas E. Oblinger

To order additional copies of this book, contact:
Xlibris Corporation
1-888-795-4274
www.Xlibris.com
Orders@Xlibris.com
65929

Contents

Foreword

In my first book, *Old Man from the Repple Depple (The story of an infantry replacement soldier in Europe in WWII)*, now available through *Xlibris Publishing* and most major booksellers, I had mentioned that history was not among my favorite subjects during my school years. Although I never considered myself to be a writer, I felt compelled to write about that time in my father's life that he seldom talked about. I needed to learn what events in his life made him the kind of man and father that I knew.

It was a task that took me twelve long years of research and writing. I finished the book in the year 2000, although it wasn't published until 2007. However, during those twelve years, I had also gathered information and facts about my own days in *Olive Drab*, but for the time being I had stuffed it all in an old file cabinet down in the basement.

Recently, when my sixty-third birthday came and went, I decided it was time to pull it all out and piece it all together. I hope to leave it to my daughter Anna Marie someday, as she may want to learn what made her father tick during her growing years.

While most Army veterans can relate to much of what I have written here, the story was also laid out for non-veterans, for family members of veterans, and for the next-of-kin of those who have experienced these things and are no longer with us today.

This is not a story about the terrible horrors of war. Instead, I tried to paint a word picture of just how hilarious life in Olive Drab can sometimes be, while mixed in with some serious moments. All I ask is that you forgive some of my inaccuracies in this story. After all, these are events that took place in the late 1960s.

I'll start with a brief background of my growing years before Olive Drab.

I was born on Wednesday, March 28, 1945. I was the third born of seven children to Raymond James and Helen Theresa (Donohoe) Oblinger. I was nine months old when Dad returned home from Europe after World War II and saw me for the first time. (I was the result of his "Pre-Embarkation Furlough" in June 1944 before shipping out to Europe.)

My brothers and sisters are:

John Peter	born May 31, 1940-(died June 11, 1953)
Raymond James, Jr.	born October 22, 1942
Mary Elizabeth	born February 15, 1947
Helen Theresa	born October 27, 1948
Michael David	born February 17, 1955
Henry Allen	born March 22, 1956

We grew up in somewhat humble surroundings. My father oiled machines for a living at the *Budd Company* in Detroit, which was a manufacturer of automobile wheels and body parts. With seven children to raise, Mom was a full-time housewife and mother. Over the years Dad was a firm disciplinarian, but he always convinced his children that we were blessed abundantly and he taught us compassion for the world's hungry and less fortunate. In general, he just taught us to live by the *Golden Rule*.

The drowning death of my oldest brother John in 1953 was devastating to me, and it left me with a horrible fear of water that lasted for many years. But beyond that, my growing years were for the most part uneventful.

As required at the age of eighteen, I registered for the Draft on April 4, 1963 at *Local Draft Board #300* for Macomb County, Michigan. This was at 25935 Gratiot Avenue in Roseville, Michigan. (Today, it is a bowling pro shop.) At that time I was 5 feet 9 inches tall with a 28-inch waist and weighed 110 pounds soaking wet.

I left *East Detroit High School* in June 1965, still short of credits for graduation, but fully intending to finish high school in due time. In July 1965 I got my first real job. I was hired and trained as a chef at the *Elias Brothers Big Boy Drive-in Restaurant* on Nine Mile Road at Jefferson Avenue in St Clair Shores. My starting pay was ninety cents an hour at that time.

I bought my first car a few months later for $60. It was a 1953 Plymouth four-door sedan. It was pea green in color with a flat-head six-cylinder engine. Then, in late 1965, I found a job with the *Detroit Plastic Molding Company* on Ten Mile Road in Roseville. Here I worked for $1.45 per hour doing general labor. Gasoline was about twenty-six cents a gallon in 1965 and cigarettes were about thirty-five cents a pack. At that time my brand of cigarettes was *Phillip Morris Commanders.*

On Thursday, 19-August-1965, I reported once again to the draft board office. But by this time it had moved farther south to its new location at 23420 Gratiot Avenue, in East Detroit. (Today, it is a florist shop.) Several of us who reported that day were taken by bus to *Fort Wayne Induction Station* in Detroit for what was then called a *Pre-Induction Physical.* By then my weight had reached 128 pounds but I still had a 28-inch waist.

Then on Friday, 1-October-1965, I finally received the dreaded, but long-awaited letter from *Uncle Sam* that began,

GREETING:

You are hereby ordered for induction into the Armed Forces of the United States, and to report at Local Board #300, 23420 Gratiot Avenue, East Detroit, Michigan on November 3, 1965 at 6:30 AM for forwarding to an Armed Forces Induction Station.

The next month seemed to fly by way too fast for me, and I really don't recall any details of my activities during that time. But as that fateful day approached, I tried to get from Dad an idea as to what I could expect in the Army. Still, Dad was reluctant to discuss any severe hardships that he had endured during World War II in 1944 and 1945.

He did however recall for me, twenty-mile hikes with an M-1 rifle slung over his shoulder and an eighty-pound field pack strapped to his back. That thought alone was enough to frighten the hell out of me. How would this 128-pound guy make it that far? Forget about dying in mortal combat, I thought. I was darn certain that I'd never even make it through *Boot Camp!*

Chapter 1

Introduction to Olive Drab

WEDNESDAY, *3-November-1965*-(6:30 AM) Local Draft Board #300, East Detroit, Michigan.

I pulled the collar up on my coat and turned my back to the cold biting wind. Others were gathered here at Local Draft Board #300, and a few more were due to show up. It was just past 6:00 AM when my older brother "Jim" dropped me off here, and the temperature this morning was 48 degrees. (Jim was actually Raymond James Oblinger, Jr., named after our father.) Still, it was windy and I wished I had worn a heavier jacket. As we shook hands and I said goodbye to my brother, I noticed that most of us gathered here were somewhat ill at ease standing around with our hands in our pockets. While pondering what the immediate future had in store for us, I nervously lit a cigarette.

As ordered in the induction letter, I had brought my Social Security Card, clothes for about three days or so in a small suitcase, and enough money to last about one month for personal purchases. Married men and/or fathers were also required to bring marriage licenses and children's birth certificates. I was feeling a little uneasy and was certain that most of the others were too.

While smoking and trying to move about to keep warm, I recalled how quiet it really was at home earlier that morning. Sitting around the kitchen table after breakfast with Mom, Dad, and Jim, none of us knew quite what to say. So, with little to talk about, I'd had a few cups of coffee before I left home. Like Dad, I had become a caffeine addict.

It was around 6:30 AM when our names were checked off a list by **Grace P. Zasa**, who was the clerk at Local Draft Board #300. Grace was a 34-year-old single woman who lived on Outer Drive Avenue in Detroit. After she signed our paper work, we all boarded a chartered bus that had pulled up several minutes earlier.

WEDNESDAY, 3-November-1965-(7:30 AM) Fort Wayne Induction Station, Detroit, Michigan.

The bus began moving slowly down Gratiot Avenue amid the early-morning rush-hour traffic. Looking out of the window, I watched other traffic as it passed by close to the bus. I stared at the faces of some of the drivers and wondered about where they were going. I was sure that most of them were headed to work on this cold Wednesday morning, and I was also sure that most of them knew what the day had in store for them. But I wondered how many of them would remember this day for the rest of their lives? I sure knew that *I* would.

After passing through downtown Detroit, we continued moving southwest about another two and a half miles and finally came to a stop at the **Fort Wayne Induction Station** located at 6053 West Jefferson at the foot of Livernois Avenue. Officially this was referred to as the **A.F.E.E.S. (Armed Forces Entrance and Examining Station).**

Authorized by Congress in 1841, the fort was built of limestone and rubble taken from many of the Lake Erie islands. Sitting on ninety-six acres of land, it was named after the Revolutionary War hero, General "Mad" Anthony Wayne, who had taken possession of Detroit from the British in 1796. The site chosen was a parcel of land at the Detroit River facing Canada, where during the Civil War it served as a training camp. During World War I it became an induction station, and then after the war it was used by the *C.C.C. (Civilian Conservation Corps).* Over the following years construction continued and by 1931, the last of the buildings were completed.

When World War II broke out in December 1941, Fort Wayne swiftly became a marshaling post for munitions produced in Detroit. Then after the war, the fort was decommissioned in 1949. In the years that followed World War II, the fort served as an Induction Station for both the *Korean War* and later *Vietnam* era service men. (Today, Fort Wayne is superintended by the *Detroit Historical Museum.*)

Not long after moving inside, we found ourselves standing naked except for our undershorts. I felt somewhat awkward standing in line on the cold, bare hardwood floors. We were given a brown paper bag in which to carry for our wallet and other personal items. There were more than seventy of us new draftees here and as I glanced around, I noticed one guy had dirty undershorts and another one had a tear in his. It made me recall when Mom always told us never to go anywhere without clean underwear. Now I knew why. I suppose for those two guys, there was a good reason. So who was I to judge?

The **Induction Physical** began for us by submitting a urine sample, and we were handed a paper cup for this. After several cups of coffee before leaving home that morning, this was not a problem for me at all. But some of the guys *did* have a problem with this. The guy standing next to me at the urinal asked if I could spare some for his cup, explaining that it was just too difficult for him to simply urinate on command. Having more than enough to do the job, I kindly obliged. Afterward, I felt about ten pounds lighter.

As I passed by each examiner, these notes were entered on my record:

Height—68 inches	Eyes—brown
Weight—128 pounds	Temperature—98.6
Waist—28 inches	Blood pressure—120/70
Build—slender	Vision—20/20
Hair—brown	

We also had a hearing test and I did OK with that too.

There was a break sometime around noon when we were all given lunch. Then afterward we got back to the business at hand. It was a complete and thorough examination as every inch, crack, and crevice of our bodies was checked. This exam also included what was called a ***Short-arm* inspection** which was an examination of the genitals. The practice actually dated back to the Spanish-American war in 1898. But the one fact that remained constant to this day was that very few men ever felt comfortable during this examination.

Eventually with the physical exam completed, they told us all to get dressed. We were then gathered into a large room on the first floor for final instructions. Here is where they told us to pass our ***Draft Cards*** forward. These cards were then collected at the front of the room and, very much to my surprise, they were simply and unceremoniously thrown into the trash basket. This dumbfounded the hell out of me. *I'll be darned,* I thought! After all the publicity about draft-dodging "hippies" burning their draft cards, the damned things were never even looked at.

Finally, we were all given an ***Army Serial Number*** and told to memorize it. To do this I repeated it in my head about a dozen times until I had it down pat—*US*

13

55-829-328. We learned that the prefix **US** referred to **Draftees**, while the prefix **RA** referred to **Regular Army** or **Enlistees.** Then we all stood for the administering of the oath. From that moment on, we were now the property of **Uncle Sam.**

It had been a long, long day to say the very least, and by 7:00 PM just before sundown, seventy-six of us boarded two chartered *Greyhound* buses that were parked out front. Each was a *Scenicruiser Model 4501* with a seating capacity of forty-three persons. I took a window seat about half way back on the right side of the bus looking forward. The temperature had risen to a welcome high of 73 degrees as the buses left Fort Wayne and headed south down Interstate-75.

Most of the guys were tired. Some hadn't slept at all during their last night at home. It may have been due to wild partying in an effort to "get it out of their system" in one form or another, or just restlessness in anticipation of all that lay ahead for them. There was some conversation between some of the guys, and several others had even dozed off.

But as for myself, I felt lonely on the drive south in spite of the fact that I was not alone. Through most of the trip, I quietly stared out the bus window counting telephone poles and stars in the night sky. It reminded me of an old prisoner's love song that Dad used to sing when I was a kid called, *Twenty-One Years*. It was about a prisoner sentenced to twenty-one years who had spent his time counting the stars and, *a million of these prison bars.*

We moved on down through Toledo and still kept on heading south. Then somewhere near Findlay, Ohio we stopped at a place called the **Post House.** It was a popular truck-stop and restaurant located on the left (east) side of the interstate. Here is where we all took a much-needed thirty-minute coffee and snack break.

As I reached into my pants pocket for money to pay for my coffee, my fingers touched the little plastic case that my aunt gave me a few days earlier. **Aunt Catherine Wolferd** was my mom's closest sister living in St Clair Shores about two miles northeast of my home. She had asked me to visit her before I left for the Army. I did so, and just before I hugged her goodbye, she gave me a small dark blue plastic folding case. In it were two miniature statues: These were of **Jesus** and his mother **Mary**. She told me that **my oldest brother John** had given them to her several years earlier before he drowned. Aunt Catherine firmly believed that if I carried them with me while I was away in the Army, God would watch over me and protect me from any harm. I loved Aunt Catherine dearly and so I gladly accepted her offer. Then I made a promise to return them to her when I came home for good.

After paying for my coffee, I went back outside and got back on the bus. Not long after that, the bus started moving again and we were soon back on I-75 continuing south. Although I was tired, I still couldn't sleep. (The *Post House* no longer exists today, but I never forgot stopping there.)

We passed on down through Cincinnati and then crossed the Ohio River into Kentucky. About twenty miles below the Ohio River we turned southwest onto Interstate-71. It was in the wee hours of the morning when we moved toward Louisville. From there the bus turned off I-71 and headed south on a highway marked US-31W which was called Dixie Highway. About thirty miles south of Louisville, we took the exit marked *Brandenburg Road / Fort Knox.*

THURSDAY, 4-November-1965—(2:00 AM) U.S. Army Reception Station, Fort Knox, Kentucky.

Leaving Dixie Highway, we took Brandenburg Road heading east into Fort Knox, and then turned southeast toward the **Reception Station** area at the eastern end of the post. This was located where 7th Avenue meets with 9th Avenue at the tall water tower. (7th Avenue was also called *Spearhead Division Avenue,* named after the U.S. 3rd Armored Division in World War II.) It was about 48 degrees outside when the bus came to a halt at 2:00 AM in front of a large orientation hall. Outside the orientation hall was a large yellow sign that read, *WELCOME TO THE UNITED STATES ARMY.* As soon as the door of the bus opened, some mean-looking sergeant stepped on and announced that we had just three seconds to get off this bus or we were going to get our asses kicked.

Stepping off the bus, the first thing I noticed was the strangely familiar smell of coal smoke in the early morning air. It was a welcome aroma as it reminded me of family visits to Swissvale, Pennsylvania when I was a kid. The next thing that caught my attention was the impeccable cleanliness of the place. Not so much as a cigarette butt or fragment of litter was in sight anywhere.

***Camp Knox* was named for Major General Henry Knox**, who was the Chief of Artillery for the Continental Army during the American Revolution. American soldiers (both Union and Confederate) had camped there as far back as the Civil War. A field artillery training center began there in 1918. Then in 1922 the post was closed following World War I, but continued to serve as a training center for the Army National Guard.

On 1-January-1932, *Camp Knox* became officially known as **Fort Knox**. In those days, camps were only occupied occasionally, while forts were usually occupied all year round. Most Army training camps and forts were located in the south, where the terrain and climate offered the very best training environment all year long. The 1ˢᵗ Cavalry Regiment arrived shortly afterward, then traded their horses for tanks and began a tank school. By 1936, the *U.S. Gold Bullion Depository* was constructed there.

In October 1940, while the rising threat of war progressed in Europe, the *Armored Force School* and the *Armored Force Replacement Center* were established there at Fort Knox. By 1943, the fort had expanded to 106,000 acres (157 square miles) with 3,820 buildings. Following that, Fort Knox was then referred to as the **United States Army Training Center, Armor (USATCA).** The Patton Museum opened there later in 1949. Then in September 1965, about three months prior to our arrival there, Brigadier General Wilson T. Hawkins assumed command of the post.

At about 2:30 AM, I was dog-tired and was sure that the rest of us were also. I began to think . . . *at any moment now, someone is going to assign us to sleeping quarters for the night so we could be well rested for whatever was to come.* But that didn't happen. Instead, we were in for an unpleasant surprise. After standing around with our hands in our pockets for what seemed like hours, we were all herded into the **Orientation Hall.**

The orientation consisted of us being told all about Army life in general and what we could expect over the next two months. We were informed about the *S.G.L.I. (Serviceman's Group Life Insurance)* of $10,000 that was available. And we were told that our pay would be $68.00 per month for a Private E-1.

It could have been worse, I thought. When World War II began, the pay for a buck private was $21 a month, hence the then often heard song called, *21 Dollars a Day, Once a Month!* Then by 1944, the Army raised the recruit's pay to $50 a month. And now, twenty years after World War II, we "buck privates" would be paid $18 more than that per month.

We were told about **contraband.** Contraband was anything that we were not permitted to have in our possession, such as alcohol, drugs, weapons (guns, knives, etc.), or anything that Army felt we didn't need. It was suggested that we dispose of it all, right there and then. A large trash container was pointed out to us in the back of the hall for this purpose. Someone among us said that there was no need for us to be thinking of home for quite a while. After all, we had **729 days and a wake-up** to go! (That would be 1,094 days and a wake-up for *RAs*.)

It was further explained to us that—*at this time only*—if we preferred, we could side-step into another branch of service such as the Air Force, Marines, Navy or Coast Guard. Or we could volunteer for Army *Airborne* training. Airborne guys were paid an additional $55 per month for what was called *Jump Pay*. Then in an effort to drive this point home, some guy in finely tailored (slightly faded), heavily starched, olive drab colored fatigues with *Jump Wings* on his chest and highly polished boots and brass, gave us a little pep talk about being part of the prestigious *Army Airborne Corps*. I'm really not sure if any of the guys in our group took advantage of this fine and tempting offer. But as for me . . . I decided to pass on it.

At about 3:30 AM we all finally left the orientation hall and moved back outdoors. Although the temperature outside was in the mid-40s, I was still uncomfortably cold in my thin summer jacket. But more than that, I was so darned tired that I was ready to drop. *Maybe now they will assign barracks and bunks,* I thought. But again, there was no such luck.

Just then, someone pointed to a long single-storey building across the road and directed all of us to *"line up at the Mess Hall over there!"* Then like a herd of wild stampeded cattle, we all made a mad dash for the building that we were directed to. As luck would have it, I was the fifth guy in line when we reached the door and was beaming with pride for having moved so fast.

After only a few minutes, a mean-looking sergeant poked his head out the door of the **Mess Hall** and barked out, *"I want you first five luggheads in here!"* For the next hour or so, I found myself cracking hundreds of eggs into a ten-gallon aluminum pot. Scrambled eggs would be the main item on the breakfast menu that morning. We (the first five guys) were fed *only* after everyone else was finished. I vowed to myself that I'd *never* be near the front of the line again. This was my first true experience with **Live-and-Learn in the U.S. Army!**

Finally emerging from the Mess Hall after breakfast, I noticed that dawn was just breaking over the water tower at the eastern end of the Reception Station. By this time, I had given up all hope of getting any sleep for the remainder of the day. I knew then that it was going to be a long, long day, and we had an awful lot to learn before it was over.

Among the first things we were taught here was that there was a proper way for **disposing of cigarette butts**. A man wouldn't dare get caught tossing a butt on the ground! The method was called **Field Stripping**. This meant that the butt, after being extinguished, had to be split open lengthwise, allowing the remainder of tobacco to blow away in the breeze, outdoors of course. Then the left over paper was rolled into a harmless little ball and allowed to fall to the ground. With filter cigarettes, that came into being some time after World War II, the spent filter was then pocketed until later when it could be disposed of properly. (I continued to practice this method over all these years, both at home and where I worked.)

The next thing we learned was that the **military operated on a 24-hour clock.** Thus 6:00 AM now became 0600 Hours (pronounced *Zero Six Hundred Hours*), 9:00 AM would be 0900 Hours, and Noon was called 1200 Hours. 1:00 PM then became 1300 Hours, 6:00 PM was now 1800 Hours, and midnight would be referred to as 2400 Hours. For me, it took an awful long time to get the hang of this, as I was not accustomed to speaking of time in terms of all those *"hundred hours."*

By mid-afternoon the temperature had risen to 67 degrees. When it came time for our **first U.S. Army haircut**, we were in for an experience we'd remember the rest of our lives. From the moment we got settled in the barber's chair, it took only sixty seconds for the barber to leave one eighth of an inch of hair on top with what we called *White Sidewalls.* When I got out of the chair, I felt as though I'd been wearing a hat all my life . . . and just suddenly lost it!

At long last when evening rolled around, we were *finally* assigned to a barracks building and given a bunk.

The old wooden **U.S. Army barracks** were made from plans drawn up by the *Quartermaster (QM) Corps* in the 1930s. These were wooden two-storey, 63 occupant structures heated by coal and painted a sick looking shade of faded yellow. Usually two platoons were assigned to each building, with two buildings to a company. (Today, very few of these old wooden buildings still exist. But the old water tower, even though it's been updated, is still there.)

After bunks were assigned to us and bedding was issued, we were taught how to properly make a bed—Army style. The top blanket had to be tight enough to literally bounce a quarter when the sergeant dropped one on it. Then finally *Lights Out* came at 2100 Hours (9:00 PM).

It was a long and exhausting day to say the very least. Many of the guys just fell in their bunk fully clothed and were asleep immediately, while some sat around and joked for a while. But as for me, my stomach began to rumble violently. I got the runs and had to make a mad dash for the *Latrine!*

The term **Latrine** is a military term referring to a toilet, shower, and washroom. We found out that in the latrine, **personal privacy was a thing of the past.** Every latrine in every wooden barracks anywhere in the U.S. was laid out pretty much the same. There was a row of toilets along one wall with no partitions between them. This made one feel ill at ease sitting on a toilet. A row of urinals hung along another wall while another wall had a row of sinks. The shower room too had several shower heads protruding from the walls. We had to become accustomed to shit, shower, and shave in close proximity to one another. It sure took some getting used to.

Over the next several days we were awakened around 0530 Hours in the morning. The daily temperatures ranged from about 43 degrees in the morning to a high in the mid-60s. But from this day onward, there would be no more wild stampedes to the mess hall. Until we were taught how to properly march, we just tried to move in an orderly manner as best we could. But we still had only twenty minutes to eat and get the hell out of the mess hall.

Throughout each day during our stay at Fort Knox, we'd often hear the distinguished sound of *Olive Drab Green* troop transport buses moving about on the post. While moving, they made an unforgettable combination of a winding-whistling sound.

We then learned how to **Police the Area.** This meant that following breakfast each morning in the Reception Station, it was time to pick up trash, cigarette butts, litter, and any other debris we could find. For this we had to gather in one long line and were told to *"extend to the right"* with arms outreached. Next we were ordered to move forward and *"pick it up!"* All the while, other groups marching by in brand new fatigues would yell at us, *"You'll be sorrrrryyyy!"* But that would change as soon as we were issued uniforms.

Our uniforms were issued in a long warehouse-type building. As we entered one end, the first thing that we were given was a **Duffel Bag.** This was a large cylindrical bag made of a heavy durable canvas cloth with the enclosure at the top. The name came from the town of Duffel, Belgium, where the thick cloth originally came from. With a capacity of about three and a half cubic feet, it included both a carrying handle and a shoulder strap.

As we passed by each "station" in the supply room, we were handed another article of clothing based upon sizes taken earlier. Each item was then tossed into the duffel bag. Finally dress shoes and combat boots were issued and we exited at the other end. The next morning, it was our turn to laugh at newly arrived recruits still in *their* "civies."

Dismounted Drill, which was formerly referred to as **Close Order Drill** back in World War II days, began here in the Reception Station. We were taught the proper way to execute the commands of *Attention, Right Face, Left Face, About Face, Forward March, Halt, Parade Rest,* and *At Ease.* With the command of *Forward March,* we were instructed to *"step off with your left foot."* Then while marching, each step was to be thirty inches in length.

Several months earlier I had mastered some of these movements of *Dismounted Drill* from instructions given by my older brother, Jim (Ray, Jr.). In February 1961 at the age of seventeen, Jim had enlisted in the U.S. Air Force, with written permission from Mom and Dad of course. After taking his Basic Training at *Lackland AFB (Air Force Base)* near San Antonio, Texas, he spent the rest of his four-year enlistment tour stationed at *Little Rock AFB* in Arkansas. While there, he met a pretty girl named Phyllis and began dating her exclusively. He married her in July 1964 and was honorably discharged from the Air Force in February 1965. Between then and my induction into the Army nine months later, he taught me many things about military life. These included the "heel and toe" pivot movement for the commands of *Right and Left Face*. He also gave me some pointers on the fine art of spit-shining boots and shoes.

We went on to learn some **Military Courtesy** and in general, how and when to salute an officer. We were told that to salute an officer was supposed to be considered as a *privilege*. But few of us ever felt that way and often tried to avoid officers or calling others to "Attention" when an officer approached.

Immunization Shots began here in the Reception Station. Most of them were administered with needles while some others came in the form of a new type of injection gun invented for this purpose. And in one particular case, the immunization came in the form of a drop of liquid on a sugar cube.

Kitchen Privilege (K.P.) began here for some of us. This was sometimes also called **Kitchen Police**. In this duty, one assisted the mess cook, peeled potatoes, washed mess trays, scrubbed pots and pans, garbage cans, and mopped the mess hall floor after each meal.

While I was here in the Reception Station one morning, some sergeant happened to catch me standing around with my hands in my pockets. This did not go over too well, and I was therefore ordered to carry a brick around with me in each hand for the rest of the day. Needless to say, I lost that bad habit fast. Once again, it was another lesson for me to *live-and-learn*.

Each day here as we learned more about life in the Army, we'd hear others marching by to the sound of *"Hut, 2, 3, 4!—Left, Right, Left!"* This was shouted out loudly by a Drill Sergeant leading them. We knew that in due time, we'd all look that sharp and move that smoothly.

Near the last day here in the Reception Station, there was a moment when I was all alone in the barracks. Knowing that the *Dress Green* jacket that I had been issued was a little too big, I took the opportunity to switch mine with another I had found that fit me like a glove. Over the years since then when I thought about it, I felt a twinge of guilt.

We eventually had our name tags sewed on our fatigues and uniforms, and this helped to make us feel more like real soldiers. Finally fingerprints were taken along with a photo for our *I.D. Cards*. We were then issued a pair of **Dog Tags** for identification. These were a pair of tags made of stainless steel and hung from our neck on a beaded chain. These tags were imprinted with our name, Army Serial Number, blood type, and religious preference if any. It was intended that in the event of our death on the battlefield, one tag would be left with the body while the other was collected along with personal effects.

The *concept* of identification tags in any form actually dates back to the Civil War, although the stainless steel tags only date back to World War II. There was a lot of speculation regarding the notch in the dog tags that appeared for many years. Some believed that the notch was intended to be jammed between the teeth in the deceased's mouth on the battlefield. But the truth of the matter was that the notch was merely intended to align the tag in the stamping machine.

Then on Monday morning, 15-November-1965, right after breakfast, we were ordered to line-up in ranks outside. A **sergeant** by the last name of **Aponte** arrived and began leading us out of the Reception Station. As we marched away, we carried our duffel bags over one shoulder, with our suitcases or "AWOL" bag in our other hand. As to why they were called AWOL bags, I have no idea to this day. **The initials *A.W.O.L.* refer to *Absent WithOut Leave*.**

From there, we marched north up Delaware Street to Sioux Street, then turned northwest cutting diagonally across an open field past the Main Post Chapel at the corner of Eisenhower Avenue and Cherokee Street.

The home of my youth - 22764 Rosalind Street, East Detroit, Michigan

Local Draft Board #300, East Detroit, Michigan (Today)

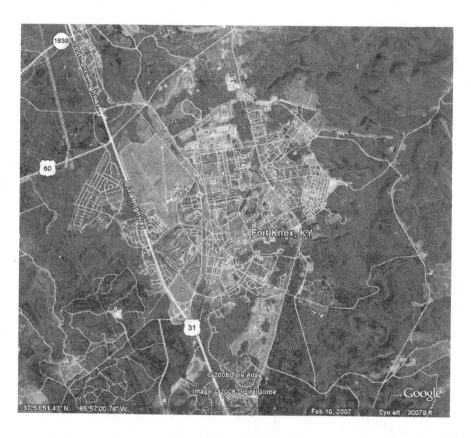

Fort Knox, KY as seen Today from 30,000 ft above

Entrance to Fort Knox, KY

Reception Station, Fort Knox, KY

US Army Military ID Card Photo, November, 1965

Chapter 2

B.C.T. (Basic Combat Training)

MONDAY, 15-November-1965—Company E, 13th Battalion, 4th Training Brigade.

About a half-mile north of the Reception Station, we arrived at our new home. This was the third barracks building north of Eisenhower Avenue, located on the east side of Bacher Street. We were now assigned to Company E of the 13th Battalion in the 4th Training Brigade. We would henceforth refer to this training outfit as *E-13-4* or *Echo-Thirteen-Four.*

It was comforting to see that the barracks here were long modern three-storey masonry buildings. Built around the late 1950s or early 1960s, they were certainly far better heated than the old wooden barracks. Each building here housed an entire training company. (These buildings are still standing today.) The main front entrance to our barracks faced south.

In short time we were moving up the front steps and into the building. I was assigned to the 4th Platoon, which was on the first floor to the right. Once inside, I was given a lower bunk about midway down on the right side of the isle. What a relief it was to finally drop the heavy duffel bag and AWOL bag.

There were four training brigades at Fort Knox. Of these, the 3rd and 4th Brigades were designated for *Basic Combat Training*. We were instructed to learn the *Chain of Command* from Brigade on down to our platoon level. It was set up like this:

CHAIN OF COMMAND

Commanding Officer (CO) of the 4th Training Brigade—Colonel A. D. Guffanti
CO of the 13th Battalion—Lieutenant Colonel John W. Norwalk
CO of E (Echo) Company—2nd Lieutenant Fred B. Hanson
Company First Sergeant—Sergeant Raymond L. Bryant
Field Training NCOs—Sergeant John E. Eickleberry and Sergeant Marion
    D. Wright
Supply Sergeant—Sergeant Fred C. Houston
Mess Sergeant—Staff Sergeant Garnet J. Broyles
Platoon NCOs—
1st Plt. Sergeant Charles R. Crump   2nd Plt. Sergeant John A. Hodges
3rd Plt. SFC Everette D. Sutton   4th Plt. Staff Sergeant Roy W. Kennard*

(*NCO* refers to a *Non Commissioned Officer* and *SFC* means *Sergeant First Class.*)

*AUTHOR'S NOTE: *Sergeant Aponte,* **the NCO who marched us over here from the Reception Station, was my platoon sergeant for the 4th Platoon during the first couple of weeks or so before he was transferred out of the company. Where he went from there, I have no idea today. Thereafter,** *Staff Sergeant Roy W. Kennard* **led the platoon for the remainder of our eight weeks.**

We all had some settling in to do and further orientation lectures to hear before the actual training was to commence on Thursday.

Thursday, 18-November-1965—**Basic Combat Training Begins.**

Our wake-up call was at 0530 Hours. This was not the gentle nudge from Mom back home, nor was it the old *Big Ben* wind-up alarm clock on my bedroom dresser. It was a loud barking voice from the doorway of our barracks. Each morning following the loud barking, the sergeant would often walk down the isle and personally shake each man from his cherished slumber. After this, came the sound of a scratchy recording over a loudspeaker outdoors somewhere in the distance. This was a recording of a bugle playing what was called *Reveille.*

For the next eight weeks, we would follow pretty much the same routine when each day began. After the wake-up call we had thirty minutes to perform what we called our S.S.S. (Shit, Shower and Shave). Then we had to make our bed (Army Style), get dressed in the uniform chosen for the day's training, and then *Fall-In* outside in four straight ranks facing south.

After roll call was taken, we were then marched around to the Mess Hall for breakfast. This was around the corner to the northwest end of our building. As each of us finished our breakfast, we'd return to the barracks and await further instructions. Soon we would *Fall-In* again outside and proceed to police the area. Then it was time to begin the scheduled training for the day.

There were 214 trainees in E Company. Of that total number, roughly 30 to 35% of them were from the area of Detroit and southeastern Michigan. Only about 5 to 7% of the company trainees were *Enlistees*, whose Serial Number prefix was *RA*, while most of the rest were *Draftees* like me with a prefix of *US*. But there were also about two or three guys in the company with the Serial Number prefix of *NG*. These guys were actually enlistees in the *Army National Guard.*

The *NGs* would receive the same eight weeks of Basic Combat Training along with the rest of us, and another eight weeks of A.I.T. (Advanced Individual Training). Thereafter they would head for home. Then for the remainder of their six-year military obligation, they would report to a training center near their home state for two days out of each month to attend *Drills*. In addition to this, they would go for two weeks of full time *Summer Camp* training in their respective *M.O.S. (Military Occupational Specialty).*

The fact that less than 10% of our total Basic Training class was black indicated that the U.S. Army still had a long way to go while working on racial desegregation.

One of three guys that I befriended here was **Wayne Lee Molner**, a guy from St Clair Shores, Michigan, whose bunk was across the isle from mine. Another friend I made here was a tall redheaded guy named **Daniel Harold Schneider**, whom we all called "Red." And the third one was a guy that I'll call **Ted Dinski**. Ted was the quiet guy whose bunk was directly above mine. Wayne, "Red", and Ted had come down on the same bus with our group from the Fort Wayne Induction Station in Detroit.

We had a lot to learn during our first couple of weeks here. We learned right away that smoking *was* allowed in the barracks, but *only* at specified times. Of course we didn't butt them out on the floor. Instead, we disposed of them in what we called *Butt Cans*. These were empty five-pound coffee cans painted red with the top cut off. These hung from support posts running from floor to ceiling at either end of the barracks. Outdoors we used *Field Stripping*, of course.

During our early days here we also learned that the **Catering Truck** (which was also called the **Maggot-Wagon** or **Gutt-Truck**) that cruised around the post after hours and on weekends, was considered as **OFF LIMITS** to us. The term *Off Limits* usually referred to a place or an establishment that we were not permitted to patronize. In our training company, any man caught coming from the *Gutt-Truck* was forced to consume *all* that he had purchased. The real problem was, often the guilty man was bringing back a load of snacks that he had not only purchased for himself, but also for others in the barracks as well.

We learned a few things about the service provided by the **Post Quartermaster Laundry** at Fort Knox. We were instructed to put our *Laundry Mark* on each item of our clothing. This mark was simply the first initial of our last name and the last four digits of our *Army Serial Number*. Therefore my mark was simply **O-9328**. Once a week our laundry was picked up, then laundered, starched, pressed, and returned. Well, at least that's how it worked in *theory*. In *reality* however, things worked quite differently.

Upon return of our laundered items, we found that about one out of every seven buttons or so was broken. As for the pressing of uniforms, they looked as if someone down there at QM Laundry tossed our clothing items on the floor and allowed a steamroller to do the pressing. To top all this off, *we* were responsible for the replacement of all broken buttons. Sewing kits containing OD Green-colored thread, needles, and various sizes of OD Green buttons could be purchased at the P.X. *(Post Exchange)*.

For those of us who chose to keep our **"civies" (civilian clothes)** rather than ship them home, we were free to include them with the laundry we sent to QM. But what a *BIG MISTAKE* that was! Among the civies that I kept and eventually sent to QM Laundry, was a black, high button-down collar, polished cotton shirt that was one of my snazziest articles of dress. But those were the days! I was sure was quite the man back then! But words alone cannot adequately describe what QM Laundry did to my prized shirt! Need I say more?

The next week I packed up what was left of my civies and sent them home. That also included my brown suede, pointed-toed, Cuban-heeled, zip-up-the-back boots. In all honesty though, I have to admit that while the boots looked quite stylish, they were actually uncomfortable to walk in and I was glad to be rid of them.

We were told about the U.S. Army's *Eleven General Orders*. These, we *had* to memorize as soon as possible. As to exactly how far back in history they did go? I have no idea. But they *do* date back to at least World War II.

They went like this:

The Eleven General Orders

1. To take charge of this post and all Government property in view.
2. To walk my post in a military manner, keeping always on the alert and observing everything that takes place within sight or hearing.
3. To report all violations of orders I am instructed to enforce.
4. To repeat all calls from posts more distant from the guardhouse than my own.
5. To quit my post only when properly relieved.
6. To receive, obey, and pass on to the sentinel that relieves me, all orders from the commanding officer, officer of the day, and officers and noncommissioned officers of the guard only.
7. To talk to no one except in the line of duty.
8. To give the alarm in case of fire or disorder.
9. To call the corporal of the guard in any case not covered by instructions.
10. To salute all officers and all colors and standards not cased.
11. To be especially watchful at night and, during the time for challenging, to challenge all persons on or near my post, and to allow no one to pass without proper authority.

Source: Department of the Army Field Manual (FM 21-13)
THE SOLDIER'S GUIDE

Each day one or more of us would be asked without prior warning, *"Soldier, what is your sixth General Order?"* Or to another, *"What is your third General Order?"* Of course if the trainee didn't immediately snap back with the correct answer, he'd be given what we called a *Shit Detail*, meaning some dirty job or another around the barracks such, as taking out all the trash. Or the *Drill Instructor* would simply order the trainee to, *"Drop down and give me twenty (push-ups)."* Early onward, it became clear to us that physical exercise was often used as punishment. We learned later that this was against Army regulations.

Close Order (Dismounted) Drill continued here with even more vigor. But each day our movements became smoother and more precise. Once we mastered the basics of these drills, we were further taught how to execute the commands of *Column Right March, Column Left March, Double Time March, Right Flank March, Left Flank March,* and *To the Rear March.* At first some of us were quite sloppy about it and occasionally got out of step, but in time we all got the hang of it and even began to feel good about it.

Immunization Shots continued here too, while we learned more about **Military Courtesy, Discipline, Sanitation**, and **First Aid**. We began rigorous daily **P.T. (Physical Training)**. This was usually in the form of *Jumping Jacks, Squat Thrusts, and Push-Ups*. We even did what they called *8-Count Push-Ups*. These were a form of exercise that combined several movements, beginning and ending in the standing position all the while including a knee-bend, a squat thrust, and a push-up.

Early in my basic training I developed a painful blister on the back of my heel. I found that the only remedy for this was to wear two pairs of heavy combat socks, then lace my boots up as tight as I could to prevent rubbing. It worked great.

K.P. (Kitchen Privilege) was assigned here too. This brought a wake-up call at 0330 Hours in the morning, as we had to report to the Mess Sergeant by 0400 Hours. One early morning before sunrise, I found myself with my head way down inside a garbage can outside in back of the Mess Hall as I was scrubbing it clean. I was a bit surprised to learn that the Army had separate garbage cans labeled for *edible* and *non-edible* garbage. I guess that *nothing* went to waste as I heard somewhere that the *edible* garbage went to many of the local farms to be used as cattle feed.

The food here was OK but nothing to really write home about. I'll admit that I *never* tried what for many years had been called *S.O.S. or Shit-on-a-shingle*. That was the G.I. nickname for creamed chipped beef on toast. Today, my wife and I both like it and have it now and then. And as for other G.I. terminology we learned in the mess hall . . . I'd also heard that ringed bologna was often referred to as *donkey dick* as far back as World War II.

The training day here was long. Other than a break for the noon meal (which the Army called *Dinner*), there were occasional breaks for us to **"smoke 'em if you got 'em"**. I remember actually feeling sorry for all the non-smokers in the company. After all, while we smokers were relaxing and enjoying a great-tasting cigarette, the other poor guys had nothing else to do but hang around and envy us. Over the years, I often wondered if some of the non-smokers back then picked up the nasty bad habit for that reason.

Anyway, our training activity would most often last until about 1700 Hours (5:00 PM) each day. Then after returning to the company area, the evening meal was provided, which the Army called *Supper*. After that, we would then return to the barracks quite exhausted.

By this time it would be 1800 Hours and the day was *still* not over. There was *Mail Call* to be held and announcements to be heard. Then barracks cleaning and other dirty chores would follow. After rifle and equipment cleaning, *Lights Out* finally rolled around at 2130 Hours (9:30 PM). This pace kept up six days a week, for almost sixteen hours a day. We also had occasional night training problems, **Guard Duty**, and weekend details called **G.I. Parties** which was a thorough and complete cleaning of the barracks from top to bottom, inside and out.

Every evening **Mail Call** was something almost everyone looked forward to. It seemed that mail from home was always welcomed as the highlight of each day. It provided a brief escape from the everyday drudgery and made life here more bearable.

About two and a half weeks into Basic Training, I noticed that **Ted Dinski**, the guy in the bunk above mine, never got any mail from home. Ted would usually gather around with all of us when mail was being handed out, but I could tell that he wasn't really as eager about it as we all were. Then out of genuine concern, I asked him one day when we were alone, why he didn't receive any mail from home. He looked around to be sure he wouldn't be overheard, and then told me quietly that no one back home knew where he was. He went on to explain that because of having only a third grade education, he couldn't even spell the name of his hometown of Pontiac, Michigan, or the street he lived on. So although he could recite to me his house number and street address, he was never really able to *write* a letter home and give his parents any details of where he was and how he was doing.

I was dumbfounded for sure. What's more, I couldn't imagine how the Army never knew about this.

Ted was single and a quiet sort of guy. Though he always tried hard, he could barely give an average performance in whatever training activities we did. And he never really excelled as far as I could recall. He wasn't the kind that would willingly draw any attention his way, and I wasn't sure if any of the others noticed his lack of mail from home.

I was touched by this, and therefore decided to help him if he'd allow me. So I asked him the next time we were alone. Once again, he looked around to be certain we weren't overheard, and then told me he'd be grateful for any help I could offer. Then I explained to him that I could "write" a letter for him if he would simply dictate to me exactly what he wanted to say. He gladly agreed.

Later that evening, we went out in the hallway and sat on the steps leading upstairs. I began the letter to his mother by first introducing myself and explaining to her that I was writing this on Ted's behalf. Then as he dictated slowly, I began writing. He sent the letter out the next day and, needles to say, he soon started to receive mail once or twice each week.

When his name was finally called during Mail Call, Ted was so excited he could hardly contain himself. But he knew he had to wait until we were alone so I could read it to him. Most of the time, we sat outside on the front steps to "read" our mail. Words alone could never describe how grateful he was to me for my help. But as for me, it felt so good being able to help him.

We had Sundays off most of the time. We were free to go to church at the *Calvary Chapel* about a block away at the southwest corner of Eisenhower Avenue and North Cherokee Street. But often after returning to the barracks from Catholic Mass, I grew bored with little else to do. Sometimes I'd go down the hall past the **Orderly Room** (Company offices) to the **Dayroom** which was our company recreation room. It was a quiet room and a great place to relax, write letters, or just listen to a radio. Occasionally I'd take a walk outside if the weather permitted and it wasn't too cold. We were allowed to go almost anywhere, but we were not permitted to leave the post.

The *P.X. (Post Exchange)* was a good place to visit. This was the Army's version of a general store. Most Army posts had one large Main PX resembling a large department store, and several smaller branches scattered across the post. Here one could purchase toilet articles, snacks, and cigarettes. Beer was also available at some of the PXs, but with only 3.2% alcohol, it didn't have much of a kick to it, and most of the guys called it *Panther Piss* or *Near Beer*.

On Sundays, phone booths usually had long waiting lines. If you talked for more than ten minutes on the phone, several lonely recruits behind you would take exception to it. Some of the guys played poker in the barracks by gathering several footlockers together to make a table. But if one wasn't careful he could end up losing the better part of his meager monthly pay.

We were trained in the use of the *U.S. Army's new M-14 Rifle*. Training with this weapon was initially introduced at Fort Knox in 1964. The M-14 was an American selective fire battle rifle manufactured by the *Springfield Armory* in Springfield, Massachusetts. The initial design of this infantry weapon began just after World War II. It was intended to replace the following .30 caliber weapons: The *M-1 Garand Rifle*, the *M-1 Carbine*, and the *B.A.R. (Browning Automatic Rifle)*. Nearly 1.8 million M-14s were produced between 1959 and 1964.

Like the M-1 before it, the M-14 was also gas operated. It had a total length of 44.4 inches including its 22-inch barrel. At 10.1 pounds with the shoulder sling and full 20-round detachable box-magazine, its overall net weight was lighter than the M-1. It had a bore of 7.62mm (.30 caliber), a muzzle velocity of 750 rounds per minute (when set on full automatic), and an effective range of 1500 feet. Its main disadvantage was that the barrel tended to rise up when set on full automatic. For that reason some thought it made a great Anti-Aircraft weapon.

During this training, we had to learn how to properly "weld" the stock of the weapon to our cheek and shoulder while aiming. The M-14 had a powerful kick when fired and was known to leave a nasty bruise if held improperly. We also learned how to properly disassemble, clean, and reassemble the rifle, sometimes even blindfolded.

We were instructed to *never* refer to the M-14 Rifle as a *gun*. Instead it was to be referred to only as a *weapon*. To drive that point home, we were instructed to hold the weapon with our right hand and grab our genitals with our left hand. Then we were made to recite the ever-popular rhyme, *"This is my weapon, this is my gun. This is for fighting, and this is for fun."* I recently learned that the rhyme actually dated back to World War II days!

Weapons Qualification always fell into three categories: **Marksman**—which was considered the minimum acceptable qualification score on the rifle range; **Sharpshooter**—above average score; and **Expert**—the highest possible score. In the end, I qualified as a *Marksman* with the M-14.

I remember while on the rifle ranges we'd hear over a loudspeaker, things like, *"Is there anyone down range?"* This was usually followed by, *"Lock and load one round of ammunition."* And let us also not forget hearing, *"Ready on the right?—Ready on the left?—Ready on the firing line!"* Lastly we'd hear, *"Commence firing!"* Then before leaving the range we had to assure the NCO in charge, *"No brass or ammunition, Sergeant!"* Do you remember picking up all the brass before we left?

I had serious thoughts back then about using this weapon in actual combat, if and when it came to pass. Could I actually kill another person with this or any other weapon? These thoughts were unsettling to me. I found myself wondering how my father handled these thoughts when he was an infantryman with General Patton's Third Army in Europe during World War II. I guess that like my father, I'd just have to trust in God's guidance, if and when the time came.

An extensive study was conducted on the subject after World War II, and the results were surprising. It was determined that most men in actual combat with an enemy, were in reality more afraid of *killing another human being* than they were of actually *being killed themselves.*

It was probably for this reason that many guys decided to "dodge" the draft. I began to feel a certain dislike for those who took that path. But I knew that I could never let my father down. Therefore I had to accept the draft, along with whatever fate it had for me.

Once we were issued a rifle, we began learning the **Manual of Arms.** We learned to execute the commands of *Right Shoulder Arms, Left Shoulder Arms, Order Arms, Port Arms, High Port, Inspection Arms,* and *Parade Rest.*

We were also instructed in the proper use of the Bayonet. For **Bayonet Training**, we were issued an *M-6 Bayonet* for use with our M-14 Rifle. The M-6 was first introduced in 1957. Including the blade of 6 and 5/8 inches, its overall length was 11 and 3/8 inches.

I was beginning to feel like a real **G.I.** now. But like it or not, we draftees had no choice in the matter. At the time, I wondered where the term actually came from. I learned years later that at first the term was used to designate anything that was of *Government Issue*. But early in World War II it, became a label used to describe draftees. The term also had other meanings. For example, if a man said that he had the "GI's," he was really saying that he had a bad case of diarrhea. If someone or some organization was "too GI," it meant that the person or organization stuck strictly to Army regulations. A "GI" was considered to be at the "bottom rung" of the military ladder.

Marching in ranks to and from the training areas or rifle ranges would take as little as ten minutes or up to an hour or so depending upon where the training took place each day. Very often it was a grueling march, and occasionally over some of the roughest terrain imaginable. We marched up a place we called *Misery Hill* and down another known as *Agony Hill.*

I have savored a few fond memories over the years that originated simply from marching in ranks. One memory stands out most in my mind today. That is while marching in ranks, one of the most unique sounds you'll ever hear in the world is **the unmistakable sound of an M-14 Rifle when it falls to the pavement below.** It gives a kind of *Clackel-Clackel* sound.—Sort of like a unique mixture of wood, steel, and plastic bound together if you could imagine. No other sound in the entire world could imitate it. Certainly not the M-1 Rifle, which was made from wood and steel only. And the M-16, which was introduced later, was made from wood, steel, plastic, *and* aluminum. No! Only the *M-14 Rifle* could make that sound.

When each day was finally over, I gave praise and thanks to God that I never dropped my weapon while marching in ranks. I could only cringe when I imagine the paralyzing horror that instantly engulfed the poor trainee whose sling broke loose, and he knew that his weapon was falling to the pavement below. And what about the reaction from the poor recruit's Drill Instructor? Can you actually imagine it?

I recall that there was one time when **we all marched in the pouring down rain** for more than thirty minutes. Then after we were thoroughly soaked to the skin and shivering, we were finally halted and told to put on our *Poncho.* I was *really* ticked off about this and believed at the time that it was totally unnecessary.

In reality though, it toughened us up for what might lie ahead for us if we were ever sent into combat.

The *Poncho* was the U.S. Army's version of a raincoat used on field marches. Dating back to World War II, they measured 66 x 90 inches and were made from a heavy cotton fabric coated with a water-resistant material. They included snap-fasteners along the edges and a neck opening in the center with a hood and drawstring. Besides rain protection, the Poncho had many other uses, including being used as a floor and ground-covering for the U.S. Army *Pup Tent.*

Incidentally, among some of the outdoor field equipment we each carried often was a *Shelter Half.* This was simply half of a pup tent, along with half of the tent pegs and poles. The idea behind this was that each man was to "pair-up" with a buddy when pitching tents.

It surprised me that our platoon sergeant, **S/Sergeant Roy W. Kennard**, was able to keep up with us on the long marches as he looked somewhat older than us recruits. But keep up, he did! And even more than that, it seemed that he never tired out like many of us. Sergeant Kennard was a 35-year-old married man from Baltimore, Maryland. He had enlisted in August 1950 and began his training at Fort Meade, Maryland. He then moved on to further training at Fort Belvoir, Virginia. By the time he was assigned as our Drill Sergeant, he had more than fifteen years of loyal and dedicated service in the U.S. Army. Roy Kennard and his wife Christine had four children back then and lived in the NCO housing quarters on post.

I recall one time **smoking a cigarette while marching in ranks!** Of course, this could *only* happen while marching near the *back* of the ranks! It happened to be raining at the time and I actually smoked the cigarette while holding it cupped in my hand under the poncho. As long as Sergeant Kennard wasn't actually looking back my way, I was OK! I simply directed my exhaled smoke down into the poncho to be dissipated below. As I recall, I only tried this once, and while I didn't get caught, I sometimes wondered what the consequences would have been if I had.

Singing was always a great pastime on long marches. I recall us all singing, *"Ain't no use in lookin' down!—There ain't no Discharge on the ground!—Sound off!"* And there was another old favorite that went, *"Here we go again,—marchin' down the avenue,—eight more weeks and we'll be through!—Sound off!"* (This changed weekly, of course.) And certainly we all remember who *Jody* was back then. He was that lucky guy back home that we all sang about in many a marching song . . . the one who was never snagged by the draft, and spent all his time trying to steal your wife, your girlfriend, or your sister.

I'm sure that many of us while marching recall hearing, *"Road Guards left and right, Post!"* This, I dreaded hearing with all my being, as I was a *Road Guard* more than once. In each platoon, there were always four ranks marching together side-by-side. The Road Guard was always the second guy from the front of the two outer ranks. Whenever the road guards heard the above order shouted out by the drill instructor, they had to literally break from ranks and then run like hell to the upcoming cross-street or road intersection ahead, and stand there holding their rifles at *Port Arms* while blocking any cross traffic coming. As soon as the entire column had passed, you'd hear, *"Road Guards, Recover!"* They'd then have to run again at a full clip in order to catch up with us and "recover" to their position in ranks. It was *extremely* exhausting to anyone who happened to be a Road Guard.

Another thing I remember about marching in ranks was wearing a helmet liner without any other head protection. I'm not referring to protection from bullets or shrapnel here. Instead I'm referring to protection from the wind and cold! On many of those ice-cold windy mornings in November and December, while marching out to the rifle ranges with only an eighth of an inch of hair on top, the helmet liner acted as a wind tunnel. Oh man, was that ever *cold!* There certainly was no doubt that my *F.T.A. (F— the Army)* attitude began here in earnest.

Other things I remember after all these years are still vivid in my mind today. Take *Classroom Instruction* for example. It was always a welcome break from the rigorous training activities and long marches. This gave us trainees a chance to catch our breath, rest and relax. But if the class happened to be boring, as was often the case, there was always the danger that one would fall asleep during the lecture. Or one might doze after the lights were turned off during one of the many training films we were shown during Basic. This, we tried to avoid at all costs. Classroom instructors took a dim view of trainees dozing in their class, and the consequences were usually harsh if we were caught.

I recall *Chow in the Field* on a few occasions when we had to eat outdoors standing at waist-high steel tables at the rifle ranges.

We learned to use the *Pugil Stick*, which was a pole about five feet long with huge padded ends. I never could figure out what we were supposed to learn from beating each other senseless with the damned things! Anyway, that was the Army!

We had *Weekly Inspections* of not only the barracks, but also our equipment, foot locker, and wall locker displays. Of course I remember getting a *Gig* once in a while back then, which was supposed to be some kind of shameful demerit. After all, who *didn't* get a gig now and then?

Although I don't recall it ever happening in my barracks, I'm sure that everyone has heard of the ***G.I. Shower.*** This was when a bunch of guys would band together and attack a fellow trainee who hadn't showered for a while. It called for dragging the offender to the showers, then scrubbing him clean with G.I. soap and a scrub brush.

A bar of ***G.I. Soap*** weighed about one pound and came in the shape of a small greenish-brown colored brick. The Army seemed to use it for cleaning everything from Mess Hall floors and walls to mess trays, mess kits, pots and pans, battle gear, laundry, and also for decontamination. Considering the fact that very few ever became allergic to it when it was used for laundry (including undergarments worn next to the skin), many considered it as a mild soap. To me it resembled the *Fels-Naptha Soap* that Mom always used for scrubbing the kitchen floor.

There was a planned ***Bivouac*** (overnight camp-out) that never materialized as I recall due to a heavy downpour of rain. *That*, I did *not* regret! There was ***Hand-to-Hand Combat Training***. And I recall the ***C.B.R. (Chemical, Biological, Radiological) Training***. That ended with the Army giving us a brief sampling of a few minutes in a tear-gas chamber. For this we had to wear our U.S. Army ***M-17 Gas Mask*** that the Army called *"Mask, Field, Protective."* The mask, introduced in 1959, was the very first "canisterless" type designed for the U.S. Armed Forces.

Let us not forget our ***Hand Grenade*** training, after which a few lucky trainees got to throw a "live" one. I sure would have enjoyed that pleasure, but such was not the case.

I also recall the ***Target Detection Range***. This was where we each had to stand behind a steel post sticking vertically about four and a half feet out of the ground with a thirty-inch horizontal crossbeam at the top. Spaced evenly along this crossbeam were four "pistol" shaped pointers. Each was randomly aimed toward the hilly and heavily wooded area ahead. The trainee was supposed to literally "point" the four pistols at four separate camouflaged "targets" in the woods. For some reason or another, I couldn't find a single target that day to save my ass. I was so frustrated. So needless to say, I scored no points for the day.

The ***Confidence Course*** had changed very little over the years. However, in World War II it was called the ***Obstacle Course***. It was another part of the training that we would always remember. We would begin with our M-14 Rifle (and a full field pack, if I'm not mistaken) and would have a certain amount of time in which to complete the grueling course. When the Drill Instructor blew his whistle, the trainee would take off running. There were several obstacles we had to climb up, swing over, slide down, jump over, crawl through, and weave around. Most of us made it in the allotted time, but a few took several tries before finishing the course.

Lastly, the ***Infiltration Course*** was among the most memorable outdoor courses that we participated in. After an orientation lecture one afternoon at the course site during daylight hours, we all returned there after dark on troop transport buses to participate in the unforgettable experience. But as luck would have it, immediately following the afternoon orientation, it poured down rain for several hours before we arrived back at the site that night.

The course was between thirty-five to forty yards in length as I recall, and there was a trench running parallel behind a short wall along the starting line. While in this trench, we had to keep our heads down until we were ordered to "move out."

When the "move out" order was given, we proceeded to leap over the wall and begin crawling forward toward the finish line at the other end with our weapon cradled in our arms. While moving forward in mud about two to six inches deep in places, we had to low-crawl around several round sandbag bunkers strategically placed throughout the course. Within these bunkers were live explosive charges that randomly sent mud and water high into the air. And of course, what goes up . . . must always come back down. We were all drenched to the skin.

Then adding to all of this realism and excitement, sitting just above the finish line was a **Browning 30-caliber water cooled machine gun** firing live *Tracer Rounds* while sweeping back and forth just above our heads and asses. *Tracer Rounds* had a coating of phosphorous orange or red paint on the tips that left a luminous trail as they passed overhead. About every fourth or fifth round or so was a tracer. During wartime use, these *Tracer Rounds* allowed the gunner to literally "trace" the rounds all the way to their intended target.

We were told earlier that day that we were expected to finish the course with a clean and dry weapon. Well . . . needless to say, that request went right out the window the very moment we leaped over the starting wall. *Nobody* that I knew of finished the course that night with a clean or dry weapon. As for myself, the moment I leaped over the wall, I fell into about four inches of water with mud below that. The muzzle of my M-14 plunged into the mud and I therefore decided to simply drag it the rest of the way.

Richard T. VandeKerchove, another draftee from my hometown of East Detroit, and a member of Sergeant Sutton's 3rd Platoon, had a better idea. He thought to himself, *Why should I go to all the trouble of crawling through all* *that mud when I can take care of it right here without all the hassle?* He quietly slipped away from the rest of us without being detected and hid behind one of the troop transport buses that brought us here. Then with his rifle in his hands, he took up a prone position in the mud momentarily while making sure that both he and his M-14 got thoroughly mud-covered. Then he stood up, waited for the right moment and slipped back into the group of guys emerging from the end of the course.

A single guy, and only eight days older than me, Rick "Van" and I must have passed each other in the halls of *East Detroit High School* many times during my last few years there, but we never really got to know each other. However, one fact about Rick was for certain. Every school-age kid in the city of East Detroit back then knew his father. *Officer Van,* as every kid knew him back then, was the Truant Officer for the city of East Detroit, and one of the most respected police officers in that city.

Rick also had a cousin in E-13-4 whose name was **Fred VandeKerchove.** Fred, who was from Harper Woods, Michigan at the time, was drafted the same day as Rick and trained with us all the way through Basic. When basic training was over, Fred and Rick went separate ways as Fred was later sent to Vietnam.

That night when we returned to the barracks, we stayed up into the wee hours of the morning cleaning ourselves and our rifles. Some of the guys just stepped into the shower naked, while carrying their weapon at sling arms. Oh, what a night that was!

In due time, we all gathered for group and individual photos. I was disgusted with the individual photo taken of me. It seemed that my clip-on necktie was not under the collar on one side and neither the photographer nor I realized it. If the photographer *did* notice it, he certainly didn't care enough to mention it to me. **Rick VandeKerchove** and a few others that pulled KP duty that day were photographed in tee-shirts and fatigues for the E-13-4 Graduation Book. I'm sure that many others were disgusted with the photos too.

Near the end of our last week here, Sergeant Kennard came into the barracks. With him he carried orders indicating where each of us would be going for *A.I.T. (Advanced Individual Training).* From Company E, a large part of our group was being assigned to the *Army Cook School* at **Fort Ord, California.** Another nineteen guys including myself from Company E were being sent to the *Military Police School* at **Fort Gordon, Georgia.**

As for myself being assigned to Military Police School? I had to admit that I felt a sense of relief about it. Though I wasn't sure about how I would do at MP School, I sure was darn glad that I wasn't being sent to Cook School in California.

Along with the nineteen of us from E Company of the 13ᵗʰ Battalion headed to MP School, Company A sent ten men, Company B sent six, and Company C sent eleven. (None were included from D Company.) **This made forty-six in all from the 13ᵗʰ Battalion.**

Very few guys failed to measure up to U.S. Army standards during Basic Training. Those who fell short of expectations had to be ***Recycled***, which meant that they were expected to retake a few weeks or so of training and graduate with a later group of trainees. I cannot recall if anyone in our company had to be recycled.

WEDNESDAY, 12-January-1966—Graduation Day!

Graduation Day came on Wednesday, 12-January-1965. The day dawned with a low of 24 degrees, climbing to a high of 48 later in the day. Many of the guys had families arriving from home to be present for the ceremony. It was certainly a day for our "Class A" dress uniforms to be worn. After all, there were awards to be handed out, after which the men later performed a *Passing in Review* as the Battalion Commander watched. I don't mind admitting that I missed all this hoop-la because of being assigned to ***Barracks/Fire Guard*** duty that day. There was no way my folks could have made the trip anyway. And I just wanted to get the heck out of there and get on a bus headed north to Detroit.

I never learned where **Daniel "Red" Schneider** went after basic, nor did I ever hear from him again. I tried recently to locate him, but my efforts there have failed me.

As for what happened to my other friend, **Ted Dinski**? I never saw nor heard from him again either. I would think of Ted from time to time over the years. While he certainly didn't come to MP school with us, I'm almost certain he would not have made it in cook school either. I couldn't imagine him trying to read a menu in order to prepare food. A few years ago I tried to locate him and/or his parents or other family members in Pontiac, Michigan, but failed in my effort there too.

I still wonder from time to time what became of these two friends.

Anyway, we all packed up and went home after that. For those of us bound for MP School, we had nine days to kill before we had to report to Fort Gordon on 21-January-1966. I never learned until much later (my last day in the Army to be exact) that these nine days would be defined by the U.S. Army as **Delay Enroute time, which was not the same as Leave time.**

Staff Sergeant Roy W. Kennard went on to make a career in the Army. During that time his list of Army assignments included service in Germany, and the Republic of Vietnam between August 1967 and August 1968. Beyond that, he also served at the Pentagon in Washington, DC. Among some of the awards he had earned were the *Purple Heart,* the *Silver Star* for valor, and the *Bronze Star.* Eventually rising to the rank of Master Sergeant, Roy Kennard was honorably discharged in September 1978. After his Army service, he returned to Maryland and became self-employed in the business of Refrigeration and Air Conditioning. With a fleet of five trucks, he and his crew did mostly mobile repair. Roy and Christine had raised five children in all before his death in November 1990.

When I stepped off the Greyhound bus in downtown Detroit, the city seemed to appear a lot dirtier than I remembered. And then it hit me.—I slowly began to notice the trash, the litter in the streets, and the cigarette butts everywhere. It wasn't really the *town* that had changed. *I* was the one who had changed. I also noticed when I got home that my old civilian clothes didn't quite feel the same anymore, and I couldn't understand why at the time. They still fit me, as I had neither gained nor lost any weight to speak of during basic. It's just that they *felt* strangely different for some reason! Many years later I learned that this was what the Army called the *Furlough Syndrome.*

But in any event, it sure felt good to be back at home again.

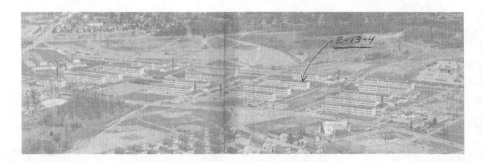

Fort Knox - Basic Training area in 1965

Fort Knox - Basic Training Area - as seen Today from 2100 ft above

Basic Training Barracks, Fort Knox

1st Lt Fred B. Hanson, C.O. of E Company

Sgt. Roy W. Kennard, 4th Platoon Drill Sgt.

SSgt Kennard

Calvary Chapel, at Fort Knox

Inside Calvary Chapel

Mess Hall at Fort Knox

Wayne Lee Molner

Bill Deeb, Wayne Molner and Paul Fillinger of E-13-4 at Fort Knox

Daniel H. 'Red' Schneider

Richard T. VandeKerchove

M-14 .30 Caliber Rifle

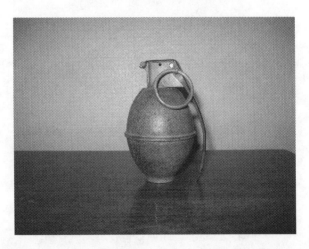

Fragmentation-Type Hand Grenade used in Basic Training

Chapter 3

A.I.T. (Advanced Individual Training)

FRIDAY, 21-January-1966—Company K, 10th Battalion, 4th Training Brigade, Military Police School—Fort Gordon, Georgia.

Those last nine days passed by way too fast for me. It seemed like I had just gotten home and had to leave again. But at least I was able to rest a little on the Greyhound bus coming south on the way down here. I kept thinking while I was at home, how much warmer the climate would be when I arrived down south in Georgia and so I was looking forward to it. I'd had enough of marching in the cold and rain. Yes, a warmer and milder southern climate was just what I needed.

On Friday, 21-January-1966, when I got off the bus at the depot in Augusta, Georgia, the temperature was still in the low forties. Oh well, I thought to myself. This isn't too bad at all for a southern state. I can sure live with this. Then I caught a local bus headed out to Fort Gordon just west of the town.

Headquarters of the Military Police School was in Building #38504 on 38th Street. This was south of Commandant Drive on the eastern most edge of the fort. The main MP School complex was bounded by 38th and 40th Streets and between Commandant Drive (which was 7th Avenue) and Academic Drive (also known as 8th Avenue). Our barracks buildings were located between Provost Avenue and 10th Armored Division Road, just southwest of and adjacent to the school area.

I reported as ordered to Company K of the 10th Battalion in the 4th Training Brigade. We would hereafter call this ***K-10-4***. It was back to living in old wooden barracks again. For the first time I noticed that the interior layout of these old wood-frame buildings was the same here too. It occurred to me that one could stumble stoned drunk into one of these buildings anywhere in the United States, and still find his way to the latrine. (Although these old barracks buildings are no longer there today, most of the single-storey buildings of the old school complex are still present and unchanged except for some added breezeways connecting a few of the old wooden structures.)

Captain William R. Waldrop commanded Company K, and our **Executive Officer was 2nd Lt. Victor A. Driscoll.** Next in command was **1st Sergeant Ernest A. Booton,** while **Sergeant William B. Bryant served as the Operations NCO.**

Camp Gordon **was originally established in 1941** in the piney woods of eastern Georgia. Located just west of the city of Augusta, it was named after Confederate Lt. General John Brown Gordon, former Governor of Georgia and twice a U.S. Senator. In World War II *Camp Gordon* served as a training camp for the 4th Infantry, 26th Infantry and 10th Armored Divisions. (My father served as a replacement in the **26th Infantry Division** in World War II.) All three of these divisions served under General George S. Patton's Third Army in Europe.

In September 1941, the *Military Police Corps* was officially organized and became a separate branch of the U.S. Army. An MP School was then set up and functioned in various locations over the next seven years.

After World War II, Camp Gordon, encompassing 56,000 acres (87.5 square miles), served primarily as a U.S. Army Demobilization and Separation Center. Then in 1948, the Military Police School was relocated there from Carlisle, Pennsylvania. At that time the Southeastern Signal School was also moved there and later during the Korean War, the 51st Anti-Aircraft Artillery was formed there. In 1956, Camp Gordon became officially designated as *Fort Gordon*.

On Monday, 24-January-1966, I woke to a morning temperature of 34 degrees outside as the training began. I thought to myself, *OK. So this is cold. But this is also the southern state of Georgia, so it can only get better from here, right?* I would sure find out in due time.

The training here was called *A.I.T.,* which meant *Advanced Individual Training.* This was the *Military Police School.* I was assigned to the second floor of one of the barracks buildings, and my upper bunk was the first one on the right side of the isle at the top of the stairs.

Not long after settling in here and making my assigned bed, I sat down on my footlocker and allowed my mind to ponder all that I was about to experience here at MP School. While I was still uncertain as to how I would perform as a military policeman, I was at the same time quite thankful that I had not been chosen for Infantry Training. I knew that Basic Training hadn't done much for me as far as weight gain was concerned, but at 129 pounds, I was at least a lot firmer than I was when I first arrived at Fort Knox forty-seven days earlier on 4-November.

Sneeze Sheets were introduced to us here at Fort Gordon as soon as we were settled in. These were our rain **Ponchos** that were hung like curtains between the bunks each night. They were intended to keep the spread of germs here to a minimum. As ridiculous as I thought these *Sneeze Sheets* were at the time, I felt that they also added a small measure of privacy.

I walked downstairs to the first floor one day to chat with **Wayne Molner**, whom I met during Basic at Fort Knox. He was bunked near the far end of the barracks on the right side of the isle. Here is where I met **Edward W. Mitchell** for the first time, also bunking on the first floor. This leaves me wondering today if we were assigned bunks in the barracks in alphabetical order with *A* through *N* downstairs and *O* through *Z* upstairs.

Ed Mitchell was a single guy from the west side of Detroit. Though he was six months younger than me, Ed was drafted one day after I was. He also took his Basic Training at Fort Knox, but in Company A. In the beginning I was a bit jealous of Ed Mitchell because his hair was a little longer. Mine was taking much too long to grow back. I still had a rough time then getting used to hair that short.

There were two other guys in this company that I befriended. These two guys (whose names I can no longer recall today) had, before their Army days, both played musical instruments in a high-school marching band from their respective hometowns. What stood out in my mind most about these guys was the fact that while we were marching in ranks, their actual movements greatly resembled (you guessed it!) those of high school marching bands, of course! I was certain that their style of marching was definitely *not* what the U.S. Army would approve of. I kept thinking that any day these guys would be noticed by the officers or NCOs in authority and would be reprimanded for it. But that never happened.

One of these guys had a girlfriend back home that he lovingly referred to as *Sloopy*. The name came from a popular Rock 'n' Roll tune of that day recorded by a group called *The McCoys* from Dayton, Ohio. Once on an overnight pass, we three guys went into the city of Augusta together, stayed at a *Quality Courts Motel*, got bored with little to see or do in town, and returned to the barracks early the next day.

If I expected eight full weeks of mild southern weather here at Fort Gordon, I was in for dire disappointment. On Sunday night, **30-January-1966**, only nine days after our arrival here, the overnight temperature plunged to a low of only **six degrees above zero!** It would be our coldest night by far here at Fort Gordon.

I was on the duty roster late that night for *Fire Watch/Barracks Guard* duty, and took my shift at the scheduled time. This meant that I had to pull a two-hour shift of shoveling coal into the furnace while still keeping watch over the barracks. It was not only a lonely job, it was also very dirty one.

The furnace room in each barrack was accessed only from the outside of the building. I had bundled up warm before going out there, and sat on a folding chair inside the furnace room. Then about every fifteen minutes or so, I'd go back inside and take a slow walk through the barracks to "keep watch" as I was supposed to.

A little later back out in the furnace room, I got restless and stood up to look around. I noticed that over the years, men who had passed through here had left their initials carved on the walls. One man's initials were dated sometime in 1944. Then I noticed someone had also carved the famous phrase, **KILROY WAS HERE!** I wondered where it originated. I learned many years later in my World War II research that Kilroy was a real person.

James J. Kilroy was a rivet inspector at the *Fore River Shipyard* in Quincy, Massachusetts during World War II. While working, he discovered that his inspection chalk marks were often missing on work he had previously checked. He learned that other workers had removed them hoping that their work would be counted twice. Upon learning this, he began writing the words *KILROY WAS HERE* after each inspection. Then as ships carrying this cargo departed for places where the war was being fought, Kilroy's name became famous everywhere. All around the world GIs started writing it, painting it and carving the phrase everywhere. Even the Germans wondered who in the hell Kilroy was.

About fifteen minutes before the end of my shift, *S.O.P. (Standard Operating Procedure)* called for me to go back inside the barracks and wake up my relief man. I did, and when he came downstairs to relive me, I happily went back upstairs to my bunk. (For the record, I do not recall today who my relief man was that night.) My face and hands were absolutely grimy from the coal dust, and I certainly needed a shower, but I was just too darned tired to bother. So deciding that the shower would have to wait until morning, I hit the sack and snuggled in under the wool O.D. (Olive Drab) blankets. As luck would have it, the overnight temperature plunged all the way down to just six degrees Fahrenheit.

Early the next morning, Monday, 31-January-1966, I was awakened by a lot of yelling, cussing and commotion in the barracks. As soon as my head emerged from under the warm and cozy blankets, I noticed that the air was much colder on my face than I thought it should be. I sprang from the top bunk, and when my bare feet hit the floor, I needed no further explanation for the all the excitement.

Every Butt can in the barracks was frozen! When I went downstairs to take the much-needed shower, I noticed further that **all the toilets, sinks, and showers were frozen too.** Sometime during the night, some poor slob, whose duty followed after mine, had fallen asleep on the job and failed to wake *his* relief man. Not only did the fire in the furnace die out, but the hot water heater eventually shut down as well.

As I recall, Captain Waldrop came into the barracks that morning and informed us that there would be no training that day. If the person responsible is reading this today, please know that I am making no judgments here. Since that day I kept thinking . . . . *But for the grace of God, it could have been* me *that had fallen asleep and failed to wake my relief man.*

Then just before Captain Waldrop turned to walk out of the barracks, the dark soot on my face and hands had caught his attention. He came over and stopped in front of me for a moment to make a comment of it and then left. I knew that I'd remember this experience for years to come. But from that day onward, no one ever fell asleep on *Fire Watch/Barracks Guard* duty.

As part of our Military Police Training, we were schooled in the proper use of the U.S. Army's .45 caliber ***Colt Automatic Pistol M-1911.*** This weapon was designed by John Moses Browning in 1911 and was used through two world wars and the Korean conflict. The sidearm weighed 2.44 pounds fully loaded including the seven-round detachable magazine. It had a very powerful kick when fired, and with a muzzle velocity rated at 800 feet per second, its maximum effective range was listed at 75 yards. But beyond that range, its accuracy was questionable. Over the lifetime of the weapon, the U.S. Military had procured about 2.7 million of them.

On 18-February-1966, I was among the three trainees who scored the lowest on the qualifying pistol range with a score of 319. But try as I might, I just couldn't seem to hit the broad side of a barn with the damned thing!

For the most part we had Sundays off here too, although I do not recall ever attending Catholic Mass at Fort Gordon. Sunday meant long lines at the pay phones here too but by this time, we all expected that.

Another memorable day stands out in my mind regarding those days at Fort Gordon. Each day when we marched over to the **Mess Hall** in ranks, we were always required to **"Ground" our equipment** outside before entering. This meant that our headgear along with any other equipment that we carried here must not be brought into the Mess Hall. Upon order, we had to place these items on the ground at our immediate right, then proceed in a single file and in an orderly manner into the hall.

On this particular morning after grounding our helmet liners outside (which was the only gear we carried that day), we proceeded into the Mess Hall as always. But this time as luck would have it, when I finished my breakfast, I happened to be the very *last* one out of the Mess Hall from Company K.

As you may have already guessed by now, there was not a helmet liner in sight. Some jerk had stolen the damned thing. I must have looked like a damn fool standing there as I spurted out a few colorful words at the air around me. I tried going back into the Mess Hall on the off chance that someone would be waiting just inside the door with it and simply hand it to me. But that didn't happen of course.

Giving up the search at the Mess Hall, I finally and went back to the barracks. Then I casually walked down the isles both upstairs and down in both barracks buildings trying to find someone with an "extra" helmet liner. And of course, that effort didn't work either.

Not long afterward, when the time came to "fall-in" outside to begin the day's activities, I stood in my usual spot near the back of the ranks. While everyone else wore helmet liners as required for the day's training, I stood there wearing my O.D.-colored baseball cap. I don't know what ever made me think that I could "get away with it." I must have stood out in the group like a floating turd in a punchbowl!

It took Captain Waldrop no more than about twenty seconds to notice me. How can I describe the look on his face when his eyes locked on mine from thirty feet away? He came directly through the ranks and stopped in front of me, with his nose only four inches away from mine. I tried to explain to the captain what had happened, but it was no use. In short, I was ordered to go to the Supply Room immediately and purchase a new one. I was so damned angry, that I could have spit nails. But I was helpless as to what to do about it. If today the guilty party is reading this, please know that I forgive you. All I ask is that you "go and sin no more!"

The **Night Compass Course** was also burned well into my memory. This training was unique. After several hours of classroom instruction during the daytime on how to navigate at night with a U.S. Army compass, we were finally given our chance to prove that we could do it.

We were brought out to a wooded area on the outskirts of Fort Gordon just after dark one night and dropped off at the edge of the woods. We were instructed that we had about thirty minutes to find our way through the woods and emerge at a pre-selected gathering point on the other side. It didn't seem like it would be too tough a task to complete as the woods were not very hilly. I believe that most of the guys felt quite comfortable about pulling it off. However, just before we were given the go-ahead to enter the woods, we were instructed that there was to be no smoking in the woods and absolutely no yelling.

Well . . . you guessed it again! The woods soon became filled with what looked like dozens of "fireflies" from all the cigarettes burning! What's more, there was a lot of hollering, *"Hey, This is the way!"* and *"Yo! Over here!"* or *"Follow me!"* I have no idea how any of the others fared on this particular exercise, but as for me . . . I scored a big "0" for the day.

We were given a military **Driver's Training** class as part of our Military Police schooling. It was here that we were introduced to the U.S. Army's new **M-151** Jeep. This was a one-quarter-ton utility vehicle designed by the *Ford Motor Company* in 1951. It was intended to replace its World War II predecessor, the **M-38.**

The new M-151 was shorter in height than the M-38. It was also wider and had a longer wheelbase. Production of the M-151 began in 1960 and ended eighteen years later in 1978 with most of them built by the *Ford Motor Company* and *General Motors*. They carried a 141-cubic-inch 4-cylinder engine putting out 71 horsepower at 4000 rpm. Weighing about 2400 pounds with a 4-speed manual transmission, it was 4-wheel drive capable and had a maximum speed of about 66 miles per hour.

We were also instructed in the proper use of the U.S. Army's **Military Police Radio.** I recall during classroom instruction that we used the name *Green Timer* as a "call sign" during class exercises. We would say over the radio something like, *"Green-Timer, this is Green-Timer One, Over."* Then we'd wait for a reply. As I recall, we practiced different scenarios with the radio until we had the procedure down pat.

But today one thing stands out in my mind after all these years about learning *Military Police Radio Procedure*: We were taught to *always* remember that a radio transmission was ended by simply saying, *"Out."* But we were *never* to say, *"Over and Out."* It was burned into my mind back then and to this day I have never forgotten it. The transmission was either turned *"Over"* to the other party, or it was ended by saying, *"Out."* But under *no* circumstances is it *ever* "Over *and* Out." How many times over the years since then have we watched old movies about the U.S. military and heard the actor recite the phrase, *"Over and Out"*? That always irritated me.

We also learned about the ***Military Police Radio 10-Codes.*** We weren't really expected to memorize the entire list as there were fifty of them in all. They went like this:

Military Police Radio 10-Codes

10-1 MP needs assistance

10-2 Ambulance needed (urgent)

10-3 Motor vehicle accident

10-4 Wrecker requested

10-5 Ambulance requested (non emergency)

10-6 Send civilian police

10-7 Pick up prisoner

10-8 Subject in custody

10-9 Send MP prisoner van

10-10 Escort / Transport

10-11 In service

10-12 Out of service

10-13 Repeat last message

10-14 Your location

10-15 Proceed to

10-16 Report by land line

10-17 Return to station / Headquarters

10-18 Assignments completed

10-19 Contact or call

10-20 Relay to

10-21 Time check

10-22 Fire

10-23 Disturbance

10-24 Suspicious person

10-25 Stolen / Abandoned vehicle

10-26 Serious accident

10-27 Radio check

10-28 Loud and clear

10-29 Signal weak

10-30 Request assistance (non emergency)

10-31 Request investigator(s)

10-32 Request MP Duty Officer

10-33 Stand by

10-34 Cancel last message

10-35 Chow / Meal (some use 10-99)

10-36 Are there any messages?

10-37 Send your message

10-38 Relief / Change

10-39 Check vehicles or building

10-40 Send back-up patrol

10-41 MP down

10-42 Suspicious gathering of personnel

10-43 Send Explosive Ordnance Disposal

10-44 Require the following items (list)

10-45 Stay clear / Avoid the following area

10-46 Latrine check (some use 10-99 or 98)

10-47 (Varies by MP Station)

10-48 (Varies by MP Station)

10-49 (Varies by MP Station)

10-50 Change to another frequency

Along with the MP Radio 10-Codes, we were also expected to learn how to properly *pronounce* the alphabet and numerals when making radio transmissions.

This was also stressed as important for us to learn. After all, we would not want to mistake the letter "B" for the letter "P" as they sounded very similar when spoken over a radio. They went like this:

Military Police Phonetic Alphabet and Numerals

A—Alpha (Al fah)	N—November (No vem ber)	1—Wun
B—Bravo (Brah voh)	O—Oscar (Oss car)	2—Too
C—Charlie (Char lee)	P—Papa (Pah pah)	3—Thuh-ree
D—Delta (Del tah)	Q—Quebec (Keh beck)	4—Fo-wer
E—Echo (Eck oh)	R—Romeo (Row me oh)	5—Fi-yiv
F—Foxtrot (Foks trot)	S—Sierra (See air rah)	6—Six
G—Golf (Golf)	T—Tango (Tang go)	7—Seven
H—Hotel (Ho tell)	U—Uniform (You nee form)	8—Ate
I—India (In dee ah)	V—Victor (Vic tor)	9—Niner
J—Juliet (Jew lee ett)	W—Whiskey (Wiss key)	0—Zero
K—Kilo (Kee loh)	X—X-ray (Ecks ray)	
L—Lima (Lee mah)	Y—Yankee (Yang kee)	
M—Mike	Z—Zulu (Zoo loo)	

Here at Fort Gordon we experienced more boring classroom instruction along with more sleeping in class. We also learned *Military Map Reading* as well as how to read military motor vehicle markings and how to become a *Trained Observer.* Our MP training continued here too with a full **18 hours of** *Hand-to-Hand Combat* instruction and *Judo Training.* I enjoyed this as it gave me the feeling that I had become 129 pounds of *deadly* lethal weapon!

We were familiarized with the paperwork associated with Military Police duties. Among some of the forms we used were:

DA Form 19-24 (1-Sep-62)—*Statement*
DA Form 19-31 (1-Dec-62)—*Military Police Receipt for Property*
DA Form 19-32 (1-Sep-60)—*Military Police Report*
DA Form 19-68 (1-Jan-61)—*Military Police Traffic Accident Investigation*
DA Form 2400 (1-Jan-64)—*Equipment Utilization Record*
DA Form 2404 (1-Apr-62)—*Equipment Inspection and Maintenance Worksheet*

And of course we were all familiar with the:

DD Form 1408 (1-Dec-62)—*Armed Forces Traffic Ticket*

Although there was absolutely nothing wrong with the old suitcase that I brought with me from home, I finally decided to buy a new AWOL bag at the PX here anyway. While AWOL bags are actually considered as small pieces of luggage, they did not in reality *resemble* traditional suitcases. It's just that by this time, many of us preferred the "classy" new look of carrying an AWOL bag, as opposed to the rather long-established dull look of toting a traditional suitcase. After all, we were proud members of America's fighting men and therefore had a tough image to live up to.

I don't really recall much about the ***Night Stick Training*** that we had. But I *do* recall being taught that the *Night Stick* was supposed to be considered as "an extension of the arm." Then we were shown how to get an irate suspect to "come along peaceably" when he was standing in front of us. We did this by utilizing a pivot of our wrist causing the night stick to whack him in the testicles!

We were also effectively trained in such things as ***Land Navigation, Riot Control Tactics*** and of course, the proper methods of ***Directing Traffic***. (Several months later I would be grateful that I never fell asleep during instruction on *Directing Traffic*.)

As the days went by here the nights were still cool, although not as bad as that night the thermometer fell to six degrees above zero. But during our last days here at Fort Gordon, the temperature rose into the 60s and 70s through the daytime.

While it may seem to some that since my induction back in November, I had become a general screw-up in the U.S. Army. This was not really the case at all. Except for the *Night Compass Course* that I certainly failed miserably, I did do *exceptionally* well in three other areas of my Military Police training. On ***Inspections*** during A.I.T., I ended up with a respectable final score of 92%.—(Not too shabby if you ask me!) On ***Driver Qualification***, I finished with a score of 99%. And on ***Land Navigation***, I totally out did myself with a perfect score of 100%.

Graduation Photos were also taken here at MP School. But I was surprised to learn that the Dress Green jackets we all posed in that day were completely open in the back. Because we were all wearing our fatigue uniforms for training that day, most of us just slipped into the dress jacket from behind for the photo. (The trousers for the dress uniform were of course not needed, as the photos were only taken from the chest up.) The brass buttons on the jacket as well as the police whistle were badly tarnished and the leather was not that well shined, but at least the white *saucer cap* hat looked great, I thought. In spite of all this however, I was still quite satisfied with my photo this time and decided to order a copy.

SATURDAY, 12-March-1966—Graduation Day.

Graduation Day dawned with a low of 37 degrees in the morning and topped off by mid afternoon with a high of 75. On this day, 128 of us from K-10-4 were handed *Special Order #62* from *HQs, U.S. ARMY SCHOOL / TRAINING CENTER, FORT GORDON.* These orders stated that we were being released from Company K, of the 10th Battalion in the 4th Training Brigade, and that we would be assigned to the **218th Military Police Company** in the Dominican Republic.

I left Fort Gordon with orders to report to my next duty station on 18-March-1965. This time, I had six days of *Delay Enroute* before I was to report to *Fort Bragg*, North Carolina.

On the bus headed north to Detroit, I took a window seat about two or three rows back on the right side when facing forward. The only aspect of this trip home that I still recall today was that another passenger (an old lady sitting across the isle from me to the far left) didn't like me smoking cigarettes, even though I was seated next to an open window. Can you remember the days when smoking was accepted nearly everywhere?

In July 1975, the Military Police School was finally relocated and moved to Fort McClellan, Alabama. During its twenty-seven years at Fort Gordon, the MP School trained some 160,000 personnel. Then in May 1999, the MP School moved once again to its present location at Fort Leonard Wood, Missouri.

Today, Fort Gordon is often called the *Home of the Signal Corps,* and is considered as one of the largest communications and electronics facilities in the world.

Fort Gordon, GA as seen Today from 30,000 ft above

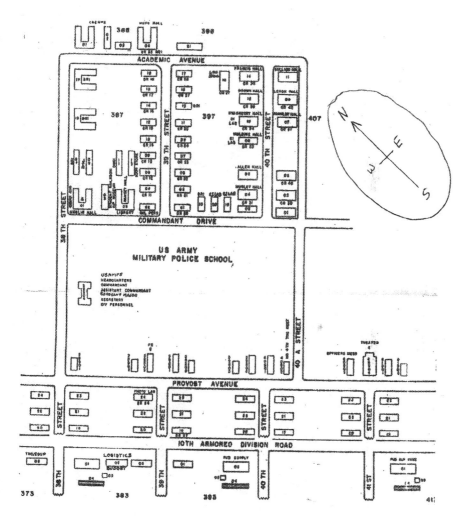

MP School at Fort Gordon (Then)

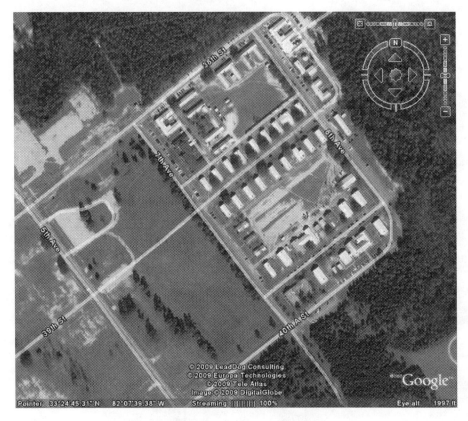

MP School Area, as seen Today from 2000 ft above

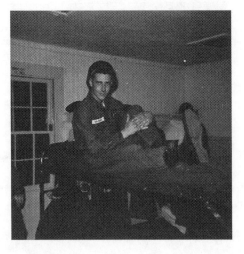

Tom O at MP School, upstairs, first top bunk on right

Thomas V. Marston at Fort Gordon

Edward W. Mitchell

M-1911 Colt .45 Caliber Automatic Pistol

ARMED FORCES TRAFFIC TICKET ☐ WARNING (See Remarks below)

The person named below committed traffic violation set forth at the time and location, and on date shown, and was issued this traffic ticket.

NAME (Last - First - Middle Initial)
JONES, Joe

RANK/GRADE	DATE OF BIRTH	SERVICE NUMBER
Sgt	31 May 40	RA 18408357

ORGANIZATION OR ADDRESS Hq & Hq Co,
41st Sig Bn, Ft Gordon, Georgia

DRIVER LICENSE NUMBER 51352   ISSUING AUTHORITY (State or XXXXX) Georgia

MAKE OR TYPE OF VEH	STATE LICENSE OR REGIS NUMBER	INSTL TAG NUMBER
4-dr sed 57 Ford	Ga. 1967-2	176

DATE (Day-Month-Year) This date   TIME 0900   LOCATION 4th Div Rd & 21st Street

VIOLATION

SPEED OVER LIMIT
X 58 mph in a 40 mph zone

5 - 10 MPH	11 - 15 MPH	OVER 15 MPH
IMPROPER LEFT TURN	NO SIGNAL	CUT CORNER	FROM WRONG LANE
IMPROPER RIGHT TURN	NO SIGNAL	INTO WRONG LANE	FROM WRONG LANE
DISOBEYED TFC SIGNAL (When light turned red)	PAST MIDDLE INTERSECTION	MIDDLE OF INTERSECTION	HAD NOT REACHED INTERSECTION
DISOBEYED STOP SIGN	STOPPED WRONG PLACE	FAILED TO STOP	ROLLED/SPED THROUGH
	AT INTERSECTION	CUT-IN	WRONG SIDE OF PAVEMENT
IMPROPER PASSING AND LANE USAGE	BETWEEN TFC	ON RIGHT	ON HILL
	LANE STRADDLING	WRONG LANE	ON CURVE
FOL TOO CLOSELY	OTHER VIOLATIONS (Describe)		
FAIL TO YIELD			

PARKING OVERTIME | PROHIBITED AREA | DOUBLE PARKING | OTHER (Describe in Remarks)

CONDITIONS THAT INCREASED SERIOUSNESS OF VIOLATION

SLIPPERY PAVEMENT	X RAIN	AREA	TRAFFIC ACCIDENT TYPE OF ACCIDENT:
	SNOW	BUSINESS	☐ PD ☐ PI
	ICE	INDUSTRIAL	☐ FATAL
	NIGHT	RURAL	
DARKNESS	X FOG	SCHOOL	PEDESTRIAN
	SNOW	X RESIDENTIAL	VEHICLE
OTHER TRAFFIC PRESENT	CROSS	HIGHWAY TYPE	HIT FIXED OBJECT
	ONCOMING		RIGHT ANGLE
	PEDESTRIAN	X 2-LANE	SIDESWIPE
	SAME DIRECTION	3-LANE	REAR END
CAUSED PERSON TO DODGE	PEDESTRIAN	4-LANE	INTERSECTION
	DRIVER	4-LANE DIVIDED	HEAD ON
	JUST MISSED ACDT		RAN OFF ROADWAY

REMARKS
Anything needing clarification - otherwise, NONE. *Sample*

NAME OF PERSON ISSUING TRAFFIC TICKET
Your Payroll Signature

ORGANIZATION AND INSTALLATION PMO, Ft Gordon, Georgia   RANK/GRADE Your Rank

DD FORM 1408, 1 DEC 62   REPLACES DA FORM 19-93, 1 NOV 54, AND AF FORM 1311, WHICH ARE OBSOLETE.   CO of violator or appropriate civil agency

NAME (Last - First - Middle Initial)
TICKET NUMBER A 762652

DD Form 1408 (Armed Forces Traffic Ticket)

Thomas E. Oblinger, MP

Chapter 4

218th *MP Company, (USFORDOMREP)*

FRIDAY, 18-March-1966—381st **Replacement Company, Fort Bragg, North Carolina.**

On Friday, 18-March-1966, I arrived at *Fort Bragg, North Carolina* at 1230 Hours in the afternoon and reported as ordered to **Building #38405.** This was located on the eastern side of the post south of Woodruff Street running between 3rd and 5th Streets. This was the HQs office for the ***381st Replacement Company.*** There were a total of 128 of us here from the graduating class of K-10-4 at Fort Gordon.

The origin of the 381st Replacement Company actually dates back to World War II. During that time U.S. Army replacement depots, battalions, and companies, often referred to as *Repple Depples* or *Repo Depos*, were set up to receive and process fresh new manpower to the front line combat units. Here too at Fort Bragg, the 381st was organized and set up in a similar manner. The 381st would be our "stepping stone" to a Military Police unit in immediate need of manpower to replace other men whose **E.T.S. *(Estimated Termination of Service)*** date was drawing near. (Most recently, the 381st was deployed by *N.A.T.O.* and served in *Operation Joint Endeavor* in Bosnia. Today, it's still active serving in the Army Reserves.)

This morning the air was cool and the temperature was in the low 40s. Once again, the six days of *Delay Enroute* just didn't seem quite long enough. But it was still good to be back home again, even if it was only for a few days. Not much was happening on this day while the afternoon temperature rose into the low 70s. But this sure as hell beat the awful cold and wet weather we endured back in *Basic* and *AIT.* We were to remain here until our final movement orders were received and transportation arrangements could be made to our next duty assignment. We therefore had to spend the night here at Fort Bragg.

SATURDAY, 19-March-1966—218th Military Police Company, (USFORDOMREP).

The next morning, Saturday, 19-March-1966, while carrying new orders along with our own *Personnel File,* we all knew where we were headed. The orders indicated that we were destined for an assignment to the 218th Military Police Company stationed in the Dominican Republic. While *Geography* and *History* were never among my favorite subjects during school years, I found myself wondering at that time where in the world the Dominican Republic was located. Though I never voiced this aloud back then, I found myself wondering how many of the others wondered the same thing. Sometime before noon we were driven by buses to **Pope Air Force Base** immediately northwest of Fort Bragg.

Officially established by the War Department in 1919, Pope Air Force Base ranked as one of the oldest installations in the U.S. Air Force. It was named after 1st Lt. Harley Halbert Pope, who was killed earlier that same year when his *JN-4 Jenny* biplane crashed into the *Cape Fear River* near the town of Fayetteville, North Carolina.

Upon arrival at Pope AFB we were immediately driven out to the edge of the airfield where the buses came to a stop near the flight line. Sitting majestically on the tarmac about fifty yards ahead of us, was a large *U.S. Air Force C-130* aircraft.

The **Lockheed C-130 "Hercules"** was among the most rugged and versatile tactical transport aircraft ever built by the United States. It was designed by the U.S. Air Force *Tactical Air Command (T.A.C.)* in 1955 and first entered service in 1960. Powered by four powerful *Allison T-56* turboprop engines and a crew of four, its length was 98 feet with a wing span of 133 feet. Its height was 38 feet at the tail and its weight (empty) was 75,331 pounds. Other statistics showed a maximum take-off weight of 155,000 pounds, a maximum cruising speed of 374 mph at 20,000 feet, with a ceiling of 33,000 feet, and a range of 2,487 miles.

The cargo bay measured approximately 41 feet in length, 10 feet in width, and 9 feet in height. Both the cockpit flight station and the cargo bay could be pressurized to maintain cabin pressure at higher altitudes. (Although fully updated now with modern technology, this fine aircraft is still in worldwide use today.)

We waited and watched while this monstrous aircraft was being loaded with all our duffel bags and AWOL bags. Following this, a U.S. Army M-151 jeep was driven up the rear tailgate ramp. It was loaded into the cargo bay and securely tied down.

We were next to be loaded on the aircraft, and I began to feel a little nervous. Not just because I had never flown on an airplane before in my life (as I had not), but because it was so unbelievably huge! *"Oh my God!"* I exclaimed out loud. *"How in the hell is this damned thing ever going to get off the ground with all of us—and all of that?"* It looked scientifically impossible to me.

We were finally moved on board and packed into the aircraft in a manner that someone referred to as *balls to the walls.* I was seated against the left side of the craft, which was called the *Port* side when facing forward. My back was to the outside wall which was called a *Bulkhead.*

In due time, we slowly taxied down to the end of the runway. While we waited there for clearance to take off, my stomach began to flutter.

After a few moments we began rolling,—slowly at first, then swiftly building momentum and speed. I was gripping my knees tightly with both hands as the nose of the aircraft lifted high into the air. It seemed as though it was standing almost vertical and before I knew it, we were airborne! I breathed a slight sigh of relief, but was still unable to relax. After about fifteen minutes or so, we had leveled off somewhere between 10,000 and 20,000 feet. (The exact altitude at which we flew is still unknown to me today.)

It couldn't have been more than thirty minutes after takeoff, and we were already out over the Atlantic. That was when I realized that I needed to take a leak. So I asked a member of the flight crew where to go for this and I was pointed in the right direction. Mounted on a bulkhead (wall) just under a porthole (window) on the starboard (right) side of the aircraft was a small urinal hidden behind a canvas curtain. As I stood there relieving myself, I was forced to hold on to the bulkhead with my free hand. Momentarily, I happened to look out through the porthole—and nearly lost my breath gasping in absolute horror!

I was staring at the far right starboard engine with its propeller standing perfectly still. And far below us . . . only ocean, as far as the eye could see! My knees nearly gave out on me as I stumbled back to the crew member that I spoke to earlier, and calmly reported my observation.

All this time, seated next to me was **John W. Patterson**, another new MP from the graduating class of K-10-4, whose hometown was Kaufman, Texas. John was laughing his ass off and thoroughly enjoying my predicament. The crew member simply and calmly informed me that I had absolutely nothing to fear and explained to me that the pilot was already aware of this small problem. He went on to state that we still had three good engines and that we were already turning back to Pope AFB.

Such was my very first experience *ever* with a "heavier-than-air" flying machine. These things in life we tend to never forget.

Many years later, when I was in the *U.S. Air Force Reserve* at *Selfridge AFB* in Harrison Township, Michigan, I had an opportunity to ride on a C-130 from there to *Eglin AFB* in Florida. This time I asked if I could observe from the cockpit. My request was granted and I stood behind the pilot. He looked quite relaxed on "auto pilot" with both feet up on the "dashboard" and arms folded across his chest. I was fascinated this time with the breath-taking panoramic view of the landscape below. But I felt no fear.

Before too long we had landed back at Pope AFB, changed planes, and were off again into the wild blue yonder. To pass the time after I had relaxed to a degree, I pulled out a paperback book I had picked up somewhere along the way and began reading. It was a collection of short stories made famous by the author, *Rod Serling*. I recall reading one called, *The Monsters Are Due On Maple Street*. To further pass the time on this flight, we were issued a box lunch that included sandwiches, a piece of fruit, a bag of potato chips, and a one-pint carton of milk. I had no complaints about this as I was getting hungry.

We flew southeast out over the Atlantic Ocean and onward through the *Bermuda Triangle*. That fact alone might have sent me off the deep end back then, but at that time I knew very little about that famous stretch of water. After a 3.7-hour uneventful flight of about 1,400 miles, we arrived at a little place called **San Isidro Airfield.** This was about 8.9 miles east of the city of **Santo Domingo in the Dominican Republic.**

As for why we were sent to the Dominican Republic, one had to know something about its turbulent history. It was a mountainous country. Its climate was mostly tropical with temperatures ranging between 74 to 95 degrees or more by day with nights a lot cooler. The average rainfall was about 60 inches per year, and its population in 1966 was 3,750,000 spread over 18,704 square miles. Its Capital of Santo Domingo alone had a population then of 522,500. About 20% of the population was Black with about 15% White and the rest was a mix of Black, White and Indian. The Dominican Republic encompasses the eastern two thirds of the island of Hispaniola while Haiti occupies its western third. The country was primarily Spanish speaking.

Christopher Columbus discovered the island of Hispaniola in 1492, and four years later in 1496, his brother Bartholomew founded the city of Santo Domingo. Throughout its violent history the country suffered many wars, revolutions, and dictatorships. The strife continued on down through the years until 1916 when the U.S. sent Marines in to restore order. The Marines were withdrawn eight years later in 1924.

In 1930 **General Rafael Leonidas Trujillo Molina** took power in the Dominican Republic by revolt, and remained dictator there until his brother Hector Trujillo took office. Early in 1960 **Joaquin Balaguer** succeeded him, but Rafael Trujillo remained the military dictator for a few more months until his assassination in May of that year.

Balaguer tried to hold his position, but there was a lot of popular unrest at the time. In 1962, an opposing group of dissidents set up a ruling council. The first free elections were held in December of that year putting **Juan Bosch** in office as the newly elected President. However, he was deposed only eleven months later in September by a military coup. Then only two months later in November 1963, U.S. President John F. Kennedy was assassinated. Immediately Vice-President **Lyndon B. Johnson** was sworn in as the 36th U.S. President. Then in April 1965, another uprising took place in the Dominican Republic to reinstate Bosch, and a civil war erupted as a result.

By this time, the U.S. had had enough. Immediately, President Lyndon B. Johnson sent the Marines in again along with elements of the 82nd Airborne Division following soon after from Fort Bragg. The U.S. Joint Chiefs of Staff would thereafter call this *Operation Power Pack.* **Their mission was to restore order and help prevent a Communist take-over of the country**, thereby preventing "another Cuba" in our hemisphere. At this time, the evacuation of Americans from the island had begun and by 17-May-1965, peak U.S. military strength in the region had reached 24,000. In order to solve this problem, the U.S. then began working together with the *O.A.S. (Organization of American States).*

The OAS Charter was first adopted in 1948 by 21 nations of this hemisphere including the U.S. and the Dominican Republic. Their purpose was to work with the U.S. to promote peace, justice, and solidarity in our hemisphere. Today 35 nations are involved in the OAS.

In May 1965, the OAS sent military forces to mediate between both opposing factions in the Dominican Republic. To carry this out, the OAS established what became known to us as the *I.A.P.F. (Inter-American Peace Force).* The IAPF then consisted of military forces from six American nations. These were: Brazil, Costa Rica, Honduras, Nicaragua, Paraguay, and the United States.

Under the IAPF, the *United States Forces Dominican Republic (USFORDOMREP)* was commanded by Lt. General Bruce R. Palmer, Jr. This force consisted of the 82nd Airborne Division (from Fort Bragg, North Carolina), the 4th Marine Expeditionary Brigade, the 5th Logistics Command, the 7th Special Forces Group, the 42nd Field Hospital (from Fort Knox, Kentucky), the **503rd**

Military Police Battalion (also from Fort Bragg), and other elements of the U.S. Army, Air Force, Navy, and Marines.

While here, the 503rd MP Battalion provided direct support for the IAPF troops on a siege and secure mission in the *"Rebel Zone."* The four-month-long civil war finally ended in August 1965, and in October of that year, the 503rd MP Battalion (leaving Company C behind) returned to Fort Bragg.

It was a bloody war for sure, but sporadic fighting continued well into 1966. In early February 1966, Company C moved from *Sans Souci* (at the eastern side of the mouth of the Ozama River) to its new location in Santo Domingo, behind the Headquarters of the USFORDOMREP. **This Headquarters was the former dictator Trujillo's old residence.**

A month later in early March, all of the personnel of Company C, 503rd MP Battalion, were redesignated as the U.S. Army's *218ᵗʰ Military Police Company.* Its mission here was to patrol the city of Santo Domingo and the surrounding areas primarily in a peacekeeping capacity.

From San Isidro Airfield, we all boarded 2½-ton trucks and took a highway headed west. (A U.S. Army 2½-ton truck was referred to then as a *Deuce-and-a-half.*) Though this highway was actually called *Avenida de las Americas* (Avenue of the Americas) on local maps, we would all refer to it as *San Isidro Highway.* After traveling about eight miles, we came to a bridge spanning the Ozama River flowing southward into the Caribbean Sea. The *Duarte Bridge* was named after *Juan Pablo Duarte (1813-1876),* who was known as the *Father of Dominican Independence.*

Shortly after crossing the Ozama River, we passed an old pink colored building on the right side of the road that had been shot up and sustained serious damage during the hostilities. Our convoy then split up, and we were never sure why this happened at the time. Some of the trucks continued on and eventually came to a stop at the Dominican Fairgrounds at the far southwestern edge of the city along the coastline. They would spend their first night there.

After moving another 2.6 miles southwest of the Duarte Bridge, the rest of the convoy (with me included) turned left into our new campsite. Our arrival at that time brought the strength of the 218ᵗʰ MP Company up to 4 officers and 209 enlisted men.

The **218ᵗʰ was set up on the north grounds of the Headquarters, USFORDOMREP.** Sitting 165 feet above sea level, this was also the location of the **Military Police Headquarters** which was referred to as the *P.M.O. (Provost Marshal's Office).* Though we often referred to this building as the *"Palace"* back then, it was not to be mistaken for the ***Dominican National Palace*** (Capitol Building) located about seven blocks over to the east.

The main gate to the 218th was on an avenue called *Avenida Dr. Pedro Henriquez Urena.* Directly across the street to the north of the 218th was a 350-bed maternity hospital called *Maternidad Nuestra Senora de la Altagracia (Our Lady of Altagracia).* The National Police Headquarters was about two blocks north from there. Close by was the U.S. Embassy within walking distance about one block southeast from there at the northwest corner of *Calle Cesar Nicolas Penson* and *Calle Leopoldo Navarro.* (*Calle* in Spanish means *Street.*)

Captain Dennis T. Ellis commanded the 218th MP Company at this time along with **First Sergeant Amos Terry.** For the next five months our new mailing address here would be written as: *218th MP Company, A.P.O. New York 09478.* (*A.P.O.* stands for *Army Post Office.*) *Our* job upon arrival here at the 218th, was to replace many of the men whose E.T.S. (Estimated Termination of Service) date was growing near.

The next morning, **Sunday, 20-March-1966, 31 more enlisted men from the class of K-10-4** arrived here including **John Patterson.** This brought the strength count of enlisted men to 240 for the 218th MP Company. This same day, 24 men in the company were also promoted to Specialist-4 (Pay grade E-4). **Captain Ellis left for home on a 10-day leave** while **1st Lt. Terrance M. Fiore assumed temporary command of the 218th** in his absence.

Captain Dennis T. Ellis was a 29-year-year old married man from Columbia, South Carolina, and was among those who came to "Dom Rep" along with the 503rd MP Battalion in May of 1965. Captain Ellis was described as an idealist, a super person and a soldier's soldier. But most of all, he was considered as being "fair and just" in his reasoning. He also believed in his senior NCOs and trusted them to run the company efficiently. And they never let him down. Dennis also loved to be involved in the company sports of the 218th.

After departing, Dennis flew back to Pope AFB and Fort Bragg where his wife Ursula was waiting to meet him. He hadn't seen her in ten months. She had driven 148 miles up from South Carolina with their two daughters to pick him up.

The **218th MP Company was originally constituted in July 1943** in the U.S. Army as the *1298th MP Company, (Aviation).* The 1298th was activated a month later at Camp Ripley, Minnesota. During World War II, the 1298th served under the 793rd MP Battalion. In February 1944, the 793rd left the U.S. for training in Scotland. Then in August of that year, they crossed the English Channel and moved into France.

Serving under the 793ʳᵈ MP Battalion, the 1298ᵗʰ MP Company performed traffic security duty for the famed **Red Ball Express** in northern France. This was a vast trucking organization set up by the U.S. Army's Quartermaster Corps, in a hasty effort to supply the fast-moving Allied armies until November 1944. (My father, PFC Raymond James Oblinger, in September 1944, drove a truck on the *Red Ball Express* in northern France before being assigned as a replacement to an infantry regiment on the front line in Patton's Third Army.)

In December 1944, the 1298ᵗʰ MP Company was sent north to protect and defend the vital Allied seaport of Antwerp, Belgium, and remained there until *V.E. Day* (8-May-1945). One month later in June 1945, the 793rd moved south to the port of Marseilles, France in preparation for shipment to the Pacific Theater. But following *V.J. Day* (2-September-1945), the battalion remained there providing security for the port. The 1298ᵗʰ then returned to the U.S. and was deactivated at Camp Patrick Henry, Virginia in October 1945.

Twenty years later in October 1965, the 1298ᵗʰ was redesignated as the *218ᵗʰ Military Police Company* and was activated several weeks later on 10-December in the Dominican Republic. Then in early March 1966, the ranks of the newly activated 218ᵗʰ MP Company were filled with men from Company C of the 503ʳᵈ MP Battalion. The 503ʳᵈ (less Company C) had just returned to Fort Bragg in the U.S. at that time.

My twenty-first birthday came and went on **Monday, 28-March-1966** without fanfare. Life moved onward for me as always.

On Wednesday, **30-March-1966, Captain Ellis returned from leave** and resumed his command of the 218ᵗʰ. The next day, Thursday, **31-March, Sergeant Amos Terry was officially promoted to E-8.**

Six days later on **6-April, Lt. Fiore departed at 1230 Hours for home on a nine-day leave.** He couldn't wait to get back to New York and see his parents on Long Island.

1ˢᵗ Sergeant Amos Terry, whose hometown was Elk Valley, Tennessee, was a 35-year-old married man with three children. He had enlisted in the Army in October 1948 and took his Basic Training at Fort Jackson, South Carolina. Later he served with the infantry during the time of the *Korean War* before being trained in Military Police. He had just recently arrived in Dom Rep on 8-August-1965.

With more than seventeen years of loyal service in Olive Drab, Sergeant Amos Terry was well deserving of this promotion. This honor was personally requested and recommended by Captain Dennis Ellis, stating that Sergeant Terry, *"has demonstrated conscientiousness and dependability . . . and has performed his assignments with interest, confidence, and enthusiasm."*

1st Lt. Terrance M. Fiore was a 23-year-old single man from Uniondale, New York. He had also accompanied Captain Ellis to Dom Rep with the 503rd in May 1965. Enlisted in July 1964, Terrance had come through the *R.O.T.C. (Reserve Officer's Training Corps)* program and entered the U.S. Army as a 2nd Lieutenant. Fiore was described as a strict and no-nonsense officer, who was a strong advocate on loyalty. Effective as of 1-February-1966, Lieutenant Fiore was responsible for the *Motor Pool, Record Management, Utilities and Utilization, Air Mobility, Training and Operations, Material Readiness,* and *Communications*. As if that wasn't enough, he was also listed on record as the *Postal Officer, Re-enlistment Officer,* and *Unit CBR Officer*.

As to why Company C of the 503rd was redesignated as the 218th MP Company—none of us new guys new at that time. It wasn't until recently after I actually began writing this story that I was able to learn the reasons for this change.

When the 503rd returned to Fort Bragg in October 1965, leaving Company C in the Dominican Republic, the (then) Battalion Commander assured 1st Sergeant Terry, that he would not forget the men of Company C when the time came around for promotions of senior NCOs. But unfortunately, this was merely a *verbal* agreement at the time. Sergeant Terry knew that enlisted ranks from Private (E-1) up to Sergeant (E-5) could be promoted at Company level, but promoting senior NCOs from E-5 and up needed approval from Battalion HQs and/or above.

Later upon learning that several senior NCOs of the 503rd at Fort Bragg had been promoted while Company C was passed over, Amos Terry became concerned. He flew back to Fort Bragg immediately in order to personally face the Battalion Commander alone. Sergeant Terry was then told in so many words that the Battalion Commander had to look out for those under his direct command there at Fort Bragg. Amos was infuriated, and told the commander that this was an outright violation of their earlier verbal agreement. Terry was certain that, had another witness been present, he might have been charged with disrespect to a superior officer.

When Sergeant Terry returned to the Dominican Republic, he decided to take the matter into his own hands. He contacted the *Department of the Army* in Washington, DC to request a change in organization. Then he placed a call to the

Third Army HQ at Fort Bragg and requested the deactivation of Company C, and permission to transfer its records back to Fort Bragg.

His request was granted. The official ***Change of Command*** ceremony took place in front of the PMO "Palace" in early March 1966, just prior to the arrival of us new guys from MP School. Except for those on duty at that time, the entire unit attended this ritual. This also included the *Provost Marshal* and other members of the USFORDOMREP command staff.

During this thirty-minute ceremony, Company C's *Guidon, Standards and Colors* were replaced by the new ones from the 218th MP Company. There were some brief remarks describing the history of the 218th as well as that of Company C and the 503rd. Shortly afterward, all of the old records of Company C were returned to the 503rd at Fort Bragg along with a few guys headed back there for their ETS. At that time the newly activated 218th Military Police Company was placed under the U.S. Army's newly constituted *16th General Support Group.*

1st Sergeant Amos Terry was a force to be reckoned with in those days. No one at that time could question his dedication when it came to the fair treatment of the men under his command.

Several weeks prior to my arrival in the Dominican Republic from MP School, Company C (prior to becoming the 218th MP Company) was employed to provide escort and security service for the **USO shows** taking place there. Although **Bob Hope** was the main attraction for the USO shows being put on in various places around Santo Domingo, the famous young and vivacious singer, dancer, and actress, **Joey Heatherton** also drew quite a following then.

On **11-April-1966**, shortly after our arrival there, the 218th was called upon for help. The earth-shaking event was a **farewell ceremony for U.S. Ambassador W. Tapley Bennett, Jr.** It was to be held at the Polo Field just west of the *Hotel Embajador* on the southwestern edge of the city. It was quite a ceremony with representatives of several U.S. forces being present. It included a demonstration by the *USA Golden Knights Parachute Team*, a flyby of several U.S. Air Force fighter aircraft, and two U.S. Army M-48 tanks passing by. The 218th was employed to maintain security for certain distinguished visitors, as well as provide traffic and spectator control before, during, and after the scheduled parade.

Situated in the northeast corner of our compound (campsite) was an enclosed temporary ***Transient Stockade*** for U.S. Army prisoners. This was just behind what was once a miniature golf course for the "palace" and measured 36 x 103 feet in total area. The stockade was enclosed by an eight-foot chain link fence and topped off with a three-strand roll of concertina wire. This is a type of barbed or razor wire formed in large coils, which are expanded like a musical concertina. Then overlooking all of this were two enclosed guard towers about ten feet in height. Within two wood-framed, **16 x 32-foot Medium U.S. Army G-P (General Purpose) Tents**, the stockade was set up to handle a maximum of sixteen prisoners. With a capacity of fourteen prisoners in medium custody and two in segregation, over its time there, the stockade usually housed an average of nine prisoners at a time.

The Stockade was initially commanded by 1ˢᵗ Lt. John T. Everett, followed later by 2ⁿᵈ Lt. Forrest Craver. It was fully approved by **Lt. Col. Billy L. Brown, the Provost Marshal for HQs, USFORDOMREP.** Men of the 218th MP Company not only manned the guard towers, but also provided supervision inside the prisoners' living quarters. Initially these guard personnel were assigned on a weekly basis, but due to lack of enough training, this was soon changed to monthly assignments.

1ˢᵗ Lt. John T. Everett was a 24-year-old married man from Knoxville, Tennessee who preferred to be addressed by his middle name Tom. Tom had married a girl named Shirley that he grew up with back home in Knoxville. After playing football in high school, he had earned a degree in education from the *University of Tennessee* where he participated in the ROTC. Just three months after their marriage, he entered the U.S. Army in August 1964 as a 2ⁿᵈ Lieutenant and was assigned to Company C of the 503ʳᵈ MP Battalion at Fort Bragg.

Shortly after his arrival in Dom Rep, Tom Everett, along with a fellow officer and close friend named **Terrance Fiore**, found themselves pulling guard duty at a place called *Check Pointe #3*. This was in the *Rebel Zone* prior to the company moving to its present location.

2ⁿᵈ Lt. Forrest E. Craver, III was a 24-year-old single man from Gettysburg, Pennsylvania who entered the U.S. Army in August 1965. He had taken his ROTC at Dickson College in Carlisle, Pennsylvania, and attended the MP Officers School at Fort Gordon. From there he went on to Airborne training at Fort Benning, Georgia. His first assignment was the 204ᵗʰ MP Company at Fort Sheridan, Illinois, before coming to the 503ʳᵈ at Fort Bragg. During his time in Dom Rep, Lieutenant Craver enjoyed scuba diving on the weekends. This took place off a small island near the Santo Domingo coast. Along with three other divers from the 218ᵗʰ, they harvested lobster and drank beer while gorging themselves on the beach.

After his Army days, Forrest Craver attended a graduate school in social work and then a law school, both in Detroit. He married a hometown girl and had two sons. In the meantime he made a career as a professional fundraising consultant.

During those years, he raised money for the *National Association of Atomic Veterans* as well as the *Agent Orange Campaign* and the *Campaign to Ban Land Mines* for the *Vietnam Veterans of America*. Today he resides in Boulder, Colorado.

As for my sleeping quarters in Dom Rep, initially I was assigned to a tent in the row running parallel to the north perimeter wall of the camp. All tents used for living quarters in this camp were of the **U.S. Army "G-P" (General-Purpose) type—Large**, about 18 feet wide and 52 feet in length (936 square feet in area) with a 12¼-foot height down the center. The side walls were 5½ feet high. Each tent housed about 18 to 20 men. The wood-plank floors in the tents came from building supplies obtained by **Sergeant Whitmill**, one of the original MPs who had come to Dom Rep along with the 503rd.

The north wall of our camp was of masonry construction about eight to ten feet high and roughly one foot thick. At the entrance to our compound was a two-piece hinged wrought iron driveway gate measuring about ten feet wide (five feet per side), and nine feet high. Just inside this gate stood a guard shack made of 2 x 4 wood framework and plywood, measuring about six feet wide, three feet deep and eight feet high with a rolled shingle gable roof. A gate guard would be posted at this gate in three shifts, 24 hours a day, seven days a week.

During our stay in this country we would be sleeping on Army-issued wood-frame canvass folding cots along with an air mattress made from rubberized cotton. For the first few days (and nights) here, we were not issued mosquito nets for our cots. This was an experience to remember. Just after dusk each night mosquitoes would come out in droves. Until we were issued these nets to cover the cots, we would literally be eaten alive by morning. I tried using my sleeping bag for a couple of nights for protection, but by morning I woke in a puddle of sweat. Sleeping bags were often referred to as *Fart Sacks* as far back as World War II primarily due to their smell.

A few days after our arrival, I was moved into a 3rd Platoon tent along the fence line on the eastern side of our compound. I took the second cot on the right just inside the door. A few weeks later, the guy in the first cot was shipped back to the U.S. and I inherited his mosquito net. After that, no one ever moved in to take the first cot and eventually I just took it back to the supply room. Thereafter I had the entire front corner of the tent to myself.

What a relief it was to finally have a net. We made wooden racks from 1 x 2-inch pine boards to be fastened at the head and foot of the cot from which the nets could be draped over for protection. The nets worked great until some joker discovered how to make a blow torch with a can of *Right Guard* spray deodorant in one hand and a *Zippo* cigarette lighter in the other. (At that time *Bic* lighters hadn't yet come into being.) All you had to do back then was to point the can at some poor victim's mosquito net while holding the Zippo under it, and strike! Then *Poof!*—You now had a gaping hole in the net about the size of a basketball. I swear these idiots must have stayed up nights figuring out how to become royal screw-ups.

It was around this time that my brand of cigarettes had changed from *Phillip Morris Commanders* (unfiltered) to *Winston* filtered. Then utilizing an empty *Fallstaff Beer* can as a Butt Can, I hung it from my cot with a bracket that I had made from a length of coat-hanger wire. That was one of many tricks I had learned from my father. Dad was a real artist when it came to creating useful things from coat-hanger wire. In fact for his entire life, he was an all around "jack of all trades."

Most of the senior NCOs of the 218th billeted in the northern most tent closest to the stockade along the eastern fence line. **The Junior Officers took up residence at the *Hispaniola Hotel.*** Built in 1956, it was located at the northeast corner of the intersection of Avenida Independencia and Avenida Abraham Lincoln about 2.7 miles to the south southwest of the 218th Compound. **The *Jaragua Hotel* housed all the Senior Officers and other "top brass" of the HQs, USFORDOMREP.** Originally built by Trujillo in 1942 for the Dominican elite in Santo Domingo, the Jaragua was located at 367 George Washington Avenue on the southern coast of the city and was the first luxury hotel in the Dominican Republic.

While in Dom Rep, I never needed to have my sleeping bag cleaned or laundered. Instead, one of the "old timers" here explained to us how to freshen up smelly old sleeping bags now and then. We were told that by turning the bag inside-out and hanging it on the tie-down ropes outside of our tent, this would allow the sun's ultraviolet (UV) rays to kill the bacteria after a few hours. He went on to explain that this treatment tended to disinfect it and leave it clean smelling. Much to my surprise, he was right! It sure worked great!

As for keeping our tents clean, it wasn't too difficult a task. I believe that each tent was issued a straw broom for that purpose, and as long as the weather was dry, we only needed to sweep the floors of dust now and then. It was the rainy days and nights that made things rough for us. At times like that, mud being tracked in was simply unavoidable. But we learned to live with it and had very few complaints. I kept thinking that in other "hot spots" in the world where the fighting was going on, many U.S. military men would give anything to change places with us.

The **latrine facilities** here were certainly not what we were used to, but they left a lasting impression nonetheless. Located just west of the stockade along the north wall under a Medium GP tent, was a deep-dug covered latrine about ten to twelve feet long. As I recall it had seating for about four to six men. I cannot recall if it was ever moved while I was there, but do I recall the smell took some getting used to.

As for urinals, there were a few located throughout the camp. One of them was just twenty feet from the entrance to my tent. Made of wood with a screen-type covering tacked at the top to keep out rodents, it was buried with about 2½ feet of it protruding above ground level. The urinals were surrounded by a four-sided canvass partition about 4½ feet high for privacy. There was concern that female personnel and/or other visitors were watching us from the HQ, USFORDOMREP "Palace" building only 40 to 50 yards away to the south.

Early onward I was assigned to pull **Line-Duty Patrol** with a senior partner. Our partners were usually guys who had been in the 218th longer than we were, and were well familiar with the city of Santo Domingo and its surrounding areas. For the most part while we were in this country, we worked in shifts of what we called *9-on-3-off.* This meant working nine consecutive days on duty, followed by three days off. For duty days it meant three days of day shift, three days of afternoon shift, and three midnight shifts.

Before each duty shift, those who would be going out on patrol had to stand an inspection that we called ***Guard Mount.*** This took place on the tennis court by the pool house. In this, like any other inspection, we had to stand at *Attention* in two ranks while the Duty Officer checked us over to be sure we had a clean shave, neatly trimmed hair, a proper clean and pressed uniform, with boots, leather, and brass all highly shined. We were also expected to have whatever equipment was required for that shift. This included such items as a police whistle, hand cuffs, a night stick, etc.

Prior to *Guard Mount,* proper weapons were issued to the MPs. Each man carried a .45 Caliber Colt Automatic Pistol loaded with one seven-round magazine. In addition to this, two additional magazines were carried in a leather case attached to the belt. But for a short period of time, the junior man in each patrol was also required to carry an M-14 rifle loaded with a twenty-round magazine in addition to his sidearm. It was decided a few weeks or so after our arrival in the 218th, that the M-14s would no longer be necessary. This was due to fewer incidents of hostility with the local population, and thereafter only side arms were carried.

During our time in the country of *Dom Rep,* **M-151 Jeeps were utilized as Military Police vehicles.** These jeeps had no heater, which made patrolling uncomfortable at night when the air was much cooler. For this reason, many of us carried our field jackets along on night patrols. While nearly all the M-151s had canvas tops, some of the guys on patrol preferred to keep the top folded down. The reason for this was that when the 503rd MP Battalion first arrived in Dom Rep, there was always the threat of snipers shooting from upper levels of buildings and roof tops. And you can't shoot back very well through a canvas top. So keeping the top down not only allowed for a better view of the MP's surroundings, it also allowed for a faster evacuation of the vehicle in an emergency, especially by rear-seat passengers if any.

However, the biggest drawback of keeping the top down was the obvious one. That is, the occasional torrential downpour of rain in that country. But by the time most of us arrived from MP School in March 1966, there was very little threat of sniper fire. Most of us therefore opted to keep the top up in an effort to stay dry.

As the junior partner on patrol, manning the **Police Radio in the M-151** became my job. We used the ***Model AN/GRC-8 (Army Navy/Ground Radio Communication)*** tube-type radios with a "pork chop" style microphone. These were mounted on the right rear passenger side and were equipped with a vertical "whip" antenna. By way of these radios, each patrol was able to keep in constant touch with the ***P.M.O. (Provost Marshal's Office)*** at Military Police Headquarters. The only drawback of these radios was their short range of transmission and reception, which was approximately ten miles.

I admit that I felt a bit silly using the radio at first. Our radio *Call Sign* for the 218th MP Company back then was *South Jury.* It was believed that this was due to the initial arrival of Military Police being sent to act as sort of a "jury" to referee the establishment of democracy on the island. However, at that time I thought that *South Jury* was simply a southern drawl mispronunciation of *South Jerry.* So, many of us therefore used *South Jerry* as the call sign. I actually recall hearing *both* versions used back then.

Many fond memories of those early patrols stand out in my mind over all these years. One of them was driving along ***George Washington Avenue,*** which ran along the southern coast of the island and the city. (It reminded me of *Lake Shore Drive* back in Grosse Pointe Shores, Michigan.) But as I recall, every night there after dusk, little sea crabs by the hundreds would crawl up out of the Caribbean and attempt to cross the avenue. Whenever the headlights from our jeep hit them, they'd literally get up and try to run like hell across the avenue. It was comical as hell to see!

Because I was never in favor of harming God's little creatures, I made every effort while driving to swerve so as not to hit the little buggers. I was not very successful at this. My senior partner at that time, a short guy who was also fluent in Spanish (I think his name was **Jose Delgado, Jr.**), exclaimed to me that he was nearly tossed from the vehicle. He requested in a civil manner that I cease and desist immediately in my defensive driving tactics. I reluctantly complied.

On another patrol he took me out to a place that everyone called the ***Pink Palace.*** This was a long, low one-storey masonry building located somewhere east of the Duarte Bridge. It was on the north side of the road as you headed east along Boca Chica Highway, which ran along the southern coast. This was one of the "better" and cleaner houses of prostitution. I have no idea as to why it was called the *Pink Palace,* as in reality the building was actually ***Blue*** in color.

There were many of these establishments throughout the city of Santo Domingo and its outskirts. Basically, when we came upon U.S. servicemen in these *Off Limits* establishments, our job here was *not* to "write them up." Instead, we were supposed to give them a stern warning and order them to return to their unit. Anytime I was along on patrols and caught subjects "with their pants down," I handled it that way. There were only a few MPs who were hard-nosed and wrote them up. It was sort of an unwritten rule with many of the prostitutes that as long as the MPs didn't harass their patrons, the MPs could partake of their professional services without charge.—Or so I've been told.

Sergeant Ron Cook and **Lt. George Martin** spent a good deal of time on patrol, policing the ***Pink Palace*** as well as many other houses of pleasure. This included one particular establishment located at ***144 Maximo Gomez Avenue.*** This was a 2-storey building located on the eastern side of the avenue as you traveled north. But at that time, this building *did* happen to be ***Pink*** in color. Ron and George also learned that a *huge* problem of *Sexually Transmitted Diseases (STD)* existed in this country. It was estimated then that about 30% of the female population there were infected.

Sergeant Ronald W. Cook, then serving his second enlistment in the Army, was a married man from Lexington, South Carolina, and often served as the ***Patrol Supervisor*** and ***Desk Sergeant*** for the 218th. Ron and many of the "old timers" here referred to us new guys as *Newbies*. In time, each of us lost that *Newbie* status and became one of the guys. From then on, Ron admitted that we worked hard, played hard, and supported each other no matter what we were doing. Cook had joined the U.S. Navy Reserve while still a senior in High School and stayed with them for about a year. In June 1962, he side-stepped from the Navy into the U.S. Army. Following Basic Training at Fort Knox, he went to Fort Benning, Georgia for Airborne School then on to Jungle Warfare training in Panama. About that time,

Ron had re-enlisted and was soon sent to Fort Bragg and assigned to Company C of the 503rd MP Battalion.

Once while out patrolling in Santo Domingo, Ron had stopped by *144 Maximo Gomez Avenue* and found a U.S. Air Force Major in a compromising situation. To avoid any serious problems in his career and personal life, the major assured Sergeant Cook that he could provide him anything he needed if the incident was forgotten. Certain that the major wasn't serious, Ron simply replied, *"I could sure use a real bed to sleep on instead of an old Army folding cot, a smelly old sleeping bag, and air mattress."* A few days later Ron got a call from the Major and was asked to meet him at San Isidro Airfield with a three-quarter-ton truck. From that day onward until he left Dom Rep, Ron Cook slept on a genuine U.S. Army bed complete with a real mattress, sheets, pillow, pillow cases, and an Olive Drab Green Army blanket. Though many asked Ron where it all came from, he was in no hurry to divulge the identity of his secret supplier.

Soon after leaving Dom Rep, **Ron Cook** was assigned to Fort Jackson, South Carolina close to his home. There he served as an MP until his final ETS in February 1968 at the rank of Staff Sergeant. Ron then returned home and worked for the *Columbia Police Department* in South Carolina, then went on to the *State Police* and retired after 35 years. During that time, he joined the *Army National Guard*, and completed *Officer Candidate School* in May 1970. But deciding that he'd make a better NCO than an officer, he chose not to accept a commission. In this last assignment he served as the *Brigade Sergeant Major* for the *218th Heavy (Separate) Mechanized Combat Infantry Brigade* and retired from the Guard in June 1994.

Today Ron has become sort of the unofficial *Keeper-of-the-Records* for our days with the 218th MP Company and the 503rd MP Battalion.

2nd Lt. George N. Martin, III was a 23-year-old single man from Jacksonville, Florida. Coming through the ROTC program, he enlisted in the U.S. Army at Fort Gordon in August 1965. Arriving in Dom Rep and placed in Company C of the 503rd in October, he was assigned as the 2nd Platoon Leader. He remained in this position even after Company C was redesignated as the 218th MP Company. George described himself as an unabashed fisherman back then who got to be pretty good with a *"Dominican Rod and Reel,"* which he described as no more than a length of *"mono-filament line wrapped on a rum bottle."* He explained that, *"with a one-ounce weight attached, you could swing it over your head, bolero style, and sling the thing quite a distance."* Sometimes he'd go fishing off the jetty at the *P.O.L. (Petroleum, Oil, and Lubricants) Terminal* at the mouth of the Ozama River where he'd catch some really nice Yellow Fin Tuna.

After leaving the 218th, Lt. Martin was sent to the 138th MP Company at Fort Jackson, South Carolina, where he was assigned as the new Post Stockade O.I.C. (Officer in Charge). After his ETS in August 1968, George Martin attended college and then made a career with the *South Carolina Department of Corrections*. Over the years George and his wife, Pat (married in January of '68) raised three children.

One night on patrol, my partner took me on a tour of the **Trujillo Family Yacht** that was docked at **Port Haina** (most of us pronounced this as **Hi-Anna**), about ten miles west of Santo Domingo. Some of the guys from the 218th pulled guard duty there. As I strolled through its passageways and peered into the lavishly decorated cabins on board, I was impressed with the 359-foot-long, four-masted luxurious watercraft. It was believed to be the largest private sailing yacht ever built at that time. It was commissioned by a U.S. stockbroker in 1931, then requisitioned by the U.S. Army during World War II and used as a weather station. Trujillo purchased the craft in 1957, restored it and named it after his daughter. (It was restored again in 1979 and today, it is renamed *Sea Cloud* by its German owner who now offers it for cruises.)

While the sea crabs made night driving along George Washington Avenue hazardous, the avenue was highly dangerous in other ways too. One night **Keith E. "Gus" Gustafson** and his partner, **James W. "Limey" Walker** were barreling along this road while on patrol. With "Gus" driving, they were traveling along a well-lit stretch of the avenue when abruptly they drove into a dark and unlit area. Suddenly, a large flatbed truck appeared in their headlights. It was up on jacks with a flat tire and no reflectors. Gus jerked the steering wheel to the left but it was too late. The corner of the truck clipped the windshield of the M-151 Jeep and tore the MP radio from its rear mount, tossing it onto the avenue.

Though "Limey's" head was in line with the corner of the truck, what saved him from sudden decapitation was the fact that he had leaned into Gus when they swerved. The corner of the flatbed had just missed him by mere inches. Luckily, another patrol happened by shortly afterward and they were brought back to the compound safe and sound, though a little shaken! The jeep, however, was history.

"Gus" Gustafson enlisted at the age of twenty-one from his hometown of West Covina, California, and took his Basic Training at Fort Ord. After his AIT at Fort Gordon (K-10-4), he came down to Dom Rep with most of us. He was married with no children at the time.

"Limey" Walker was another story. Born in England in 1945, he came to the U.S. at the age of sixteen and enlisted in the U.S. Army at the age of eighteen. He joined the *82nd Airborne Division* and came to Dom Rep with them in May 1965. While there, he had participated in most of the earlier hostilities. After returning to the U.S. on emergency leave, his ETS came up and he left the Army. Not long after that, he made a decision to re-enlist. But this time instead of going Airborne again, he opted for the *Military Police Corps* when he heard that the next class from Fort Gordon was being assigned to the Dominican Republic. Walker then took his MP training along with us and returned to Dom Rep with our Graduating Class of K-10-4.

Often while on patrol in the hills, or when driving out beyond the city in either direction, we'd find **"shanty towns"** scattered here and there. In these places there were many homes made from plywood, corrugated steel, cardboard, tar-paper, and many other less-than-permanent materials. Another such impoverished area was on the southeastern edge of the city along the west bank at the mouth of the Ozama River. I often wondered back then and even today how they could live like that. It served to remind me how blessed a life I really had.

I also remember once in a while hearing some locals yelling at us, *"Yankee Go Home!"* I've always wondered, even to this day, why they couldn't understand that we were there for their benefit.

Not long after I arrived in Dom Rep, I received a *Kodak Model #110 Instamatic* camera from home. It was great little camera that cost Mom and Dad less than $10.00. Today, I wish that I had taken many more photographs with it than I did. But today that is what we call *20/20 hindsight!*

Besides line-duty patrol at the time, I was occasionally chosen for other jobs in the 218th. More often than not, I'd be assigned the duties of **guarding the Main North Gate** to the camp. This wasn't bad duty at all. It wasn't strenuous but it *was* quite boring, especially at night. It was too difficult to read after hours as there was no light in the Guard Shack. Occasionally, I'd bring reading material during daylight hours, but I had to be careful. I didn't want to get caught reading when I was supposed to be guarding. Inside the shack there was a small wooden milk crate providing the only place for any of us to sit.

I remember sometimes hearing babies crying while on duty there. The sounds, which could be heard during any hour of the day or night, would be coming from the maternity hospital across the street from our camp. Looking up at it from the gate, it was easy to see it was primarily a white four-storey building with a three-storey wing on the eastern end of it. (Today, it still looks pretty much the same as it did in 1966.)

Another guy who manned the main gate here from time to time was **Thomas E. Marston**. Tom was a newlywed from Astoria, New York. He had taken his Basic Training at Fort Gordon, but during the several days before MP School began there, he went home and married Debbie. It was a marriage that would stand the test of time.

Once I was on the Duty Roster to man a *Security Check Point* along one of the designated hot spots in the city. That too, was a boring and dull job. It was a day shift when my partner and I were dropped off there and not much was happening. An M-151 was already parked there so we sat in it while watching the traffic and pedestrians moving about us. I got restless after sitting there for hours with my .45 caliber side arm and an M-14 rifle. So seeing nothing to report, I decided to take the jeep for a turn around the block just to break the monotony. I found out that the clutch pedal was not working and was lying on the floorboard. That didn't deter me. So after making sure that the transmission was in neutral, I went ahead and started it anyway. Then after using my foot to kick it into low gear, it lurched forward with a jerk. From there without a clutch, shifting went OK as long as I did it slowly and smoothly. After coming around the block I returned to our spot without incident.

I pulled *C.Q. Runner Duty* for one night only while in Dom Rep. (*C.Q.* stands for *Charge of Quarters*). We always had a *C.Q.* and a *C.Q. Runner* after hours. The C.Q. was sort of the "man in charge" of the *Orderly Room* when the Commanding Officer, Executive Officer, First Sergeant and Company Clerk were out, usually on afternoons and midnights. Our Orderly Room was the tent in which the company's main office and headquarters were housed. Besides assisting the C.Q. with whatever tasks that needed to be done, the *C.Q. Runner's* job was to periodically "run" and wake up anyone scheduled to go on duty at various hours. It wasn't too bad a job as far as boredom goes.

On this particular night I sat at the desk of **Jackie A. Webster, our Company Clerk.** He was the one who typed the daily *Morning Reports* (*DA-Form-1*), for the 218th. I got to use a typewriter for the very first time in my life at this desk, and even managed to type a letter or two before morning by using the old "hunt and peck" method. (It's a method I still use today! I was recently rated at about 22 words per minute without mistakes on a word processor.)

Jackie Webster was a single guy from Pennsylvania who was also part of the 218th MP Company's softball team. As of mid-July 1966, the *DomRep*Dispatch*, a weekly newspaper put out by the *USFORDOMREP* and distributed every Friday, reported that the 218th was in fifth-place out of thirteen teams in league standings with five wins and four losses. (Later after returning to Fort Bragg, Webster would join the softball team for Company C of the 503rd and later still, try out for, and make the *All Army Team* traveling with them as a Third Baseman.)

Several local civilian children and ladies in the area did work for us. **House Boys**, most between the ages of twelve and 15 years, came by a few times per week to pick up our boots to shine and return them later in the day. However, one of these houseboys was an elderly black gentleman named *Salvadore* with white spots here and there on his body. The guys called him "Spots" for obvious reasons. The **Laundry Ladies** who served us seemed to do a fine job most of the time. Once a week they'd pick up our laundry and return it the next day or so. I was more than pleased with their work and never had a complaint. I still didn't complain when **Tom Kranch,** a friend and fellow 218th MP from Lancaster, Pennsylvania, got back a pair of my undershorts one time along with his returned laundry, but that was a rare occurrence.

Many of the guys who did line-duty patrol asked the ladies to use extra heavy starch in their fatigues. After trying heavy starch once, I found that I didn't like it as it made the uniforms felt like stiff cardboard and way too scratchy for me. Some of the guys bought their own iron at the PX and cans of spray starch to add to the already stiff cardboard. There was no question that they looked sharp while standing at Guard Mount, but they also looked uncomfortable, like stiff robots to me.

Doyle W. "Gabby" Hayes, an enlistee and single guy from Florence, Alabama, was one of those "spit-and-polish" types. His fatigues were so stiff from all the spray starch and extra ironing that he often needed help getting into them. Then further help was needed in getting up on his feet in order to prevent breaking the crease in the trousers. Once on his feet, he'd walk out stiffly on "stovepipe" legs to stand Guard Mount.

"Gabby" was a gas station worker before his Army days. After enlisting he had taken his Basic at Fort Benning, Georgia and his AIT with us at Fort Gordon. While with the 218th MP Company, Hayes pulled line-duty patrol, raided a few whorehouses, did traffic control at a pontoon bridge site, and guarded supply ships at Port Haina.

During our later months in Dom Rep, the C.O. and others came up with an idea that was supposed to encourage the guys to look "sharper" than ever before. This was set up so that the sharpest looking MP standing at Guard Mount each day would be called the **Super Numero** (or some such name as that), and would be given the day off as a reward. For sure, **Doyle Hayes** won this title several times in a row. Others who have also claimed that title from time to time were: **Steven "Durwood" Pack** from Winston/Salem, North Carolina, **Thomas M. "the Yankee" Pierno** from New York City, **John Patterson** of Texas, and **Rick VandeKerchove** from East Detroit, Michigan.

"Durwood" Pack was a single guy who had taken his Basic Training at Fort Jackson, South Carolina before attending MP School at Fort Gordon with most of us.

Many of these guys, after winning the *Super Numero* title, would immediately go back to their tent and resume the spit-shining of their boots and leather gear. They'd even add more spray starch to their fatigues, and iron them some more. After winning the day off several times in a row, Pack and Pierno were no longer allowed to participate, but were still required to pull their shift of duty. This was truly an unfair ruling and soon afterward I believe the *Super Numero* idea was dropped.

Ed Mitchell too, was among some of the sharpest and cleanest MPs at Guard Mount with his leather and brass highly shined, but he never won. This was for two reasons primarily. Ed never had his fatigues tailored back then and he never used spray starch or additional ironing of his fatigues. But as for me, I preferred light starch which gave me a neat and clean appearance without looking too sloppy or too stiff. Ed billeted in the last (southernmost) 3rd Platoon tent along the eastern fence-line. His cot was on the right side about half way back from the door.

Prisoner Escort Duty was another job that was well liked by those who pulled it here. I was never assigned to this duty but I heard that it was a relaxing and enjoyable break from the daily routine. About once per week two men were picked to escort prisoners from our stockade here at the 218th back to Fort Bragg, North Carolina. It was usually a three or four day assignment. It involved being transported to San Isidro Airfield, returning to the *CONUS (Continental United States)* via C-130 to Pope AFB, and delivering the prisoners to the Post Stockade at Fort Bragg. The men of the 218th would then spend a night or two at Fort Bragg on unofficial R&R (Rest and Reorganization) and return to Santo Domingo. **Sergeant Ron Cook** pulled this duty three times and was able to visit his home in South Carolina on two of the three occasions. When guys on Prisoner Escort Duty stayed at Fort Bragg, they usually bunked at the *Transient and Casual Quarters* located on the eastern side of the post.

Ron Cook also pulled ***Classified Courier Service*** for the HQs, USFORDOMREP on a few occasions. This duty required a *U.S. Security Clearance.* In this capacity, Ron was assigned to carry sealed classified documents and personally deliver them to a certain individual at Fort Bragg. This duty *also* brought with it two extra days of unofficial R&R.

Shortly after I arrived in Dom Rep, my **church attendance** seemed to go by the wayside. This was due primarily to the varying times of my work shifts. It wasn't something I'd planned, although I had inquired as to where Catholic Mass and/or other church services would be held. I never told my folks about this back home, as I preferred to not worry them needlessly.

It wasn't more than a month or so after I arrived in Dom Rep that I learned of an opening for a position in the *Arms Room*. **The Arms Room was commanded by S/Sergeant Ozell Roby, Jr.,** who was also in charge of our *Unit Supply Room*. He had just returned from thirteen days of emergency leave on 17-April. The Arms Room was merely a 16 x 32-foot medium GP tent. In the Arms Room were three large heavy *Conex Containers*. These were six-foot high cubicles made of corrugated steel. They served as cargo containers in which all of our weapons and ammunition were stored. The job called for being there during various duty hours as it was manned twenty-four hours a day, seven days a week.

In short time I grew to really like this job. What's more, the job only required clean fatigues daily. As I wasn't really into all the spit-and-polish that went with line-duty patrol, this job seemed to be "right up my alley." Besides issuing weapons to the MPs going on duty and checking them in when they came off duty, my job was to keep the Arms Room clean and organized. This I enjoyed. It gave me plenty of "free time" to do many other things.

To pass the time, in the Arms Room, I began to read a lot of books that were always passed around. I also wrote many, many long letters while sitting there on midnight shifts. I found that I preferred midnights for this reason. One letter I recall writing took twelve full sheets of yellow lined legal pad filled on both sides. And *that* letter was to someone I had never actually met yet. She was a close friend of a girl I knew back home. (A few days or so after I got out of the Army, we dated only one time but we never really hit it off.)

I had a portable transistor radio that I had bought from another guy who was shipped back to the States on ETS. On midnight shifts I enjoyed listening to all the "oldies" on *A.F.R.S. (Armed Forces Radio Service)* **in Santo Domingo**. The D.J. for the *Night Sounds* oldies then was a PFC named Jim Scanlon, and Herb Nesmith was the station's Program Director.

While my duties involved the issuing weapons to the MPs going out on duty and checking them back in upon their return, it was *not* my job to clean them. It was the patrol MP's own responsibility to clean his weapon before returning it. At first I was somewhat lenient on this rule and did not enforce it. But when Sergeant Roby told me one day that I'd have to clean them if they didn't, I quickly changed my attitude and got hard-nosed about it. Some of the guys didn't like it and made vocal their objections, but in the end they complied. I sure hope today that none of them hold grudges.

One time while working the Arms Room, a guy brought to me a brown paper bag that he had rolled up under his arm. The bag contained a lot of loose .30 caliber M-14 rifle ammunition that he wanted to turn in. He was soon to go home on ETS he explained, and simply wanted to "wash his hands" of the stuff. I seem to recall there were about 150 or more rounds in the bag. Because it was all unaccounted for ammunition, I wasn't quite sure what to do with it.

Really, I should have turned it in to Sergeant Roby, but because I had promised that I would not divulge where it came from, that option was out of the question. So I mentioned it to a couple of guys (whose names escape me today) and a day or so later we borrowed a jeep, drove out into the boondocks somewhere in the hills north of Santo Domingo, and shot it all off. That sure felt great and it was the only time I went up into the mountainous area north of the city.

Charles J. "Chuck" Gheldof, whose hometown was Ferndale, Michigan, was another guy who had come through Basic and AIT with me. I learned that for about three months here in Dom Rep, he carried a plastic toy replica of a Colt .45 caliber automatic pistol when he went out on patrol. It happened belong to the 10-year-old little brother of Chuck's girlfriend at the time. You'd have had to look pretty darn close to realize that it was just a plastic toy. I was amazed at how "real" it actually looked. His reasoning was that he was tired of having to clean his weapon every time he came off duty. I kept wondering, what if he actually *needed* the real thing? *Then* what would he do? Or what if he got caught with it during Guard Mount? But in the end, he pulled it off smoothly and was never discovered with it on duty.

After his ETS in November 1967, Chuck Gheldof returned home to Michigan and his old job at *Alameda Gage Corporation,* and remained with them for twenty-four years until they moved to the West Coast. Chuck then stayed behind and tried other avenues. Today, he and his wife Marcia are owners of several rental houses and two apartment buildings. After raising two children, they now reside in Walled Lake, Michigan.

On **Wednesday, 27-April-1966, Captain Dennis T. Ellis was released from duties with the 218th MP Company and assigned to the HQs, USFORDOMREP.** Here he served as the *Military Police Operations Officer* while working for **Colonel**

F. P. Field, the Chief of Staff. While Dennis Ellis was sure going to be missed, the company would still be in capable hands. In his place, **1st Lt. Terrance M. Fiore** once again assumed command of the 218th.

On **Tuesday, 10-May-1966, I was promoted to PFC (Private First Class)** along with sixteen other guys while twenty-two others were promoted to Specialist-4. Nine days later (on 19-May), ninety more men of the 218th were promoted to PFC. I felt great about the promotion as there would be no more slick-sleeve uniforms for me. The standard pay for a PFC back then was $121.00 per month.

Now with all this extra money to burn, like a lot of others in the 218th, I decided to have my fatigues tailored. The standard issue fatigue slacks had a seventeen to eighteen-inch circumference around the bottom of the leg. I asked the civilian seamstress here to taper that down to fourteen inches. After a bit of reluctance on her part (as she was told by someone in authority *not* to do so), she finally gave in and complied.

Many other thoughts came to mind over the years since then. I fondly recall that one day **a dog wandered into the compound and I befriended it early on.** From thereafter it followed me just about everywhere I went, even to the mess hall. When I came out it would be right there happily accepting my bacon, sausage, or any other scraps of food that I could spare. It would lick my face to wake me in the mornings. So it didn't take long for me to become attached to my new friend. But sadly that attachment was destined to be short lived.

Outside the Arms Room, about twelve feet away under a shade tree, was a six-foot-long picnic table where I occasionally sat cleaning weapons or doing paperwork. While sitting there one hot sunny day, I suddenly realized that a jeep was parked near the table and blocking my view to the Arms Room. I decided to move it. When I started the jeep and backed it up, I accidentally backed over the dog that was lying in the cool shade under it.

It took the poor thing about ten long minutes to suffer terribly and die. All I could do was stand there and watch it. By this time a crowd had gathered around, and although my gut was torn to pieces, I had to be a tough guy and not show it. Days later some of the guys began to rib me about it, calling me *Killer* and other things. God, I missed that little four-legged friend for a long, long time to come.

John H. Osborne, Jr. was a guy from Royal Oak, Michigan, who had also come through Basic and AIT with me. He told us once that over in the Mess Hall, **Sergeant Dave Stewart** was serving egg sandwiches at night after hours to MPs coming off duty. The only stipulation was that the MPs would only be served if they were still in uniform. John was right about that, and I took full advantage of this one night after coming off an afternoon shift from the Arms Room. The sandwiches were excellent, and this reminded me of how much I missed Mom's fried egg sandwiches back home.

Staff Sergeant David S. Stewart was our Mess Sergeant in Dom Rep and was known as a gentle soul. As far as Army cooks went, he was considered as a pretty darn good one. He was able to do such wondrous things with powdered eggs by mixing them with various ingredients, that you hardly knew they were powdered. Whenever **Lt. Martin** came back from a fishing trip with a mess of tuna, Sergeant Stewart was always more than happy to broil them up and serve them to all the guys on movie nights in the camp.

But David Stewart had a personal side that many of us new guys in the 218th were unaware of back then. Having come to Dom Rep earlier with Company C of the 503rd, Sergeant Stewart had seen first hand what the turmoil in this country had done to its young children. He knew the war had turned too many of them into homeless and hungry orphans, and he was touched deeply by this. He made up his mind right then and there to do whatever he could to help them. To do this, he began by gathering food from the mess hall that he was quite certain wouldn't be missed. Later he added clothing along with any other supplies that he could scrounge and began donating it all for the children's benefit. In due time, news of this had gotten around the company, inspiring many others to offer their help.

Funds were soon raised by voluntary contributions from the men in the unit, and they decided to sponsor a **home for abandoned and homeless children.** This all took place somewhere east of the Ozama River in the *Sans Souci* area before the company moved to its present location behind the HQs, USFORDOMREP. Help later came in the form of food purchased and given to the home along with crib mattresses and pillows. Soon the U.S. Army Engineers stepped in and made all the needed repairs on the plumbing and appliances in the home. Further help came in the form of school supplies such as pencils, paper, crayons, and other things from **Sergeant Ozell Roby**, who had obtained them with the help of **Sergeant Bill Whitmill.** In the end, this gained favorable publicity for our unit.

We had a **Dayroom** in the 218th that included both a **Pool table and a Ping-Pong table.** It was sure great to have. This Dayroom was another 16 x 32-foot medium GP tent stretched over a 2 x 4 wood frame with a wood plank floor.

There was one guy in particular that I recall whose name escapes me today. He looked quite ordinary and spoke with a southern drawl, but he sure was a hell of an *ace* at the pool table. He wasn't loud or boastful as I recall, and like me, he wasn't the spit-and-polish type either. Though he was always dressed clean, he evidently used either very little or no starch in his fatigues at all. But every time he got on that pool table, he ran the show from then until the end of the evening. He sure loved the game of *8-Ball* and I do not recall anyone ever beating him at the game.

The only time I ever played against him was one time when we were both alone there. I wouldn't play him for money, of course, and that was certainly OK with him, as he told me he needed the practice anyway. Although I never became great at the game of *8-Ball,* he sure taught me a few pointers back then.

Samuel W. Dickson was our Company Barber in Dom Rep as well as later at Company C, of the 503rd. After pulling line-duty patrol there for a short period of time, he was able to put his barber talents to work for us in the 218th. Sam was a single guy drafted from the small town of New Matamores, Ohio on the southeastern edge of the state. Prior to his Army days, he attended a Barber College just across the state line in West Virginia.

Then after his ETS, Sam Dickson cut hair for a short period of time in Ohio. But with the "long-haired hippie era" coming on strong in the late 1960s and early 1970s, he found out that the need for men in his profession was dwindling fast. So he decided to seek a life's work elsewhere. He then found work at *Western Electric* and retired from there in 2001. Sam is still single today and lives in Columbus, Ohio.

My tent (or at least my little corner of it) survived one of the worst tropical storms that hit the Dominican Republic during our entire stay there. Every day as I came in and out, I took a moment or two to give a little extra tug on the tie-down ropes supporting my corner of the tent. Some of the guys thought I was wasting my time and didn't mind saying so, but I kept up the ritual just the same. That habit sure paid off in spades! In a photo I took one day, it was easy to see that my right front corner of the tent was straight and snug.

Sure enough, one night during high winds and a heavy torrential downpour, the entire tent fell in on its occupants. That is, of course, all except for my snug little corner. What had happened was this: The roof of the tent always sagged between all the other poles where it was never kept tight. And the weight of rainwater in these "valleys" is what did the job. Because I kept my corner snug and tight, there was no sagging valley for the rain to collect in. While all the others were scrambling around in the dark trying to fight their way out from under the heavy wet canvas, I was still dry and comfortable in my little corner of the world. I sure as heck got the last laugh that night and no one ever ribbed me about it again.

I later learned about a **boat trip that night from Port Haina to Puerto Rico** for a few of our 218th guys who were caught in the storm. About ten miles west of our compound after dark, these same heavy rains and hurricane-force winds that brought down most of my tent, had also washed out a bridge across the Haina River near Port Haina. The hurricane season in 1966 ran from June through November in the Caribbean with no fewer than eleven tropical storms that year.

A large civilian freighter ship had docked at Port Haina while off-loading military supplies. This was just across the harbor from Trujillo's Yacht which was docked there on the opposite side. Two men from the 218th MP Company were providing pier security for the docked supply ship, while two others were on town patrol in Port Haina. What's more, two more guys were assigned to a roving patrol that day, although these last two MPs were supposed to be patrolling elsewhere.

Four of the six guys were **Thomas Marston,** a married man from Astoria, New York; **James Simone,** a single guy from Detroit, Michigan; **David Champion,** single, from Marquette, Michigan; and **James Axente**, also single, and from New York City. (The names of the last two were unavailable.) When the hurricane broke out in force, all six of them were invited by the ship's crew to come aboard in an effort to get safely out of the storm.

During this powerful storm, the ship broke loose from the dock when its mooring cables snapped. Then unable to get its engine running, it began spinning end-over-end, striking the breakwater in the harbor several times. In due time the ship, while still without power, was ousted out of port by the fast-moving tide. Out in the Caribbean after getting the engine started, the Captain was unable to re-enter the port due to the violent storm. He then opted to move on to his next port-of-call.

The ship then sailed for a day and a half to Puerto Rico some 250 miles to the east, arriving at Old San Juan. Then after about two or three days, the U.S. Army Special Forces sent one small aircraft to pick up the six guys from there and return them to the 218th. This event was never mentioned in the daily Morning Reports. Nor were any of the six MPs listed as AWOL. They were simply asked to report on all that had happened to them, and that was the end of it.

As for other memories, **I never had a problem with the chow in the 218th** but I *do* recall the mess trays we used always had a perpetual film of greasy scum. No matter how many times we washed them, we could never seem to eliminate that film. We were each issued a mess tray when we arrived in Dom Rep, and we were also responsible to wash them ourselves after each meal. The trays were about 10 x 13 inches in size, and made from some kind of molded resin. Along with these trays, we used our own canteen cups for coffee or milk with each meal. Most of us drilled a hole in the edge of the tray, and then by fashioning a hook from coat-hanger wire, we hung them in our tent.

Ron Cook warned us once about eating food from the local restaurants and other eating establishments saying that one never knew what he was being served. He went on to explain that it might have been a parrot, monkey, snake, dog, or even a rat.

We had an MP Lounge in our compound. This was set up in the far southwestern section of our camp just behind the Motor Pool. It was also in a tent (GP Large) stretched over a 2 x 4 wood framework with a plywood floor and walls. **Sergeant William D. Whitmill** built the lounge with the help of his close friends, **S/Sergeant Richard D. Plummer** and two Dominicans whom Whitmill called *Ace* and *Tom-Tom*. After about a month of construction, the lounge opened for business.

Born in 1936, **Sergeant Bill Whitmill** was a 29-year-old married man initially from Toledo, Ohio. He enlisted in the U.S. Navy in 1955 and served until 1961, then traveled the country and was once a police officer in North Las Vegas, Nevada. Joining the U.S. Army in November 1963 while still single, Bill took his Basic at Fort Ord, California and his AIT at Fort Gordon. After marrying Ellen in 1964, they moved to Fayetteville, North Carolina. There he served with the 503rd MP Battalion at Fort Bragg, while coming to Dom Rep with Company A in May 1965.

Initially, Bill worked checkpoints in Santo Domingo as a Corporal and pulled road patrol along with Dominican counterparts. Soon after arriving in Dom Rep he was pulled off MP duty by Captain Herbert Langendorff (C.O. of Company A at that time), and put in charge of the MP Club. It was a club set up near the 503rd HQ at Sans Souci, where only beer and soft drinks were served. No hard liquor was permitted at the time. This was due to the fact that officers' lounges and NCO clubs in Dom Rep had to abide by strict rules from higher command. But when our lounge was later built in the 218th MP compound, it was kept private and therefore open to all ranks, and fully stocked with hard liquor.

In order to obtain the liquor, Bill had to make a deal with a friend of his serving with the U.S. Army Special Forces in Dom Rep. They wanted a lounge too, but couldn't get command approval for liquor. They had a two-engine Caribou aircraft that was used on various missions. Whitmill promised to supply his friend with all the booze he needed if they agreed to fly him back and forth from San Juan, Puerto Rico now and then as necessary. There, he would purchase the liquor and other bar supplies from a U.S. Air Force NCO Club. This cost Bill a fifth of scotch for each of the two pilots for each round trip. After the booze was brought back, it not only stocked the MP lounge, but was thereafter used to barter for many goods or services needed by the 218th.

Bill had bartered booze for lumber and nails as well as many other building supplies from the U.S. Army Engineers at the Dominican Fairgrounds. All the while, his friend **Dick Plummer**, bartered for the barstools somewhere in downtown Santo Domingo. Plummer had run the lounge at times while also tending the bar.

As the walls of the club were also made from plywood, Whitmill and a few of the guys took the time to give the walls a scorched look using blowtorches. Someone placed an actual casket along the bar to hold the beer for a while. It was an insulated aluminum casket used for the transporting of military deceased.

Our lounge had three pinball machines and even a jukebox with a lot of good tunes. One favorite tune of mine that I recall hearing often there was *Surfer Girl* by the Beach Boys. Bill's wife, Ellen, supplied the 45rpm records for the jukebox. She had gone to many of the local radio stations back home in Fayetteville, North Carolina and asked for donations of records for the 218th. Sergeant Whitmill had no idea where the jukebox and pinball machines came from other than the fact that they were delivered by way of a *deuce-and-a-half* one night without explanation. The cost was three cases of beer.

After leaving Dom Rep, Bill Whitmill became a Drill Instructor at Fort Jackson, South Carolina and served there until May 1967. He then attended O.C.S. at Fort Knox, Kentucky and graduated in October of that year. From there he took an officer assignment with the Provost Marshall's Office at Fort Stewart, Georgia. Then in May 1969, he was sent to Vietnam as a replacement officer. In Vietnam, Bill was assigned to 2nd Squadron, of the 1st Armored Cavalry Regiment, eventually becoming the C.O. of HQs & HQs Troop.

In June 1970 he returned to the U.S. and was assigned to the G-2 Section of the XVIII Airborne Corps at Fort Bragg. Then in July 1971, Bill was released from active duty as a reserve officer and once again assumed the enlisted rank of Staff Sergeant. He then served with the 21st MP Company attached to the P.M.O. at Fort Bragg. While there, he attended College through night school. By the time of his graduation, Whitmill had risen to the rank of Sergeant First Class (E-7).

In 1972, Bill came to Fort Leavenworth, Kansas as the assistant to the Commandant for one year. Leaving Kansas, he served one year in Korea and returned to the U.S. at Fort McPherson, Georgia. He retired from the U.S. Military there in June 1976.

Then returning to North Carolina, Bill Whitmill worked as a Deputy Sheriff for Cumberland County. He then worked for the *North Carolina Prison System* and eventually became the Assistant Superintendent. Later Bill worked for the *North*

Carolina Motor Vehicle Division and finally retired in 1991. Today Bill and Ellen Whitmill reside in Hope Mills, North Carolina and have raised two children.

Another of our bartenders at the 218th was **Vernon V. Schwieterman**, a single guy from Celina, Ohio. Vern was drafted in November 1965, took his Basic Training at Fort Jackson, South Carolina, and his AIT at Fort Gordon. Arriving in Dom Rep in March 1966 with many of us from the MP Class of K-10-4, Vern tended bar for most of his time in the 218th.

Among his favorite memories of Dom Rep was one particular night after a party and cook-out at the MP Lounge. Vern recalls that it was a festivity given for the company officers shortly after he had taken over as a new bartender. No enlisted men were allowed in, but as usual, a few slipped by. Some local ladies were bussed in later that night after the lounge closed.

Some time later when the party fizzled out, Vern and several others began cleaning up the lounge. They found out that there were still several steaks leftover outside buried in the barbecue sauce. He and a few others fired up the grill and enjoyed the best steaks ever. All this commotion woke up a Signal Corps radio repairman who was sleeping close by. At first he was angry about it but after one bite into a juicy steak, the anger swiftly faded.

Two local girls named Nelly and Consuelo worked as waitresses in the MP Lounge during the later months there. **Nelly** was the older of the two and spoke fairly good English, while **Consuelo** was younger and spoke no English at all. They were actually hired by (and paid through) the main NCO club which was about five or six blocks away from our compound. **Vern Schwieterman** always drove over there and picked them up each night that they worked in our lounge, and dropped off there again after closing.

Later after returning to the U.S., **Vern Schwieterman** was assigned to the 503rd MP Battalion where he pulled duty in the Motor Pool as the Rations Truck Driver. After his ETS in November 1967, Vern married Judy in 1971 and spent the next thirty-plus years in the printing industry until it dried up. Then in 1985 they moved to Florida. While there, he went to school, studied air conditioning and found a job with the *Pinellas Florida School System*. He did A/C repair and enjoyed it very much. Currently residing in Largo, Florida, Vern and Judy have raised two children.

Richard T. VandeKerchove was another guy who helped build the MP lounge. Rick "Van" was not only drafted the same day as me, but we also went through Basic and AIT together. Upon arrival in Dom Rep, Rick spent most of his time pulling line-duty patrol, but like me, was also occasionally assigned other duties too.

Among some of the other assignments he was scheduled for, was being a nightshift guard in the Transient Stockade at the 218th.

On one particular night, Rick was stationed inside the Segregation Section guarding prisoners held in the two 6 x 12-foot cells there. He was unarmed except for the keys to the cells that he held. Rick was darned tired due to the fact that he had already pulled an eight-hour shift of duty earlier that day, and consequently fell asleep while sitting there. As luck would have it he was caught sleeping on duty and was given an Article-15 reprimand. However in due time, the Article-15 was erased from his record by the Company Commander because VandeKerchove had won the *Super Numero* award three times in a row.

Rick VandeKerchove, after leaving Dom Rep in August 1966 with the same group as me, was also assigned to Company C of the 503rd MP Battalion at Fort Bragg where he continued pulling line-duty patrol.

After his ETS in November 1967, Rick settled in Warren, Michigan and went to work as a Production Manager for the *Travco Corporation* near his home. In 1974 he moved to Alexandria, Virginia and took a job there for about seven years. In 1981 he moved to Cincinnati, Ohio. By this time, Rick and his first wife had split up and he was now married to Tammi.

In Ohio, he ran a plant that built and/or modified special mobile units for commercial or military use (NASA, DEA, FBI, Army, etc.). That career lasted for ten years until serious cut-backs and down-sizing caused him to be cut loose. Between 1991 and 1997, he took a job in Indiana for a company that built modular homes and was later transferred to run their North Carolina Division. Later in 1997, Rick and Tammi moved back to Ohio. Today, still living in Batavia, Ohio, Rick has one son from his first marriage and one daughter through Tammi.

Of several **signs and posters displayed in the lounge**, I recall two in particular. One behind the bar read, *Don't wait for the shrimp boats . . . I'm coming home with the crabs!* Another one hanging above declared, *He who enters covered here, buys this bar a round of cheer!* I got caught entering "covered" once when I was too slow to remove my hat. Fortunately, it didn't cost me much as there were only three or four others in the lounge.

I remember drinking *Fallstaff* **Beer** from sixteen-ounce cans, but I was *never* able to finish the entire sixteen ounces. I never was much of a drinker. Even today, I can only finish about three twelve-ounce beers before my face goes numb. We also had a brand of beer then called **Black Label** from the *Carling Brewing Company.* As for hard liquor, occasionally I'd have a **7&7** back then. But beyond that, I didn't do much drinking as it usually only got me into trouble.

For example, one night **Samuel Quinones** and I wandered down to the MP Lounge. Sam happened to be fluent in Spanish and operated as our interpreter for the 218th. Because our particular barmaid was a local girl and spoke no English, Sam naturally did the ordering for both of us. I asked him to order a 7&7 for me. After ordering his drink, he told the girl in Spanish to make mine a double. From that point on it didn't take long. About half way through the drink, my lips started to go numb. After a few more sips, my entire face began to feel like it belonged to someone else. Needless to say, I was totally smashed, and Sam was enjoying every minute if it.

Shortly afterward, I began wandering back to my tent, but on the way I decided to drop in on my friend **Ed Mitchell** to see what he was up to. Staggering in, I must have made a complete ass of myself. I honestly don't recall who or how, but someone literally picked me up and bodily tossed me out through the door. I faintly recall a sensation of flying when a tree suddenly jumped into my flight path. I remember my torso hitting the tree and falling to the ground below with one hard thud. I do *NOT* recall wandering back to my own tent and cot. But nevertheless, I sure as hell remember waking up there. And I also recall the crashing hangover the next morning.

We also had an in-ground **swimming pool** within our compound, and what a welcome pleasure it was to have. It was quite large and fan shaped as I recall. It was narrow at the shallower end and wide at its deeper end. Its depth ranged from two to ten feet and had a low as well as a high diving board. I was told that the water was pumped in through underground pipes from the Caribbean about a mile to the south. We heard that **Kim Novak** had been known to swim naked in this same pool. She was a very popular Hollywood starlet at the time who often dated Trujillo's son and lived here at the family Palace for a while.

Our Lifeguard in Dom Rep was Carl M. "Mike" Hagemeister. Mike was a 23-year-old single man from Garden Grove, California. Early after his arrival in Dom Rep, he had pulled line-duty patrol once. Then shortly thereafter, an NCO offered to send him to lifeguard classes. He took full advantage of this and from then onward, his full-time job for the 218th MP Company was to be our lifeguard.

I finally learned to swim here at the age of twenty-one. Actually, I only learned to dog-paddle. I'd been terrified of water all my life, ever since my older brother John drowned at the age of thirteen in 1953. I was only eight years old at the time. So while here in Dom Rep, I was in no hurry.

Once while I was "learning" here, someone from under the water grabbed my ankle. I got terrified immediately and panicked. Thereafter it took a lot of patience on my part, and a lot of hours of "getting my feet wet" when no one else was around. Often I'd waited until long after dark (on my nights off duty, of course) and practiced alone until I got comfortable in the water. I was totally frightened at first. But dangerous as it was without a lifeguard, in due time I gained experience and confidence and was soon jumping off the low board every day.

Only *once* did I go off the high diving board. But it wasn't actually by choice. All I did was climb the steps to the top out of sheer curiosity, just to get a feel of how high it was. I never really intended to actually jump from there. Upon finally reaching the top, I looked down. It sure *felt* like I was a thousand feet in the air. When I turned around to start back down the ladder, another guy had just reached the top and informed me, *"You ain't gettin' down this way!"* So after some nervous hesitation, I turned around and took the plunge. Oh my God! That was a long, long, long way down! But never again to this day did I *ever* get near a high board. I'll stay with the low board every time.

Carl Hagemeister also had an artistic talent that didn't go unnoticed by his friends and superiors. He was often called upon by the C.O. to make up bulletin boards, special signs and many other unique projects for the 218th and later for the 503rd MP Battalion.

Memories still flood my mind now and then. Such as cigarettes that sold for $1.50 per carton at the **PX which was located in the *Jaragua Hotel*** in Santo Domingo. I also remember buying a $25.00 U.S. Savings Bond and sending it home each payday with a letter to Mom and Dad. Then there was the unpleasant job of **trucking our garbage down to the sea** and dumping it there. I went along on this chore once and that was enough for me.

Brian R. Bryan was another MP who found that trucking the garbage down to the sea was a "real eye opener" experience on his first trip there. It bothered him deeply to witness local Dominican children and adults digging through our dumped garbage for something to eat.

Brian Bryan was a single guy from Wapakoneta, Ohio who, prior to being drafted, had just begun a career as a Tool and Die Maker. Then drafted in November 1965, he had taken his Basic Training at Fort Gordon as well as being part of our class of K-10-4 there at MP School. In the 218th MP Company, he pulled line-duty patrol most of the time. While in Dom Rep, he enjoyed the natural beauty of the country and the overall friendliness of the people in spite of the very difficult conditions many of them faced. Brian also had a *Kodak Instamatic* camera and took many photos with it.

Another unpleasant job was the **Sand Detail.** I was not part of this, but **Gus Gustafson** and a few others were assigned to this task early one afternoon. They went to a place that was called ***Red Beach.*** This was where the U.S. Marines first landed in April 1965 near Port Haina. They were told to load sand to be brought back to the compound. The sand was utilized in various places around our camp, especially at the entrance to the Arms Room. There was a large sand-filled bucket there that was used for the clearing of weapons.

At Red Beach they hated the idea of shoveling sand all afternoon, so when they noticed a local man not far down the beach with a shovel, they asked him if he'd like to make a few bucks. The man grinned and eagerly replied, *"Si!"* So the guys all dug deep in their pockets and came up with three dollars in paper currency, a handful of coins, a couple of brass police whistles and a few packs of smokes. The man was so elated with the fortune he was offered for the job, that he worked harder and faster than the guys had anticipated. Nevertheless, they hung around the beach anyway and killed several more hours before heading back.

I recall there were always long lines to stand in **if you wanted a hot shower.** These showers were located back behind and just west of the Mess Hall. I waited in that line only once or twice back then, but then if the line was too long, a person was apt to end up with a cold shower anyway. After that, I opted for the cold showers over at the pool house as there was no waiting at all required. It was only the shock of those first few seconds of cold water hitting you that was really tough to take. But after that, I was able to shower swiftly in about one and a half to two minutes. Can you imagine trying that now after all these years? Ahh, but we were young and brave back then.

Once or twice a week we had **movies in the compound**. It was like an outdoor drive-in movie theater, but without automobiles. At the northeastern end of the tennis court was a large 8 x 16-foot movie screen made of plywood and painted white. The screen was set up off the ground on fifty-five-gallon drums. We brought out folding chairs, blankets, milk crates and other items to sit on while gathering around the tennis court on those nights. One movie I recall back then out of all that were shown was called, *Your Cheatin' Heart (The Hank Williams Story)* starring George Hamilton and Susan Oliver.

In some of the local establishments, restaurants and sandwich shops we'd see American shows on television. I still remember seeing the old TV police series called, *Highway Patrol* in black and white starring Broderick Crawford. His lips were moving on the TV screen, but all you heard was a strange voice in Spanish. About ten minutes of that was really all I could take.

Thomas R. Kranch, my friend from Lancaster, Pennsylvania, showed me a nice place to eat called *Vicki's*. It was a small hamburger joint a couple blocks east of our compound on the same avenue. It had a carport and a large open window. Her parents owned the place along with Vicki, who had had just gotten back from a boarding school in New York. She had a couple of cute older sisters who helped out there. They served *Pepsi-Cola* and good hamburgers. It was one of the very few food establishments that Kranch and I trusted for safe food.

Tom Kranch was single and had worked briefly in his father's electronics business before being inducted. He had taken both Basic and AIT at Fort Gordon, Georgia.

A couple of guys caught a large rat in a trap under their 3rd Platoon tent one day using leftover pizza from a local establishment as bait. Then they put the rodent in a small cage, gathered around a fifty-five-gallon drum of water and drowned the poor thing. (These guys preferred to remain nameless for the purposes of this story.) As I walked by that day I noticed the cage was submerged in the water with the poor rodent's nose only a half-inch below the surface, and the priceless life-saving air above. Even though I wouldn't want it living in or under my own tent, I still felt sorry for the damned thing.

Tarantulas were among other unwelcome critters inhabiting the Dominican Republic. (I just recently learned this.) These were referred to as the **Giant Hispaniolan Tarantula.** Reportedly, they had large bodies, eight hairy legs and fangs measuring more than three quarters of an inch in length. First off, let me state for the record here that I have *never* encountered one of these creatures during my entire stay on the island. If I *had*, I'd have *certainly* remembered the experience all these years! (The mere *thought* of it gives me the willies today!) But they were certainly well remembered by **Mike Johnson** of the 2nd Platoon, who recalled killing them with his nightstick now and then. He even once put one in the battery box of his jeep and told the mechanic at the motor pool that the battery was bad. Can you imagine the mechanic's reaction to meeting the hairy thing face-to-face?

Michael G. Johnson was a single guy from Seattle, Washington. He had taken Basic at Fort Ord, California and AIT at Fort Gordon with us.

Lt. Terrance Fiore recalls encountering one of the tarantulas in the street one day while being out on patrol. When his partner stopped the jeep so they could get a better look, it reared up at them as if to say, *"OK, big guys, give me your best shot!"* **Sergeant Ron Cook** recalls them as just another nuisance. He claimed that occasionally one of these hairy creatures would get into your boots while you were sleeping. If he had mentioned that to me back then, I'd have damn sure taken his word for it. He recommended shaking your boots upside down just to be sure before pulling them on. Ron also recalled **light green frogs** that would make weird sounds and would jump up on things and stick. I don't recall these either. (Maybe I *did* serve in Dom Rep with my head in the sand! Who knows?)

Back in the southwest corner in front of the MP lounge, our Motor Pool was set up in a Quonset Hut. Behind there in that area between the Motor Pool and the MP Lounge, there was a *"hole in the fence"* where local prostitutes gathered to ply their trade. Ranging in age from thirteen to about forty-five, they sort of walked along the fence line separating the 218th from the back yard of the all-girls school building to the west of us. The going rate in those days for their services was usually five dollars . . . . Or so I've been told.

We were able to make **long-distance phone calls from Dom Rep to our homes in the U.S.** around this time. This came about one night while **2nd Lt. George Martin** worked as the *Duty Officer* and his partner, **Sergeant Ron Cook** served as the *Patrol Supervisor*. They happened to drop in that night to **144 Maximo Gomez Avenue.** There was no question that this address had become a hot spot in the nightlife of the city. This time they found a senior NCO involved in a less-than-flattering circumstance. Lt. Martin gave the NCO one of his sternest reprimands and told him to get dressed and get back to his unit.

Several days later that same NCO recognized Lt. Martin in the lounge at the *Hispaniola Hotel.* He couldn't thank George enough for keeping their last meeting quiet, explaining that it would have ruined his career as well as destroyed his marriage. He then asked George, *"Is there anything that I could do for you to express my gratitude?"*

Then he explained further to Lt. Martin that he was one of the senior NCOs in charge of the **U.S. Military Overseas Switchboard** in Dom Rep. In short time, a long-distance phone system was set up in our compound. It allowed us at the 218th MP Company to make calls home from our Orderly Room to the U.S. each night after hours. A U.S. Signal Corps communication van was always parked next to the "Palace" on the opposite side from the PMO. It was used primarily for calls during the daytime from the HQs, USFORDOMREP back to the XVIII Airborne Corps HQ at Fort Bragg and the Pentagon in Washington, DC.

Once the system was in place at the 218th, calls were then placed from our Orderly Room to the Fort Bragg switchboard. From there the calls would be patched through to the nearest U.S. Military base to our call's final destination back home. At that point, the call was again forwarded to its final intended objective. We were, however, expected to pay for any "collect" call charges from that nearest military base to our call's final destination.

Those of us who wanted to take advantage of this, needed to put our name on a call list. Calls were placed this way usually after business hours and this went on all night sometimes. I took advantage of this once. On that particular night, I was awakened by the C.Q. Runner and told that my call was coming up next.

In my case the call was placed through *Selfridge Air Force Base* about fifteen miles northeast of my home. I was allowed only ten minutes on the phone, but it was great to hear a familiar voice from home. It was a tremendous morale factor for many of us back then.

At one point, word had come back through the grapevine that the Signal Corps guys who had set up the system, expected the 218th MPs to cut them a lot of slack regarding traffic offenses, bad bar behavior, and/or visits to houses of prostitution. **Lt. Terrance Fiore** got wind of this problem developing and passed it on to the others at the 218th. When the MPs of the 218th didn't comply with the expectations of the Signal Corps, many of the calls failed to materialize at all or would come through in the wee hours of the morning, local time back home. But in time, the problem was worked out and all was OK after that.

Terrance Fiore scheduled a call once to his girlfriend in college back home. When the call came through to the pay phone in the hallway outside her college dorm at 2:00 AM, he wasn't too popular after that.

On Wednesday, 1-June-1966, free presidential elections were held in the Dominican Republic. It was a contest between **Juan Bosch** and **Joaquin Balaguer**, but with 57% of the votes, **Balaguer easily won the presidency.**

The next day, **Thursday, 2-June-1966, 43-year-old Captain Daniel G. Scheuermann assumed command of the 218th MP Company** while **Lt. Terrance Fiore returned to the U.S. on ETS.**

After about one year in Dom Rep, **Lt. Tom Everett** was sent back to the U.S. in early June 1966. He was then assigned to the 502nd MP Battalion Headquarters at Fort Carson, Colorado and finally left the Army in August 1969 as a Captain.

Following his ETS, **Tom Everett** attended a Theological Seminary in Texas before returning to Knoxville, where he spent three years as the pastor of a local Baptist church. Then beginning in 1975, Tom spent the next twenty-nine years doing inner city ministry providing food, clothing, and a place to belong with a listening ear for those who needed one. After retiring in 2004, he enjoyed two fellowships, each of them a semester in length at the Harvard University in Massachusetts. Today, he still enjoys hiking and mountain climbing. Tom and Shirley have raised two children and still reside in Knoxville, Tennessee.

On Monday, 13-June-1966, Captain Scheuermann was officially promoted to Major per Special Order #113, HQs, Department of the Army, Washington, DC. The order was signed by Harold K. Johnson, General, U.S. Army Chief of

Staff. It stated that the date-of-rank was to be listed as of 2-June-1966. A veteran of World War II and Korea, Major Scheuermann was born in Rock Island, Illinois on February 28, 1923. His wife, Myrtle was born in Illinois on January 17, 1923.

I got an *"Article-15"* while in Dom Rep. **An Article-15 was a written reprimand for misbehavior or disobeying an officer or NCO.** It was considered as *Non-Judicial Punishment* under the *Uniform Code of Military Justice (U.C.M.J.)* and was intended for minor disciplinary offenses only. In this case Sergeant Roby, who was my immediate supervisor, had instructed me to clean the conex containers in the Arms Room. Though I made a noble effort to do so, I evidently failed to do this to his satisfaction and was written up for it. Sometimes these reprimands came with the loss of pay and/or reduction in rank. The Article-15 didn't cost me any rank, but it sure *did* cost me $30 per month for the next two months.

I learned that a soldier may refuse to accept the Article-15 and demand a trial by court-martial instead. But I chose to accept it without a fight. This did *not* mean that I was admitting guilt. It merely meant that I was allowing our C.O. to decide my guilt and choose whatever punishment he deemed appropriate. In hindsight, Sergeant Roby was right. My bad-ass attitude was alive and well back then. What I *didn't* know at the time was that this attitude of mine would come back to haunt me again several months later.

I never knew it at the time, but my being given that Article-15 was never mentioned in the daily Morning Reports. On 15-June-1966 however, two others were given an Article-15, but these guys were also busted down in rank. These *were* recorded on the Morning Report I believe, only because of their reduction in rank.

Another guy came to me one day and explained that he was "getting short" and was due to head back to the U.S. soon on ETS. He asked if I'd be interested in **buying his old guitar.** So I gave him $10 for the guitar and $2 more for a new set of strings that he had. At that time, I could scarcely strum three chords on the thing (*C, F,* and *G7*). Then as luck would have it about two or three weeks later, my cherished guitar fell off a conex container in the Arms Room and broke at the neck. Well, that sure ended my short career as a singer and musician for a long time.

On Friday, 1-July-1966, the most cherished memory of my Dom Rep days took place. This was the day that the newly elected Dominican President, Joaquin Balaguer was sworn into office. The ceremony was also to be attended by **U.S. Vice-President Hubert H. Humphrey** who was visiting for two and a half days from Washington, DC. For the 218th MP Company, this was to be the most critical security mission of all. That was ensuring the safety of the U.S. Vice-President.

But there was going to be a problem that day. The festivities were going to be delayed for a short period of time—about 3 minutes to be exact—by me!

That afternoon, I was standing at a dirt crossroads in a rural wooded area on the outskirts of the city directing traffic. I was dressed in clean and pressed fatigues, but with medium starch this time instead of my usual light starch. My 218th MP helmet liner was gleaming in the sunlight and resting squarely and smartly on my head. I wore an MP armband, and my boots, pistol belt, and holster were highly spit-shined—at least to my own satisfaction. And I was well prepared.

Earlier that day, I had gone over in my mind all the training that I'd had back at Fort Gordon about the proper procedure for directing traffic. So there I stood, watching the intersection from both directions. All was quiet except for the sounds of insects and other wildlife in the woods around me. Being in a rural area, traffic here wasn't exactly what we back home in Detroit called "rush-hour" traffic, and I started to get bored.

Then after some time, a military convoy approached me from ahead. Because it was the only traffic approaching that I could see at that moment, I raised my right arm and gave the lead vehicle the "come ahead" signal. The convoy moved toward me, then passed by and continued on through my intersection. It was quite long as I recall—about thirty or more vehicles.

About a minute or so later while this convoy was still passing, another convoy approached me from my right. This second convoy had several military vehicles along with a few civilian vehicles and one limousine. I turned and again raised my right arm high in the air. But to *this* second convoy, I gave the "halt" signal while the first convoy continued on through.

Abruptly, a young 2nd Lieutenant exited the lead vehicle of this new convoy and came up to me. With a stern look on his face he told me that I needed to break the convoy already passing and allow his entourage to pass immediately.

I started to sweat. I began to think, *Oh shit! Did I screw up?* I took a moment to collect my thoughts and rack my brain. I was *certain* that we were taught that under *NO* circumstances do we *EVER* break up a military convoy already passing. It seemed quite simple to me. Therefore I informed the lieutenant that I would allow his convoy to pass just as soon as possible. Then in a courteous tone of voice, and with all due respect, I asked him to please return to his vehicle. His immediate reply to me was, *"Look here PFC, Do you have any idea who you are holding up here?"* I said, *"No Sir, I do not."* He went on to explain to me that I was holding up the U.S. Vice-President from getting to an important function.

Silently I thought to myself, *Oh my God! This can't really be happening to me!* I still wasn't totally positive that I was doing the right thing. But as long as the deed was done, I thought, what else could I do now? So aloud, I once again asked the young officer to please return to his vehicle. He was ticked off to say the least and told me while taking my name down, that I hadn't heard the last of this. But he returned to his vehicle as I asked without further confrontation. Now mind you,—this entire scene took a mere three minutes!

Immediately after the first convoy passed, I turned to my right again and gave the second convoy the "come ahead" gesture. As the lieutenant passed by me in the lead vehicle, I gave him as snappy a salute as I could. But he merely ignored me as he passed and did not return my salute.

When I got back to the compound later that day, I was still not sure what backlash I would get from it all. But surely enough, immediately upon my arrival I was informed that the C.O. wanted to see me in the Orderly Room right away. *Well,* I thought to myself, *I guess this is it! I'll face it as best I can and take whatever comes.* Then I reported to **Major Scheuermann** "on the double" and was quaking in my boots when he returned my shaky salute.

As it turned out, the Major told me that, not only did I do the right thing out there, but he was also *glad* that I stood my ground, stuck to my training, and handled it the way I did. He went on to say that he was proud of how I'd handled it. To this day, I've always regarded that experience as my proudest day in Olive Drab. What a day to remember!

In the end, the complete inauguration ceremony was executed without incident. As a result, the entire 218th MP Company was showered with high praise from the Vice-Presidential Staff for their excellent performance.

Major Daniel G. Scheuermann would be warmly remembered by several others from the 218th MP Company as well. **Lt. Forrest Craver** recalls him as being a friendly guy, a great joke teller, and often filled with laughter. He also recalled that the Major loved to have a beer with his junior officers after hours in the lounge at the *Hotel Hispaniola.* He noticed the Major always used an ivory cigarette holder (or filter device) whenever he smoked.

Lt. George Martin recalled that when the Major first arrived at the 218th, he resented being assigned to service in Dom Rep. In fact, he was so bitter about it that it became a concern among his junior officers. Major Dan Scheuermann had apparently been the victim of a devastating and ill-deserved *Officer Efficiency Report* some years prior, resulting in his being passed over for promotion a couple of times. Lt. Martin also recalled that Dan seemed preoccupied with "... *that* *damned Spottswood,"* a person who may have been the one responsible for nearly ruining his career. Anyway, when the promotion order finally came through, he'd already had his *Field Officer's Cap*, complete with the "scrambled eggs" and wore it proudly with his fatigues.

George Martin went on to explain **Scrambled Eggs** as this: the regular round "saucer" cap worn by lieutenants and captains had a plain bill, like those of enlisted personnel. However, the hats for "Field Grade" officers (i.e., majors and above) were adorned with fancy gold braid that many thought resembled scrambled eggs. It was regarded as an important rite of passage for career officers. A *Field Grade* officer was above Company level but under the rank of General.

After his promotion, George noticed that the Major seemed to quickly develop a good working relationship with his junior officers and senior NCOs. They all soon came to appreciate and respect him. Like a dark cloud that had suddenly been lifted from above him, Dan Scheuermann became a man whom George and many others greatly admired. The image that stuck with George all these years was that day when the Major stood tall and proud with that majestic hat and ivory cigarette holder.

1ˢᵗ Sergeant Amos Terry apparently knew in advance of the upcoming promotion of Dan Scheuermann. He therefore put a call through to a friend of his stationed at Fort Lee, Virginia. He asked this friend (a Sergeant Major named Charles Samples) to purchase for him a Field Officer's saucer cap (with the scrambled eggs), and asked that it be shipped to him right away. Sergeant Terry paid his good friend $29.00 plus postage for this favor and then presented the cap as a gift to Captain Scheuermann a little in advance of the actual promotion.

Lawrence C. Schlaud, from Grand Blanc, Michigan, was on duty with his partner during the time of Vice-President Hubert Humphrey's visit to Santo Domingo. They were assigned to a checkpoint at an intersection along George Washington Avenue. This was the known route of the expected VP motorcade. Before too long a procession of vehicles began passing by that included a long black limousine convertible in which Humphrey was seated in plain sight. Larry got a short glimpse of the VP and even saluted as the motorcade passed by. Whether the VP noticed his salute, Larry had no idea, as the salute was not returned.

"Larry" Schlaud, a 21-year-old and unmarried, was drafted on 4-November-1965. After taking his Basic Training with the class of C-13-4 at Fort Knox, he had come through AIT with many of us from K-10-4 at Fort Gordon. While in Dom Rep, Larry worked only one night shift in the Arms Room and spent all his other time in uniform pulling line-duty patrol.

During his time in Dom Rep, **John Osborne** (the guy from Royal Oak, Michigan, who also came through Basic and AIT with me) recalled pulling guard duty at a floating pontoon bridge when the Vice-Presidential motorcade came around for a visit. He also recalls another time when he had an extra handful of unaccounted-for .45 caliber pistol ammunition with him while out on patrol. He spent the ammo shooting at a fish he swore was the size of his leg, missing every time of course. Then he had to explain the gunfire to a couple of Nicaraguan soldiers nearby, all the while knowing only six words in Spanish.

On 1-July-1966, with a new Dominican President in place and peace finally restored in the Dominican Republic, the U.S. was finally able to breathe a sigh of relief. Planning then began for a full withdrawal of all U.S. forces from the country.

A week later on **Friday, 8-July-1966,** the Adjutant Generals Office of the United States Forces, Dominican Republic issued *Order #7-18* entitled, *Movement Order, Permanent Change of Station.* It stated that the 218th MP Company was to be *released from USFORDOMREP* and assigned to *Commanding General, Third Unites States Army, duty station: Fort Bragg, North Carolina. Company strength: 4 Officers, 176 Enlisted Men.* Then on 22-July-1966, orders were drawn up by Major Daniel Scheuermann stating that *Personnel Out-Processing* of the 218th was to begin. The 218th MP Company was to head back to the U.S. in three phases.

One morning around mid to late July, **John Patterson** was on patrol with his partner, **Leslie "Glenn" Roark,** a single guy from Jena, Louisiana. They had taken a prisoner from the stockade to *Sick Call* at an Army Medical Clinic nearby and were returning him to the 218th. Glenn said that he would sign the prisoner back in and release him while John waited outside.

Because weapons were not permitted inside the stockade, Glenn took the .45 caliber Automatic pistol out of his holster, ejected the magazine, and handed them to John, and then led the prisoner inside. John stuck the magazine in his pistol belt while holding the pistol in his right hand behind his back, and struck up a conversation with **Steve VanDerSluis**, one of the stockade guards on duty that day. They were standing on the concrete slab at the entrance to the stockade chatting away when, without thinking about it, John unconsciously pulled the hammer back on the .45 and squeezed the trigger. Big Mistake!

The accidental discharge of the weapon sent Steve and John jumping about three feet in the air. In a matter of seconds, everyone in the free world was on the concrete slab facing two somewhat shaken MPs looking white as sheets asking, *"What in the hell just happened here!!?"* Apparently the weapon was *not* cleared, and neither John nor Glenn was aware of it.

Immediately John asked Glenn why he hadn't cleared the weapon before handing it over with a round in the chamber. Glenn replied that he had never chambered a round that day and that the weapon was just as it was when he checked it out from the Arms Room that morning.

When the smoke and dust finally cleared away, John was ordered to have his *"ass in the Major's office first thing in the morning."* Having recently been promoted on 19-May-1966, Patterson felt certain that his days as a new PFC would be swiftly over at sunrise in the morning.

Steven VanDerSluis was a single guy from Los Angles, California, and just recently assigned to the 218th on 29-June-1966 from the class of F-10-4 at Fort Gordon. Because of being assigned to the 218th in late June, he had earned the nickname *Rookie.* Upon hearing the gunfire, others in Steve's tent exclaimed, *"Oh my God, the Rookie has finally shot somebody!"*

Much to the surprise of John *and* Glenn, the only repercussions from the incident amounted to no more than a "slap on the wrist" for Patterson. *That was far too easy,* John thought silently. Aware that something just didn't add up, he was damned determined to look into it and get to the bottom of it . . . and he did.

He went to the Arms Room and checked the written log of weapons issued for each shift that week. Then backtracking, John found the serial number of the pistol in question listed after the name of one of the company's NCOs. The NCO in question had a reputation for carrying a pistol on patrol with a round in the chamber, which was considered a serious no-no!

It's never enough to simply eject the magazine from the weapon with the thumb release button. One had to also retract the slide in order to properly clear the chamber. This was fully the responsibility of the MP coming off duty to clear and clean his weapon before checking it in.

Apparently the anonymous NCO had checked his weapon in with the forgotten round still in the chamber. But even more serious than that was the fact that this *also* went unnoticed by the man on duty in the Arms Room, whose job was to see that all weapons were cleared and cleaned before he placed them back on the weapons rack. So when Glenn Roark checked out the weapon in the morning, he simply inserted the new magazine, naturally assuming that the pistol was already cleared.

Many of my fellow MPs thought that working in the Arms Room was an unimportant task in comparison to pulling line-duty patrol. But I knew full well that the job carried a lot of responsibility. This would never have happened if I were the one on duty in the Arms Room when the weapon was checked in. It's not that I am blowing my own horn here. It's just that I took my job in the Arms Room very seriously back then. Yes, I was a goof-off with a lousy attitude at the time, but I'd learned early on to be hard-nosed about seeing that weapons were cleared and cleaned. John was certain that the whole incident was being "swept under the carpet." He had good reason to feel that way, as thereafter not another word was ever spoken of the incident.

Near the end of our days in Dom Rep, **Dennis L. Wood**, a married man from St. Clair Shores, Michigan, was assigned to a Check Point along with his partner somewhere in the city. Dennis had married a girl named Jean in September 1965 about five weeks before he was inducted. It was a morning shift and they were under strict orders from the *PMO* to report any massive crowd movements in their area.

Sometime between 0900 and 1000 Hours in the morning, they observed a huge crowd slowly gathering in the streets not far from their position. As the angry crowd grew in numbers, they began yelling over and over again the old often heard, *"Yankees go home!"* Dennis believed that this event was triggered by the incident of the day before when a shoeshine boy from the 218th was seriously injured. It was an accidental gunshot to the head by a man from the 82nd Airborne Division.

After a few moments, Wood thought that he heard some gunfire, but amidst all the noise of the crowd, it was difficult to be certain. He *did* however, notice smoke rising into the air above the mass of protesters. Complying with their orders of that morning, they radioed in and reported the location of the disturbance. Then they "high-tailed it out of there!" Dennis reasoned that two MPs against several thousand irate civilians would not have been a fair fight. They were sure glad to get back in the 218th compound.

On Monday, 15-August-1966, I was among thirty men leaving Dom Rep in *Phase I*. By early afternoon we had arrived at San Isidro Airfield and boarded a C-130. In short time we were airborne and heading north. (The second and third phases would leave Dom Rep on 26-August and 20-September-1966 respectively.)

*   *   *

The U.S. intervention in the Dominican Republic had cost 237 casualties, both U.S. and Latin. Of that figure, the U.S. had suffered 27 KIA (Killed in Action), 172 WIA (Wounded in Action) and 20 Non-Combat Dead. In terms of money, the estimated cost to the U.S. was about $311 million for aid and military expenses. But we had accomplished our objectives. Mainly, the U.S., along with the IAPF operating under the OAS, had restored peace and prevented a Communist takeover of the Dominican Republic. Though that hard-won peace would be on shaky ground for some years to come, the U.S. has never had a reason to intervene there again.

Those of us, who were there and served in the *United States Forces Dominican Republic*, have earned the right to wear a special shoulder patch on our left shoulder. We called it the *"FIP-OEA"* patch. (For those who are unfamiliar with the meaning of *FIP-OEA*, they are the initials for the Spanish words that translated read, ***Inter-American Peace Force—Organization of American States*.**) The patch also includes the "rocker" under it that reads **USFORDOMREP.** It may not seem as impressive as the famous *Screaming Eagle* patch of the 101st Airborne Division known around the world, or the *AA* patch of the 82nd Airborne Division. But I'm darn proud to have been there and was proud to wear it.

I'm also proud to have been awarded the ***Armed Forces Expeditionary Medal.*** This was awarded to *"members of the Armed Forces of the United States who, after 1-July-1958, participated in U.S. military operations; U.S. military operations in direct support of the United Nations; and/or U.S. operations of assistance to friendly foreign nations."*

Today, the Dominican Republic, especially its capitol of Santo Domingo, is among some of the hottest tourist spots on the planet. It offers white sandy beaches, impressive mountain ranges, and spectacular views of rivers and water falls. There are many fine restaurants to dine in and several excellent luxury hotels to choose from.

These include the old famous and familiar **El Embajador**, fully updated and modernized. It has 286 rooms with stunning views of the city, lovely gardens and the Caribbean Sea. Another old familiar place is the **Renaissance Jaragua Hotel and Casino** located on George Washington Avenue. This five-star hotel was totally rebuilt in 1987 and newly renovated again 1999. With ten floors and 288 rooms, it also provides a fabulous view of the Caribbean. The **Hispaniola Hotel and Casino** today is a moderately priced, five-storey Hi-Rise with 165 beautifully decorated tropical guest rooms, surrounded by stunning tropical gardens.

There are only two main drawbacks when visiting Dom Rep today. Recently, **John and Debbie Patterson** along with **Wayne and Julie Molnar** made a short vacation trip there. I was told that the local water is still not drinkable and that the hotels ask that their guests not flush the toilet paper. They actually provide a separate receptacle for this. You can certainly draw your own conclusions!

The old *HQs, USFORDOMREP* "Palace" is no longer there today. In its place, a beautiful fountain was constructed in 1973, but it no longer works today. This and the rest of the old palace grounds today make up the *Plaza de la Cultura*, a cultural center that includes four museums. On the very same grounds that our 218th MP Company compound had set up, stands the *Museo del Hombre Dominicano* (Museum of the Dominican Man). The school building that was just west of our compound is still there, but is now occupied by the *Museo Nacional de Historia y Geographica* (National Museum of History and Geography). However, I was glad to learn recently that the old *Maternity Hospital* we all remembered still exists today across the street from all of this.

As for me, being there in 1966 was an experience I'd never forget. These days I often think of my life back then in the Dominican Republic and Santo Domingo, and I admit that I too would love to visit there once again some day.

AUTHOR'S NOTE:

During my research on this story, I found that I had something in common with a U.S. Army officer who was serving in the Dominican Republic at the time I was there. *Lt. Colonel Richard Irving Paul* (born in November 1921) was a *U.S. State Department Representative* serving with the *Presidential Relief Mission* in the Dominican Republic in 1965. Richard Paul's father, *Major General Willard Stewart Paul,* during World War II, was the commander of the U.S. 26th Infantry Division serving under General George S. Patton's Third Army in Europe. Back then, my father, PFC Raymond James Oblinger, was an Anti-Tank Gunner in the 1st Battalion, 104th Regiment of the 26th Infantry Division. During World War II, Richard I. Paul was a young junior officer serving in the G-1 Section of his father's 26th *"Yankee Division"* HQs in Europe. He was also a veteran of the Korean War.

Being fluent in Spanish, Richard I. Paul trained military personnel from many Latin American nations between 1958 and 1961. I had first made contact with Richard Paul during my World War II research, at which time he was more than helpful in offering personal information about his father that I used in my first book. It was then that I learned that he had served in Dom Rep while I was there. Just recently, when I tried to contact him again for more info about his Dom Rep days, I was saddened to learn that he had died at the age of 86 in March of 2008 in Kerrville, Texas.

US Air Force C-130 'Hurcules' taking off

US Air Force C-130 'Hurcules' over water

US Air Force C-130 at San Isidro Airfield in Dom Rep, 1965

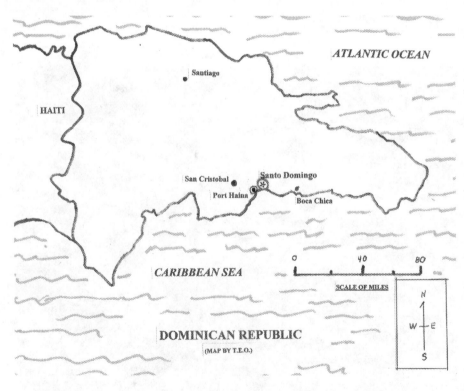

Dominican Republic

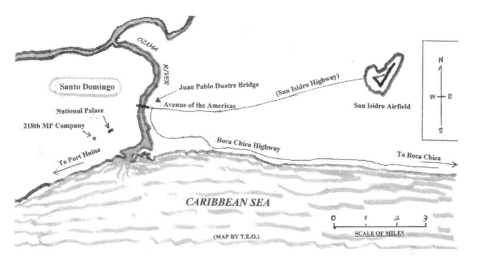

Santo Domingo & San Isidro Airfield—Dom Rep

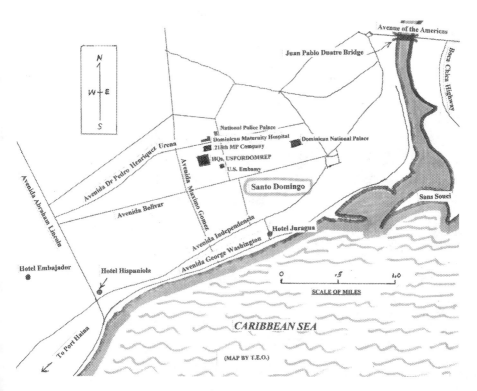

Santo Domingo, Dom Rep

Santo Domingo as seen from the east side of the Duarte Bridge

Bombed out buildings in Dom Rep

218th MP Campsite as seen from above the Maternity Hospital
across the street to the North

218th from above (2)

"If it crawls, it's a Dominican cockroach. If it flies, it's a Caribbean mosquito. If it stands up on its hind legs, run like hell!"

Army Times Cartoon

HQs, USFORDOMREP & PMO (1)

HQs, USFORDOMREP & PMO (2)

HQs, USFORDOMREP & PMO (3)

218th MP Helmet Liner (1)

218th MP Helmet Liner (2)

Early tent foundations at 218th compound

My 3rd Platoon Tent in Dom Rep

1st night inside my 3rd Platoon Tent

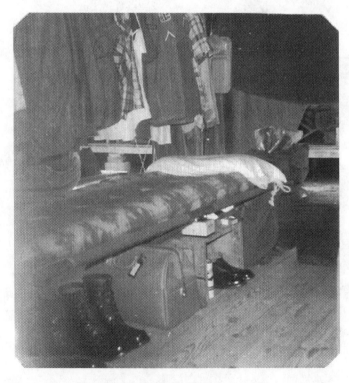

My living space

Tom O & 3rd Platoon tent

Tom O, MP

Tom O at Check Point in Santo Domingo

218th Main Gate & Guard Shack (looking out)

218th Main Gate (looking in)

Standing Guard Mount Inspection

Guard Mount (2)

Guard Mount (3)

Guard Mount (4)

Guard Mount (5)

Our Movie Screen

Ed Mitchell

Ed Mitchell (2)

Ed Mitchell (3)

Ed Mitchell (4)

218th Motor Pool (1)

218th Motor Pool (2)

218th Motor Pool (3)

Photo # 3: Aerial view of Transient Stockade. (1) Stone wall on north boundary of campsite (2) Chain-link fence on east boundary of campsite (3) Guard Towers (4) Concertina wire (single strand) around exterior of stockade (5) Stockade inner barrier (6) Medium custody compound (7) Maximum custody compound w/two segregation cells (8) Compound entrances (9) Administrative section (10) Latrine.

218th Transient Stockade & Latrine (from above)

Photo # 7: 218th Transient Stockade, Exterior view, South side, Medium custody compound.

218th Stockade (1)

218th Stockade (2)

218th Stockade (3)

Lt Tom Everett & 218th Stockade

Bob Franklin (center) standing Guard Mount

Brian R. Bryan

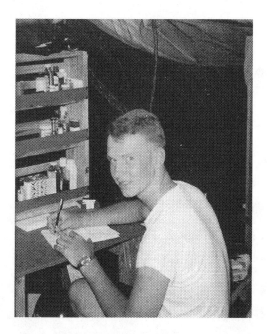

Brian Bryan (2)

Brian Bryan (3)

Brian Bryan & Soldier from Paraguay

Carl M. Hagemeister, our Life Guard in Dom Rep

MPs Goofing Off

218th MP Baseball Team

Dennis L. Wood

Dennis Wood (2)

Dennis Wood (3)

Dennis Wood (4)

Dennis L. Wood & James J. Simone at work

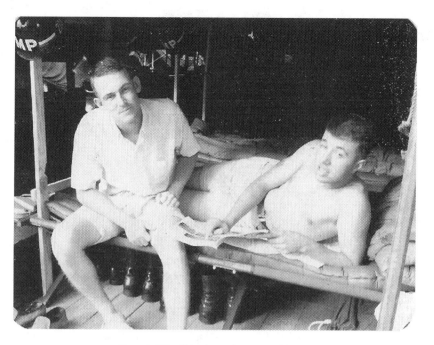

Dennis Wood & Jim Simone at leisure

John W. Patterson

John H. Osborne, Jr.

Doyle W. 'Gabby' Hayes

Downtown Santo Domingo

Another street in Santo Domingo

Country Road & Old Wooden Bridge

Country Road & Oxen

Shanty Town along the west bank of the Ozama River

Another Shanty Town

Another rural town

144 Maximo Gomez Avenue (as it looks Today)

Entrance to San Isidro Airfield in Dom Rep

Former MP HQs & Helicopter Pad at Sans Souci, Dom Rep

Fort at Sans Souci—2nd Location

Duarte Street at Check Pointe #3 in Santo Domingo

Washed-out bridge at Port Haina

Washed-out bridge at Port Haina (2)

Pontoon bridge near Port Haina

Guard Shack near pontoon bridge

Frank J. 'Lurch' Opyt on duty at bridge

Pontoon bridge

Pontoon bridge (2)

Pontoon Bridge (3)

Pontoon Bridge (4)

Another bridge in Dom Rep

George Washington Avenue looking west along southern coast in Santo Domingo

George Washington Avenue looking east
(as seen Today from the top of the Hilton Hotel)

Keith D. 'Gus' Gustafson

'Gus' Gustafson (2)

Gustafson & Partner on Patrol

Hotel Embajador in 1966

Hotel Embajador (Today)

Hotel Hispaniola (Today)

Hotel Jaragua (south side) in its early days.
Photo courtesy of the Renaissance Jaragua Hotel and Casino

Hotel Jaragua in 1966 (north side)

Hotel Renaissance Jaragua (Today)

Hotel Renaissance Jaragua (Today) -
Photo courtesy of the Renaissance Jaragua Hotel & Casino

John Patterson & Stephen 'Durwood' Pack

Larry S. Develbiss

Lawrence C. Schlaud & Mr. 'Spots'

James W. 'Limey' Walker & 'Gus' Gustafson

Drying Laundry in Dom Rep

Looking East & West at the southern coast of Santo Domingo

Lt. Everett & Driver—'Yankees Goo Out'

Michael G. Johnson

Michael L. Moots

Mike Scheitel & Partner

Dominican National Palace in Dom Rep (Then)

Dominican National Palace (Today)

Bronze statue of Christopher Columbus pointing north in Santo Domingo

Cathredal of Santo Domingo, the oldest Church in the West Indies.
Built in the 1500s

MPs John Patterson, Wayne Molner, Edwardo Placencio
along with Dominican National Police

'Red Beach' in Dom Rep

Row of tents along east fence

Samuel W. Dickson, our Barber in Dom Rep

Sam Dickson at the Zoo in Dom Rep

Sand detail at Red Beach in Dom Rep

Sgt Bill Whitmill tending bar at Sans Souci

Bill Whitmill in the new 218th MP Lounge

Bill Whitmill & Friend

Bill Whitmill

Sgt Richard D. Plummer & Sgt John T. Flack

Dick Plummer, taking a much needed break

Sgt Robert E. Gooch & Pool Table in DR

Sgt Ronald W. Cook

Ron Cook at PMO in Dom Rep

Ship 'Sea-Land' at Port Haina

Ship 'Sea-Land' at Port Haina (2)

Shoe Shine boys in Dom Rep (1)

Shoe Shine crew (2)

Sugar Plant at Boca Chica

Sgt Ozel Roby, Jr.—Supply Sgt for the 218th MP Co
and later the 100th MP Battalion

Inside the 218th MP Lounge

218th MP Lounge (2)

218th MP Lounge (3)

218th MP Lounge & Officers
(Tom Everett, Dennis Ellis, Terrance Fiore, George Martin)

First Sergeant Amos Terry & Lieutenant Tom Everett of the 218th MP Company

Rick VandeKerchove (with sunglasses) on left, Jim Simone on center,
Arnold Rohrbeck on right in MP lounge

1st Sgt Amos Terry & Rita Hager (in 2008)

Swimming Pool in Dom Rep (Empty)

Swimming Pool & Pool House

Swimming Pool (1)

Swimming Pool (2)

Timothy P. Doyle & partner goofing off

Tom Everett & 'Joe'—Interpreter from the Virgin Islands

Tom Everett & his friend (a Shoe-shine boy)

Tom Everett & Terrance M. Fiore

Tom Everett in 218th MP Company Orderly Room

Tom Everett on the wall at Sans Souci

Thomas R. Kranch

Tom Kranch (2)

Tom Kranch (3)

Tom Kranch (4)

Tom Marston & Mike Scheitel

Tom Marston at Port Haina. (Trujillo's yacht in background)

218th Arms Room

Tom O at Arms Room

Tom O at work in Arms Room

Tom O & M-60 Machine Gun

Ed Mitchell outside of Arms Room—
(Orderly Room in background)

218th Arms Room on Left, Mess Hall on Right

Tom O at leisure

Tom O on duty

Boca Chica Beach in Dom Rep

Town of Boca Chica (Then)

Main Street in Boca Chica (Today)

Boca Chica (Today)

Trujillo's family Yacht

Trujillo's Yacht (2)

Trujillo's Yacht (3)

Trujillo's Yacht (4)

Vernon Schwieterman

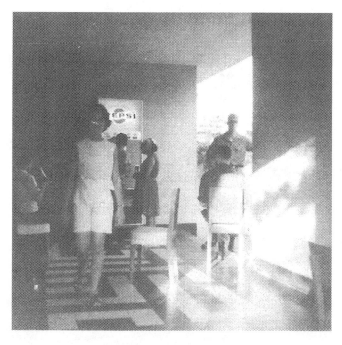

Vicki's Restaurant in Dom Rep

Wayne Lee Molner

Wayne Molner (2)

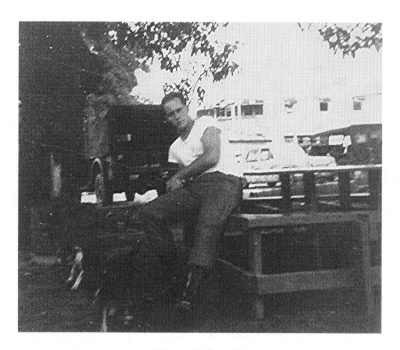

Wayne Molner (3)

Wayne Molner, John Patterson and Honduran soldiers on patrol in DR

Un Peso Oro (a Dominican One Dollar Bill)

USO Show & Bob Hope, in Dom Rep, December, 1965

The USO Show also included Joey Heatherton and other entertainers

Leaving Dom Rep, 3rd Phase, LST 1163

Leaving Dom Rep, 3rd Phase, LST 1156

Awaiting Convoy from Little Creek, VA to Fort Bragg, NC

Convoy to Fort Bragg

Chapter 5

Company C, 503rd MP Battalion

MONDAY, 15-August-1966—Company C, 503rd MP Battalion, Fort Bragg, North Carolina.

By early evening we had arrived back in the U.S. and touched down at **Pope Air Force Base.** From there we had a short ride south into Fort Bragg, North Carolina and we were soon dropped off at Building #2-1105 in the central area of the post. This was the barracks for the *503rd Military Police Battalion* located at the northeast corner of Macomb and Reilly Streets. Housing the entire battalion, it was a long, three-storey red brick building with a gable roof built sometime between 1927 and 1931. Company C occupied the westernmost end of the building. (This building is still there today.) The temperature on that evening there was still in the low 70s.

Camp Bragg **was born in 1918** about fifty miles south of Raleigh and ten miles north, northwest of Fayetteville, North Carolina. At that time about 127,000 acres of sandy soil and pine tree woods were set aside there and designated as a U.S. Army installation. (Today, that area has expanded to 161,000 acres spread over six counties. It includes seven major airborne drop zones, four impact areas, eighty-two ranges, sixteen maneuver areas and two Army airfields. Within this area, the main proper of the post encompasses 12,160 acres (19.0 square miles).

The camp began as a field artillery site named in honor of Confederate General Braxton Bragg, an artillery officer and native of North Carolina. In September 1922, Camp Bragg became officially known as *Fort Bragg* and twenty years later in 1942, Army Airborne training began there. Though all five World War II airborne divisions (the 11th, 13th, 17th, 82nd and 101st) had trained at Fort Bragg, the 82nd

Airborne Division was assigned there upon its return from Europe in 1946. In 1951, the XVIII Airborne Corps was activated there and Fort Bragg soon became known as the *Home of the Airborne.*

Lee Field House, the gymnasium on the northwest corner of Longstreet and Reilly Road, was completed and dedicated in 1951. It was named in honor of Major General William C. Lee, former commander of the 101st Airborne Division, who was considered as the *Father of the Airborne.* Then constructed in 1958, *Womack Army Hospital* was a nine-storey medical facility. With a 500-bed capacity, it was dedicated to the memory of PFC Bryant H. Womack, a combat medical corpsman from Mill Spring, North Carolina who gave his life in the Korean Conflict while saving the lives of others.

During the late 1960s and on through the days of the Vietnam War, the strength of Fort Bragg exceeded 57,800 troops. Today, Fort Bragg and Pope Air Force Base (adjacent to the north) make up one of the largest military complexes in the world.

The *503rd Military Police Battalion* **was originally constituted in February 1922** in the U.S. Army's *Organized Reserves* as the *303rd MP Battalion.* Its HQs at that time was set up at Harrisburg, Pennsylvania. After sixteen years, the battalion was inactivated in January 1938, withdrawn from the Organized Reserves, and was then allotted to the *Regular Army.*

In June 1940, the battalion was redesignated as the *503rd MP Battalion* and during World War II, was activated in February 1943 at Camp Maxey, Texas. The 503rd then served in all five campaigns of the *E.T.O. (European Theater of Operation)* and was inactivated in March 1946 at Camp Kilmer, New Jersey. After World War II, the battalion was awarded the *Meritorious Unit Commendation* for its dedicated performance in Europe. From June 1946 through November 1947, the 503rd was activated for a short tour of duty in Italy. Then in February 1949, the 503rd was called to active duty once again and assigned to Fort Bragg, North Carolina.

In March 1965, the 503rd was deployed to Selma, Alabama for what would be called *Operation Steephill XIII.* While there, the battalion provided security measures to protect participants of the *Freedom March* that was making world news at that time.

Only two months later in May 1965, the 503rd was called upon again and sent to the Dominican Republic as part of a peace-keeping force where it soon earned its second *Meritorious Unit Commendation.* On 24-October-1965, with the end of hostilities there, the 503rd (less Company C) returned to Fort Bragg. Company C then stayed behind and became the 218th MP Company for the remainder of its time in Dom Rep.

Then on **Thursday, 18-August-1966**, just three days after my return from Dom Rep, the **218ᵗʰ MP Company was redesignated again as Company C of the 503ʳᵈ MP Battalion. Major Daniel G. Scheuermann was still listed as the Commander of C Company.**

When we arrived here at the 503ʳᵈ, we were instructed to choose a bunk and get settled in. I happened to pick a cadre room on the second floor along with another MP whose name I cannot recall today. This worked out great for a while until the rest of the company returned later from Dom Rep. We were then "tossed out" of our cadre room and forced to pick whatever bunk that was left in the barracks bay. But the room was nice to have while it lasted.

It was here at Company C of the 503ʳᵈ that I noticed "the handwriting on the wall" so to speak. I always enjoyed reading, even if it *was* in the form of **graffiti on the latrine walls!** While standing at the urinal one day taking care of business, I noticed some graffiti that I never forgot after all these years. One author had written, *Don't look up here! The joke is in your hand!* Another inscription read, *No matter how you jump and dance, the last few drops go down your pants!* And still another modern-day thinker of that time wrote, *Please don't throw cigarette butts in the urinals.—It makes them soggy and hard to light!* When I read that last one, I laughed so hard I could hardly hit the urinal I was aiming at.

Within a few days after my arrival at Fort Bragg, I decided to put in for **my first real *Leave of Absence*** (formerly called a *Furlough* during World War II days). But this time I decided that my mode of travel would be different. There would be no more traveling by *Greyhound* bus for me. Now that I had twice experienced being a passenger aboard an aircraft, I decided that *that's* the way I wanted to travel from now on. My ten-day leave was granted and I was on my way to Detroit. This would however, be my first real flight on a *civilian* commercial airplane.

I arrived at the ***Fayetteville Municipal Airport*** sometime after midnight as my flight was scheduled to depart at exactly 1:45 AM. The airport was located about sixteen miles south of Fort Bragg (four and a half miles south of downtown Fayetteville), about halfway between *State Highway 87* and *U.S. Highway 301*. The airport first opened in late 1949 with grass runways and was originally named *Grannis Field* in honor of the late Ed W. Grannis, who was killed in a plane crash a year earlier. He was also the contractor whose construction company built the project. Recently, with $4 million in local and federal grants, further improvements at the airport had begun in early 1966.

Sitting 189 feet above sea level, the airport looked much smaller than I had anticipated. I'd been to Detroit's *Metropolitan Wayne County Airport* (which is actually located in Romulus, Michigan) on several occasions in the past to pick up family members coming to Detroit. So I naturally thought most airports were pretty much the same everywhere like some of the Greyhound bus terminals I've seen. However, the entire Fayetteville Airport Terminal building looked to be about the size of the old East Detroit High School gymnasium back home. But who was complaining? Certainly not me.

Piedmont Airlines began operations in 1948 as a regional airline, based at Winston-Salem, North Carolina, and had served Fayetteville since September of the following year. Early Piedmont routes were operated utilizing the *Douglas DC-3* aircraft (of World War II vintage), and then later the *Martin 404* was introduced that I would become well familiar with. Recently by 1966, these service routes included North and South Carolina, Virginia, West Virginia, and, since 1955, Washington, DC. (Later in 1989, the airline was absorbed by *U.S. Airways,* but today still flies under the name of *Piedmont.*)

At the ticket counter inside I asked for what was called a **Military Stand-By** ticket. This meant that as long as I was in uniform, I would fly at half-price unless my seat was needed for a full-fare paying passenger. The regular passenger fare for Piedmont Flight #820 to Washington, DC was $25.95, which meant that my bargain priced stand-by fare would be $12.98. It was a gamble for sure, but then again, this wasn't Detroit's Metropolitan Airport with its inevitable long lines at the ticket counters. While being handed my Boarding Pass, I was told by the ticket agent (who was pointing to her left) that my flight would depart from *"Gate #2 out that door."*

When I went outside, I saw a chain-link fence about four feet high and about thirty feet long. There were three chain-link, swinging gates along its length, with each prominently marked as (you guessed it) *Gate #1, Gate #2,* and *Gate #3.* So I thought to myself, *OK, so this ain't Detroit's 'Metro' Airport, but hey!—I'm on my way! And I'm travelin' in style this time!*

The aircraft was a *Martin 404.* It was powered by two *Pratt & Whitney* prop-type radial piston engines, each cranking out about 2400 horsepower. It could carry a crew of four and up to forty passengers at a cruising speed of 225mph. Its maximum speed was 312mph at a ceiling of 29,000 feet. But on these short hops of 284 miles from Fayetteville, North Carolina to Washington, DC, that altitude was seldom reached. The *Martin 404* was 74.6 feet long and 28.4 feet high with a wingspan of 93.25 feet.

Even at this time of night, the plane looked tired and worn out. And there was darn good reason for this. Produced sometime between 1947 and 1953, the aircraft had to be between thirteen and nineteen years old. In fact, Piedmont had just begun plans to phase out the Martin 404 within the next year.

As I continued walking toward the plane, I started getting nervous and was beginning to get second thoughts about air travel. But having come this far, I decided to go for it and went up the stairs at the back end of the plane. When I reached the top I was greeted with a reassuring smile from an attractive *Stewardess* as I entered the aircraft. This was in the days before they were called *Flight Attendants*.

As it turned out, there were quite a few seats left when the two engines were started. Once started, they seemed to spit and sputter a little as they warmed up. Knowing this was adding to my nervousness and discomfort. I had chosen a window seat just behind the wing on the right (starboard) side of the isle. This was about midway back from the cockpit cabin door. It was about 1:45 AM (0145 Hours) in the morning when we had taxied into takeoff position.

The engines revved up and we started rolling and accelerating down the 4,800-foot runway. When I looked out the window I couldn't believe my eyes. I thought, *Oh No! This couldn't be happening to me twice!* (I was recalling my first experience with an Army C-130 aircraft.) Now shooting out the back of the starboard engine, was a trail of flames about fifteen to twenty inches long. Nervously, I got the attention of a Stewardess and with a shaky finger, pointed out to her that the aircraft was on fire.

After a quick glance out the window to see what I was concerned about, she very calmly assured me that this was quite normal and that there was really nothing to worry about. Then noticing how calm *she* was about it, I decided to take her word for it and try to relax for the remainder of the flight. At that time of night there really wasn't much to see looking out the window. Just a few faint lights from the world far below. So I decided to just sit back, relax if I could, and light up a cigarette.

As we neared our destination in Washington, DC, the pilot took a long banking turn around the city, giving us a magnificent view of the Capitol in all its shimmering beauty at night. Circling from a few thousand feet above, I was able to recognize many of the famous landmarks from photos I'd seen over the years. The flight took two hours and thirty-one minutes. At exactly 4:16 AM we touched down as scheduled at *Washington National Airport*.

Here, I had a "lay-over" until about 7:30 AM when I'd catch the next flight out in the morning heading up to Detroit. For the remainder of my time in the

Army, I flew either **Northwest Orient** or **United Airlines** between Washington, DC and Detroit. At that time, **Northwest utilized the Lockheed L-188 Electra** aircraft for their run between DC and Detroit. This aircraft was powered by four Allison turboprop engines, had a crew of six, with a capacity for up to eighty-eight passengers and cruised at about 400mph. **United Airlines then utilized the Vickers Viscount (Type 800).** Introduced in 1950, the Vickers had a crew of four, and a capacity of seventy-five passengers. It was also powered by four turboprop engines, each sporting the famous *"RR"* initials of *Rolls-Royce.* I remember thinking at the time how comforting it was to know that the engines were manufactured by a name that was trusted around the world.

On the morning flight out from DC to Detroit, our altitude was always higher than that of the Piedmont flight coming in. This flight of 405 miles usually took about an hour and a half.

As dawn began to brake in the sky over southern Michigan, I had my very first look at the world from above the clouds. It looked like a soft blanket of white cotton below and seemed awesome beyond description. On this flight too, the pilot gave us a panoramic view of the city of Detroit. Approaching from about 5,000 feet or so, he circled above the city before touching down at "Metro" Airport west of there in Romulus.

Anyway, I was sure glad to be back at home again. And I also noticed that my father was especially glad to see me. Though he tried to hide it, I could tell that he had worried about me. Mom tried to scold me for not calling home a few days ahead of time, telling me that I didn't give her a chance to clean up the house for my arrival. Of course, my reason for not telling her was that I wanted to surprise her. Mom's home cooking sure was a welcome change from the bland menus in the Army mess halls.

As it turned out in the end, I *never* got bumped from a military stand-by flight. I'd heard that many of the guys did. But I had also decided that for the remainder of my time in Olive Drab, I would always schedule my leaves to begin about ten days or so *after* the major holidays. That way, there would be no long lines of homesick guys wanting to go home for *Easter, Labor Day,* the *4th of July, Memorial Day, Thanksgiving, Christmas, New Years,* and so on. And best of all, I was always able to surprise Mom.

On Tuesday, 23-August-1966, Major William C. Robbins assumed command of the 503rd MP Battalion. This would be a temporary assignment until a more permanent position could be made for him.

On Friday, 26-August-1966, the second group of guys left Dom Rep via Air Force C-130. The 218th had already been redesignated as Company C of the 503rd MP Battalion. My friend **Ed Mitchell** was among this second group returning to the States. The trip from San Isidro Airfield to Pope AFB and Fort Bragg was for the most part a quiet and uneventful experience for them. Upon arrival, Ed was assigned to a bunk on the second floor at the 503rd.

On Tuesday, 13-September-1966, 1st Lt. Louis Silverhart was assigned as the new Commander of Company C upon his return from the Dominican Republic.

Two days later on **Thursday, 15-September-1966,** two American soldiers of the 82nd Airborne Division were killed in the Dominican Republic. A 21-year-old man from New York and a 20-year-old guy from Wisconsin were shot in the back by a passing terrorist on a motorcycle. This took place while the soldiers were dropping off their laundry for the last time before being sent back to the states. It was at a downtown laundry facility in the old *Rebel Zone* of Santo Domingo. While one of the men died instantly in the street, the other was severely wounded and died four hours later at a Dominican Army Field Hospital.

John Patterson, along with his partner of Company C (the former 218th MP Company) were dispatched by **Ron Cook** at the PMO to help load the body of the wounded man in the ambulance, and provide a police escort to the hospital. After the death of the soldier, Patterson was subsequently asked to help pack the body on ice for transport back to the United States.

John firmly believed that this was a totally senseless shooting. In fact it seemed just as senseless as the fragmentation grenade that was thrown into a hamburger joint a few nights earlier when he was on patrol. He learned that a little boy had died later as a result of injuries incurred during the incident. It seemed obvious to John that while many of the Dominican people wanted all the *Yankees* to go home, it sure as hell seemed like many of them still wanted the *Peace Force* to stay. But President Johnson was confident that the "powers to be" in the Dominican Republic could continue to hold it all together and make it work. And in time, they did just that.

The next day, Friday, 16-September-1966, Major Thomas W. Adair took command of the 503rd MP Battalion at Fort Bragg in place of Major Robbins. Major Robbins was then transferred to assume command of the 100th MP Battalion which was soon to be activated elsewhere on post.

Early on **Tuesday, 20-September-1966, the remainder of Company C departed from the Dominican Republic.** To oversee this departure, **Sergeant**

Ron Cook was appointed as the *NCOIC (NCO in charge)* of the 123-man rear detachment leaving Santo Domingo. The group convoyed to Port Haina and began boarding two large flat-bottomed *U.S. Navy LSTs (Landing Ship, Tank)* which had run up on the beach to be loaded. One of the ships being loaded was the *USS 1163(Waldo County)*, which was built in Mississippi and commissioned in 1953. The other one was the *USS 1156 (Terrebonne Parish)*, built in Maine and launched in 1952. Most LSTs measured 384 feet in length, 55 feet in width with a 17-foot draft. They were rated at 2500 tons empty and 5800 tons fully loaded. They were capable of a respectable 14 knots in speed with a troop capacity of up to 395 persons.

Tom Marston had driven to Port Haina that morning in a jeep with a trailer. He recalled what a hassle it was trying to back them up the loading ramp into the ship. But eventually he got it loaded and the ships then steamed out of the port. After three days "on the high seas" they finally docked at the *Naval Amphibious Base* of Little Creek, Virginia, just east of Norfolk on the southern shore of Chesapeake Bay. After spending the night there, they assembled in the morning and convoyed about 200 miles southwest and arrived in North Carolina at Fort Bragg.

Assigned to the 503rd MP Battalion, we were entitled to wear the *Third Army Patch*. The reason for this was that the 503rd operated under the authority of the U.S. Third Army, whose headquarters was at Fort McPherson, Georgia. This was the major command for all Army units in the southeastern portion of the U.S. at that time. The **XVIII Airborne Corps** was a subordinate command under Third Army in which the 503rd MP Battalion operated, as well as the 82nd Airborne Division at Fort Bragg. But only a few of us that I knew back then wore the airborne patch.

The Third Army patch was a distinctive round blue patch with a red stripe just inside the circumference. In the middle of this was a large letter "A" in white thread.

The proper way to wear it was to move our *FIP/OEA (USFORDOMREP)* patch from our left shoulder to the right. Patches worn on the left shoulder were what we called ***Unit*** patches while those worn on our right shoulder were often referred to as ***Combat*** patches.

Upon his return to Fort Bragg, **Sergeant Amos Terry had remained as the 1st Sergeant for Company C, of the 503rd MP Battalion.**

A few weeks later, the former 218th MP Company began a period of reorganization while preparing for movement to Vietnam in Southeast Asia. As far as I know, only a few guys from the 503rd volunteered to go along with the 218th. **Jim "Limey" Walker** was one of them.

Not long after his arrival in Vietnam, **Jim Walker** left the 218th MP Company and transferred to the 101st Airborne Division. There, he joined the *Long-Range Reconnaissance Patrols (LRRPs)* of 101st and remained with them for the remainder of his tour in Vietnam. Then after six full years in the U.S. Army, Limey returned to the United States and finally left Olive Drab for good. He worked in law enforcement for a while and then opened an auto service station. Later he joined the *Federal Protective Service*. After quitting government service in 1980, he became a Private Investigator in Houston, Texas. Since his retirement, Walker has published a book about his life in Olive Drab called *Fortune Favors the Bold*, available in paperback through *Random House/Ivy Books*.

I learned that now and then a few of the guys in the 503rd who were going home on leave, would choose hitchhiking as their mode of travel. And just the thought of doing so seemed to fascinate me at the time. I was no stranger to hitchhiking back then as I had done it often back home before my Army days. So I seriously considered the idea myself and thought quietly, *What a great way to see the country up close!* I had heard that **Carl Hagemeister** was still asked to use his artistic talents here at Company C for various posters and signs. So I then asked Carl if I could hire his sign-making talents, and he agreed.

He made me up a colorful sign on a bright orange-colored poster board. It was about 12 x 24 inches in size. One side of it read: *D E T R O I T* in large bold letters, and the reverse side featured the words: *FORT BRAGG, NORTH CAROLINA.* In those days, wearing the *Class A* dress uniform while carrying that poster would have assured me swift rides each time I put my thumb out.

As things turned out, however, I never did use the poster. I just didn't have what it took to try hitchhiking that far. And to this day, I cannot recall for the life of me, what I ever did with the poster. I sometimes wonder what adventure I missed out on by not trying it just once.

Carl Hagemeister, not long after returning from Dom Rep, married Christy while at home on leave. After his ETS, he returned to California and became self-employed in automotive painting and pinstriping. He later began a furniture manufacturing business that he still runs today called *Vintage Gardens*. Carl and Christy have five children.

Back at Company C of the 503rd, I found myself pulling line-duty patrol again. While many of the MPs of the 503rd utilized M-151 jeeps, some of us rode in "real" police vehicles! These were 1963 Olive Drab Green four-door *Chevy* sedans, powered by six-cylinder engines with three-speed "stick shift" transmissions, not exactly designed for high-speed police chases. In fact, it was my opinion back then that an M-151 Jeep could outrun the Chevys *any day of the week and twice on Sunday!*

For my very first patrol assignment at the 503rd, I was paired up with a sergeant whose last name was **Comstock**. During that patrol, I was driving (as I was once again the junior partner) and we stopped a vehicle that was speeding on post. Seeing as how the subject was a sergeant who was only doing about five over, I thought I'd give this guy a break. In my past, I had been given a break by police back home, so I thought, *"do unto others as . . . "* But Sergeant Comstock wouldn't have it. He insisted that I write the guy up. This was the one and *only* traffic citation *(DD Form 1408)* that I ever wrote as an MP. I began to wonder then if being a good MP meant that one had to shed all compassion and understanding for human problems. I didn't like being that way at all.

While on one patrol, I found a drive-in snack bar complete with Car-Hops. This was a few blocks west of the 503rd off Longstreet Road. The *P.M.O.* at Fort Bragg was off Knox Street and the *Post Information Center* was on the north side of Randolph Street just west off Highway 87. Most MPs assigned to work at the "Info Center" found it to be easy and enjoyable duty.

While the Chevy sedans had heaters, the M151 jeeps here (just as in Dom Rep) did not. Later during the winter at Fort Bragg, **John Patterson** of Company C recalled one night when the temperature dipped down to nineteen degrees Fahrenheit. Without a heater, the canvas top and sides of the M151s at Fort Bragg did little to protect the MPs on patrol from the cold, wind, and rain. On nights such as this, John and his partner had to park the jeep, turn off the radio, and burn a can or two of *Sterno* to keep warm.

Sterno was what we called **Canned Heat** at the time. This was an odorless fuel made from denatured and jellied alcohol. Invented in 1900 around the turn of the century, its name came from the original manufacturer: *S. Sternau & Company* of Brooklyn, NY. Sold in any PX at the time, *Sterno* came in small cylindrical eight-once cans. It was designed to be burned directly from the can for up to two hours. Its primary use was in the food service industry, but the average Military guy found it to be useful as an emergency heat source.

I pulled *C.Q. Runner* duty again for one night only here at the 503rd, and the procedure was the same here too as it was in Dom Rep.

On Monday, 10-October-1966, after just seven weeks with the 503rd MP Battalion and Company C, I was transferred to duty at the *Post Stockade*. For this duty, I would be assigned to the *22nd MP Platoon* of the *100th MP Battalion*.

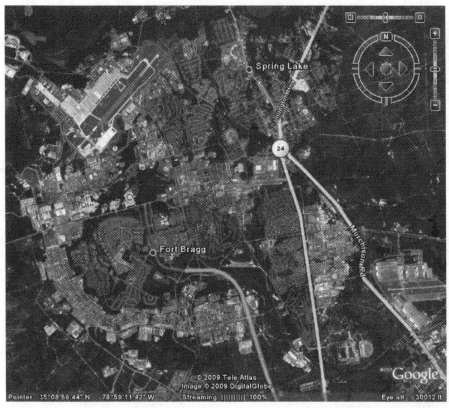

Fort Bragg, NC & Pope AFB, as seen Today from 30,000 ft above

503rd MP Battalion Building (Today)

2. By direction of the Secretary of the Army, under the provisions of paragraph 203, AR 672-5-1, the Meritorious Unit Commendation is awarded to the following unit of the United States Army for exceptionally meritorious achievement in the performance of outstanding service during the period indicated:

THE 503D MILITARY POLICE BATTALION

The citation reads as follows:

The 503d Military Police Battalion distinguished itself by exceptionally meritorious conduct in the performance of outstanding service in support of military operations in the Dominican Republic from May 1965 to January 1966. Throughout this period, the members of this Battalion demonstrated fortitude, professional skill, courage, and outstanding devotion to duty in providing military police support to the Commanders, United States Forces, Dominican Republic, 82d Airborne Division, the 5th Logistical Command, and to the State Department of the United States. Despite the hazardous situations, often under hostile fire, the men expeditiously met each commitment. Cheerfully, willingly and competently they worked hours far beyond those normally expected, insuring that all combat elements through the Dominican Republic had the best military police support. Of particular merit was the manner in which members of the Battalion established and operated checkpoints to control the flow of vehicles and pedestrian traffic entering and exiting the United States Forces controlled lines of communications and International Security Zone, in order to prevent the flow of arms, ammunition and other items of contraband which could be useful to the rebel forces or harmful to the interests of the United States Forces. When called upon to assist in demilitarizing the rebel zone, members of the Battalion successfully performed what was probably their most delicate mission during the Dominican Republic operations, the escorting of 1500 armed rebels who had previously been members of the Dominican Armed Forces, from the rebel zone through the city of Santo Domingo. The outstanding achievements of this Battalion contributed immeasurably to the success of the significant objectives of the Organization of American States in the Dominican Republic. The professional competence, devotion to duty, and esprit de corps displayed by the members of the 503d Military Police Battalion during this critical period reflect great credit upon themselves and the military service of the United States.

503rd MP Battalion Citation

503rd MP Helmet Liner (1)

503rd MP Helmet Liner (2)

Armed Forces Expeditionary Medal

Shoulder Patches

Ed Mitchell at the 503rd MP Battalion

Ed Mitchell (2)

Company C, 503rd MP Battalion Front Door

Fayetteville Municipal Airport (postcard from early 1950s)

Piedmont Airlines—Martin 4-0-4 Aircraft

Company C, 503rd, looking northeast out the back door in Winter

Anton M. 'Tony' Vavrica

John Patterson, Frank Burgos & Andy Rodecker at Fort Bragg

Robert E. Franklin, Company C, 503rd

Bob Franklin & Gus Gustafson at Company C, 503rd

Company C, 503rd Baseball Post Champs, 1967

Company C, 503rd visit to Fort Gordon for training

Tim Doyle, Mike Scheitel, Tom Marston and Gerald Clarkson goofing off

Stephen 'Durwood' Pack & Frank 'Lurch' Opyt

Carl Hagemeister with Company C, 503rd

Ed Mitchell, Carl VandenElzen, Gus Gustafson at the 503rd

Tom O, visiting Ed Mitchell at the 503rd

Other guys from Company C, 503rd

Jim Simone & Bob Franklin, Fort Bragg

Lee Field House—Recreation Center at Fort Bragg

Womack US Army Hospital at Fort Bragg

Post Theater across from the 503rd MP Bn at Fort Bragg

Chapter 6

22nd *MP Platoon, (100th MP Battalion)*

MONDAY, 10-October-1966—22nd Military Police Platoon, (100th MP Battalion).

On Monday morning, I arrived at the 22nd Military Police Platoon. This was just south of Butner Road between Armistead and Hamilton Streets in the northeast section of Fort Bragg near the small town of Spring Lake.

The 22nd MP Platoon was assigned to serve under the **100th MP Battalion**, which was soon to be officially activated on 25-November-1966. **Major William C. Robbins** (former Commander of the 503rd MP Battalion from 15-June through 24-July-1965 and from 23-August through 15-Septembe-1966) was assigned as the Battalion Commander. It was said of Major Robbins that he was a fair-minded commander who conducted himself with style. **The 100th MP Battalion HQs was located in Building # 9-T-2647.**

Other units that would serve under the 100th MP Battalion during this period were the **112th, 118th, and 174th MP Companies** along with the **483rd, 901st, and 545th MP Platoons.** These units were widely diversified in their organizations and functions. **Sergeant Joseph A. McCallister served as the Battalion Sergeant Major, while SFC Billy J. Watson (a veteran of the 218th MP Company in Dom Rep) became the Operations Sergeant. S/Sergeant Ozell Roby (my old boss from the 218th MP Company) handled the Battalion Supply Room.**

Again, I was back to living in an old wooden barracks building heated by coal. I began to feel at home in these older buildings as they seemed to proudly reek of World War II history. At first I was assigned to the first floor and the last bunk on the right at the far end of the isle. Then in time I was moved up to the second floor and was able to choose the first bunk on left at the top of the stairs. I would come to deeply regret that choice many months later.

The history of the 100th MP Battalion also dated back to World War II, when it served under the U.S. Seventh Army in the E.T.O. (European Theater of Operation). After World War II, the battalion was deactivated near Paris, France on 12-November-1945. Then, twenty-one years later, on 25-November-1966, the 100th was again reactivated here at Fort Bragg per *General Order #448, HQs, Third U.S. Army.* It was then attached to the HQs, XVIII Airborne Corps.

The mission of the 100th MP Battalion at Fort Bragg was to be three-fold. Its main responsibility was to provide Provost Marshal and Military Police services of widely varying character, including investigation of crime. Secondly, it was to increase the capabilities of fixed strength units where increments of less than company size were called for. And lastly of course, the battalion would provide command and administrative personnel for Military Police composite units.

PFC Mark Horvath was among some of the first new members assigned to the HQs Detachment in the newly activated 100th MP Battalion. His assigned role here was that of a Battalion Legal Clerk. Mark was a single guy and former student from Cleveland, Ohio. Drafted in June 1966, he took his Basic Training at Fort Benning, Georgia, and then attended AIT at the *Clerk Typist School* at Fort Knox. Following completion of AIT, he was among the three men assigned to the U.S. Navy and sent to the *Naval Justice School* in Rhode Island. While there, Mark was trained on the "gray audio-graph recording machine" that was utilized to record transcriptions of Summary Special and General Courts-Martial proceedings. Upon completion of this training, he was then reassigned back to the Army and sent to Fort Bragg.

After a brief orientation by Major Robbins, Mark was asked if he had any questions. So with nothing to lose, he asked for, and was darned surprised to receive, a one-week leave. While with the 100th MP Battalion, Mark put his training to work. He summarized proceedings (which had to be letter-perfect) which were held at the Staff Judge Advocate (S.J.A.) Building at Fort Bragg.

Mark Horvath stayed with the 100th MP Battalion until his ETS in June 1968 at the rank of Specialist-5 (E-5). He married Mary in August 1969, attended college on the *GI Bill* and received a Bachelor's degree in Psychology. After working forty years in the roofing business, he and Mary still reside in Independence, Ohio, and have raised two daughters.

The *Fort Bragg Post Stockade* was located on the northeast corner of Armistead and Letterman Streets. Being a member of the 22nd MP Platoon, I would thereafter be assigned to permanent duties there. Sitting at 285 feet above sea level on nearly twelve acres of land, the Post Stockade was about a three-minute walk just south of my barracks at the 22nd MP Platoon. The buildings there were also of old wooden construction, and the property on which the stockade sat was divided into two "compounds."

The front **Administration Compound** occupied the southern half of the property. Surrounding this compound was a single chain link fence that was twelve feet high and topped off by concertina wire. The main front gate (that we called Gate #1) faced the parking lot along Letterman Street to the south. A sidewalk running directly north from the main gate to Gate #2 divided this compound into two parts. To the left of the sidewalk was the Orderly Room with the Supply Room directly behind it to the west. To the right of the walkway were two other one-storey buildings housing a small medical dispensary, a Chapel for religious services, and a large open room used for meetings and receiving visitors on Sundays.

Beyond Gate #2 was the inner **Prisoner Compound** enclosed by two parallel chain link fences. These fences were also twelve feet high with ten feet of space between them, and filled with several coiled strands of concertina wire. This inner compound included three two-storey barracks buildings for the housing of prisoners, a one-storey maximum-security cell-block building and the Mess Hall. Until other arrangements could be made in the 100th MP Battalion, we of the 22nd MP Platoon would take our meals here also.

The Orderly Room had an administration desk just inside the door with a holding cell on the left. Down the hall to the right were the mailroom and the office of the Stockade Commander. **The stockade was commanded at this time by Captain Wallace A. Walker.** Captain Walker would also serve as the S-4 Officer for the 100th MP Battalion from January through June 1967 and Battalion Executive Officer from 12-June through 16-July-1967. Several months later, following after Captain Walker, **Captain Lawrence E. Seng** would take command of the stockade.

The stockade housed U.S. Army as well as Air Force prisoners (from Pope AFB just northwest of there) and occasionally Marine Corps and Navy detainees. I learned that more than **80 percent of the prisoners detained here were serving time for going AWOL, with a surprisingly large percentage of these being Enlistees over Draftees.** The usual punishment for going AWOL back then was what we called *Six and Two.* This meant **six full months of Stockade confinement and two-thirds loss of pay.** This term of confinement was to be considered as "Bad Time" that had to be made up after the prisoner's release.

There were several jobs here at the stockade that we'd all get to experience. This list of jobs included **"Turn-Key" at Gate #1; "Turn-Key" at Gate #2; Maximum Security Cell-Block Guard (A-Block); and Prisoner Compound Guards (for Blocks B, C, and D).** The 82nd Airborne Division furnished the three Tower Guards and one Walking Guard. Here too in the 22nd MP Platoon as in Dom Rep, we would again be working shifts of *9-on-3-off.*

One of the two **jobs I enjoyed here most** was being the *Turn-Key* at Gate **#1,** which was guarding the main front gate to the stockade. This gate was located midway along the southern perimeter fence of the stockade, facing the gravel parking lot of crushed cinders along Letterman Street. The guard shack (just outside the gate) measured about 5 x 8 feet, with the narrow side facing the gate. It had two large windows on either side, with a two-foot square window in the door. Not only did this shack have electricity and lights, but it also had an electric space heater that made a world of difference on the many cold winter nights to come.

Inside the guard shack at Gate #1, a table measuring 2 x 5 feet was placed to the left of the door along with a metal folding chair. There was also an intercom system between there and the Stockade Orderly Room. The intercom was mounted on the wall opposite the table. For the men of the 22nd MP Platoon, this gate was the only duty in which the guard was armed. For this, he carried a .45 caliber Colt Automatic Pistol (M-1911). I would spend many memorable and lonely days and nights at this gate.

Among the main duties of manning Gate #1 was watching the front perimeter of the facility. In addition to this, the guard was also responsible to "shake down" prisoners as they were escorted into the stockade. This was sometimes referred to as "searching" or "frisking" prisoners before allowing them to enter.

There was a correct and proper way for MPs to perform this task. Often in Hollywood movies we'd see a suspect or prisoner being "patted down." This was unacceptable in the Military Police Corps. We were instructed to literally "crush" the clothing of our subject using our hands along the length of the arms, around the torso, down the legs, and even the hair on his head, inside his hat, and around the collar. But . . . Hollywood had *their* method and we had ours.

Understandably of course, reading while on duty at the stockade was not permitted. But often rules were made to be broken. Using the interior light was not allowed after dark unless for official use only. However, it wasn't hard to read at night by the light coming in the window from the illuminated parking lot. The only drawback of this job was that in order to use the latrine, one had to use the intercom and call for a relief man.

The stockade perimeter was observed twenty-four hours per day, seven days per week from **guard towers in three corners along with one walking guard covering a blind spot on the northeast corner.** This blind spot, which could not be seen from the towers, ran along a curved section of the railroad tracks of the *Cape Fear Railroad.* Men of the 82nd Airborne Division manned these four positions, each armed with a twelve-guage pump-action shot gun.

I never really liked manning **Gate #2.** This gate was located between the Administration and Prisoner compounds. While both gates had guard shacks, only Gate #1 had a heater. To make matters worse, there was also no electricity, lights or even a chair at Gate #2. Needless to say, this made nights there almost unbearable at times, especially during the winter. The guard shack there was about four feet square with windows on all four sides including the door.

One cold night while on duty at Gate #2 during the winter, I found another way to keep warm. I'd stand by the window inside the furnace room of the first building to the right of the guard shack. From there I had a clear view of the gate and anyone approaching from inside the prisoner compound. But because this was about thirty feet from the gate, the "Brass" didn't approve of this, and insisted that the guard remain "at his post" in or close to the gate shack.

Larry Schlaud was another friend of mine from the 22nd MP Platoon who pulled duty at the Stockade. He too, had been assigned to the 22nd MP Platoon from Company C of the 503rd after returning to Fort Bragg from Dom Rep. Most of his time here was spent pulling shifts as a *Turn-Key* at Gates #1 and #2.

After his ETS in November 1967, Schlaud returned back home to Michigan and went to work for the *Buick Motor Division* for a short time. Then in late 1969, he left Buick to attend the Junior College in Flint. Following that, he became a Sales Representative for the *Lorillard Tobacco Company* (America's oldest tobacco company) and retired there after thirty years in January 2000. Larry remained single until he met a wonderful girl named Maria from Saginaw, Michigan and married her in 1997. They reside in Flint, Michigan and are still going strong today.

Being a **Compound Barracks Guard for Blocks B, C, and D** wasn't bad duty at all. For these jobs, the guard carried a clipboard with the names of the prisoners in his charge and disciplinary "write-up" forms for prisoners breaking the rules. He was responsible to supervise prisoner activity and see that the barracks were cleaned each day before his shift ended. He also had to see that the trash was taken out daily along with the ashes from the furnace rooms.

While pulling this duty, I often felt as though I was being helpful to the inmates. Frequently I would sit with them when time permitted, chatting with them and listening to their gripes and problems. And they sure had plenty of gripes and problems. A few of them even confided in me now and then with their innermost personal problems.

In one instance, I was passing through the barracks on a midnight shift in this compound while most of them were sleeping and I came across one guy sitting up on his bunk, unable to sleep. So I sat down and chatted with him for about an hour or so. During that time, he told me all about his turbulent life back home before being drafted. He stated that his wife had recently left him, which was the main reason that he went AWOL in the first place. And now, deeply troubled with his life, he admitted to me a strong urge to "go over the fence" again and escape from there.

I reminded him just how foolish that would be to attempt. I explained that the guards had a responsibility to stop an escape attempt by using their weapon if needed. But this did little to ease his mind.

So I finally told him that if he really felt that he *had* to make a run for it, he should at least make the attempt while I was on duty at Gate #1. This caught him off guard and he raised his eyebrows in surprise. I went on and explained to him that the tower guards utilized twelve-gauge shotguns. This meant that they had a better probability of hitting a moving target with the spread of buckshot. On the other hand, because the guard at Gate #1 carried a pistol, hitting a moving target was a bit more difficult.

I explained to him further that if I were the guard on duty there, I'd have to make it "look good for the Brass," of course. That is, I would shout the command of *Halt* three times as required of me by *S.O.P. (Standard Operating Procedure)* before sending two warning shots over his head with the pistol. Then as further required of me, I would certainly "aim" for the legs to stop him. But of course, because I had scored so poorly on the pistol range, his *best* chances were certainly with me.

In short, I was telling him that if he had the fortitude and the ability to make it to the front fence line, I'd say that he has sure earned his freedom. But instead of aiming for the legs, I'd send the third round either over his head or into the gravel of the parking lot. In that way, I'd be protecting my own butt, while protecting his too.

I had to realize after all, that this was *not* heated mortal combat in a hostile country. Nor did he pose any threat to our national security. Instead, he was just a lonely guy who happened to get foolish and go AWOL, which resulted in his ending up in the stockade. Under those circumstances, there was absolutely *no way* I would actually "drop the hammer" on him if he came over the south fence line on my shift.

As it turned out in the end, he never made the attempt. As far as I know, he finished out his time and was eventually set free. As to how his personal life actually turned out, I'll never really know. Nor will I ever know if my chat with him on that night ever really made a difference in his life. I would like to think that it did. So I think of him too now and then whenever I reminisce about those days, and I often wonder how he is doing today.

Occasionally, I'd find **contraband** in the possession of a prisoner. My responsibility here was clear-cut. I was to confiscate it and write him up for disciplinary action. Certainly, if the contraband were weapons or drugs, I would unquestionably comply, of course. But in most cases, the unauthorized contraband turned out to be only adult books or porn magazines. In my opinion, these posed no threat to me, to the prisoner himself, or any of the others. Here too, it was clear to me that our national security was still in good hands. So in one instance that I recall off hand, I just simply told the prisoner to keep it out of sight, even from me. I explained to him that if *I* got caught allowing him to keep it, I'd be in a heck-of-a-lot more trouble than him.

At first, these prisoners were unsure of my real intentions. Then as time passed by and they got to know me, they began to relax whenever I was around and learned to trust me. One of them was even dumbfounded when I asked him if I could read that book when he was finished with it.

In time, word got around among the prisoners that **PFC Oblinger was an OK guy.** Very seldom did I ever have trouble getting them to do what needed to get done. I simply earned their respect, and I got it.

Once during the cold weather on a late afternoon shift, the ashes needed to be taken out from the furnace room. The prisoners had just finished showering after a long and hard day of chores and were ready for "lights out" at 2130 Hours (9:30 PM). I asked for two volunteers. Because this was the dirtiest chore there, they were reluctant to comply with this and they let me know it vocally.

Knowing that it was my responsibility to see that it got done, I asked once again. This time I stated that if there were no volunteers, I would be forced to pick the "volunteers" myself. Finally, one of them spoke up and said to the others, *"Hey, come on you guys. PFC Oblinger has been pretty good to us. Let's give him a break. I'll volunteer, but I need one more of you jokers."* Moments later, I had another volunteer.

I believe that because I treated them with respect, compassion and understanding while still being firm when needed, I got a lot more out of them than many of the other guards. And they in turn covered my butt and made *me* look good in front of my own superiors. I was damned proud to have their trust, respect and obedience.

On early mornings just before our midnight shift ended, our job was to wake the inmates for morning Reveille, head-count, and roll call. I usually handled this by calling loudly from the doorway of the barracks. Then while moving down the isle in the barracks, I would wake each man individually by nudging him. I've never even once had a problem with this method.

However, I recall one older sergeant with a real hard-ass attitude whom we worked with (and whose name escapes me today). On one particular morning, *Sergeant Hard-Ass* came to me and informed me that we will wake the prisoners using *his* unique method. He handed me a police whistle and told me that he would enter the barracks from this end and that I was to enter from the other. Then immediately upon his hand signal, we were to simultaneously blast our whistles.

I couldn't believe what he was asking of me, and I objected to this with all my being. But it was to no avail. Needless to say, the unsuspecting victims sprang from their bunks with looks of absolute terror on their faces.—It was a look that swiftly changed to pure hatred.

I was pissed off as never before, and I swore to myself that I'd never pull that stunt again, no matter what it would cost me. That sergeant instantly destroyed all I had worked hard to accomplish. The next chance I got, I apologized profusely to the men and assured them that I was not responsible for what happened. Understandably at first, they refused to listen to me. But after a few weeks they finally came to believe that I was not at fault. Although it took a long time to restore their trust in me, it was never quite the same after that.

Their confinement was not always easy time, as often they had hard and dirty jobs to do. But when they earned it with good behavior, they would be moved to **D-Block** on what was called ***Parolee Status.*** Here they were allowed to go for work details outside the Stockade. Of course, armed guards toting twelve-gauge shotguns escorted them, but these Parolees appreciated a chance to get outside the fence, even if it was only for the day.

Occasionally, Parolees would go "over and above the call of duty" for a reasonable price. During my time with the 22nd MP Platoon, we received all new wall lockers for our barracks. But they were still packed in cardboard boxes and needed to be assembled. But for the price of a few packs of cigarettes, I was able to have one of the prisoner parolees assemble mine for me.

As luck would have it, I never did pull duty in D-Block or with the Parolees. I never knew why and I never really asked. I guess it never really bothered me.

Working the Maximum-Security Cell-Block (A-Block) was the job I preferred most at the stockade, especially on midnight shifts. As you may have noticed by now, I much preferred midnights to any other shift, as there was less "brass" around to look over my shoulder. This cell-block building was in the southwest section of the prisoner compound, just opposite the Mess Hall. There was a wooden desk to the right just inside the door, and a storage room to the left. The middle section of the building contained the actual cells. There were about ten cells as I recall placed back to back, with five cells on each side. This allowed a four-foot wide corridor along both sides of the building from the front to the back where the latrine was located.

These cells had no bunks. Instead, each cell had a mattress-sized platform made of three 2 x 12-inch boards. This was supported by a frame of angle iron, permanently mounted about five inches off the floor.

Manning the cell-block was a two-man job. Because A-Block was the *maximum* security block, no prisoner was to be allowed out of his cell unless both guards were present. Then only *one* prisoner at a time was allowed out. Furthermore in this block, prisoners were not permitted to have belts, shoe strings, or boot laces, as these could be used if the prisoner chose to hang his self. The highest risk inmates were permitted only undershorts and T-shirts, as other articles of clothing could also be used for hanging in desperate situations.

When shaving was allowed, a special safety razor was used. It was designed in such a way that the blade could not be removed without a special tool. This tool was kept by the guard in a drawer at the desk. There was concern about high-risk prisoners using the blade as either a weapon or for slicing their own wrists.

Each prisoner in the cell-block (except high-risk inmates, of course) was only allowed three ten-minute cigarette breaks per day out of his cell. Needless to say, this was damn rough on heavy smokers. The guards recorded these breaks and all other activities in the daily log kept at the desk. An entry was made in this log for every event or happening that took place in the cell-block. For example, a note in the log might read, *0700 Hours, All is quiet.* or *0830 Hours, Prisoner Smith, John D, US 12-345-678 was given a 10-minute smoke break.*

Here too, I expressed understanding and compassion. I was a smoker too and I knew how asinine that ten-minute cigarette rule was. So I thought of ways to give them longer breaks, with the exception of the high-risk inmates, of course. And again, once they got to know me, the prisoners were more than cooperative. For example, I might call out from the desk, *"This floor needs to be mopped. Do I have any volunteers?"* Upon hearing this, a few would yell from their cells, *"I'll do it!"* or *"I'll volunteer!"* Then right after I assigned the chore to a prisoner, another would ask, *"Hey, I noticed the windows need cleaning too. Can I do them when he's done with the floor?"* Needless to say, I had no problem keeping the cell-block building exceptionally clean on my shifts.

As long I allowed only one prisoner at a time out his cell, he was permitted to smoke while taking all the time he needed to do a great job. If no cleaning needed to be done, I'd still allow one of them at a time out of his cell. At times like these, they'd merely sit with me up front at the desk and chat for a while. Sometimes we even played cards at the desk. Never once did I ever have a problem that I couldn't handle while working in A-Block.

I actually recall occasionally coming in for duty on my shift there and receiving applause from the cells when they recognized my voice. This was *not* because I was anyone special. It was because they knew that on my shift, they'd be treated with respect, fairness, and compassion.

Please, don't get me wrong. I don't mean to imply here that everyone else I worked with in the 22nd MP Platoon was not doing his job properly. In reality, it was quite the contrary. The fact was, nearly *everyone* I worked with (except for maybe one or two) did a fine and commendable job. It's just that I believe I went the extra mile to be more than just a guard to the prisoners. I also became their friend. Yes, I was firm with them when I needed to be. But being a hard-nosed bad-ass was *not* a job requirement here.

While working in this cell-block, I'd heard about a former guard who had a *real* bad-ass attitude. Evidently he had worked here long before I was assigned to the 22nd MP Platoon. I'd heard that one winter night here, he took a garden hose and hosed down all the cells because he thought they were making too much noise after lights out. I never could understand why some guards (not many) had to be hard-nosed bad asses. To my thinking, I always strove to *"do unto others"* and I still do. It's a matter of the old saying, *"You can catch more flies with honey . . . "*

Three times per day, meals were brought in to A-Block for the prisoners from the Mess Hall. The highest risk and most dangerous inmates were restricted to a diet of only 1500 calories a day. This tended to soften even the hardest prisoners. As far as I can recall, we didn't have but only one or two on this diet during my entire length of service there.

There were many times that this cell-block job was hilarious. At least once every hour, *Standard Operating Procedure* called for the log entry to include the results of **Tower Checks.** An intercom system was also set up in A-Block that ran between the desk there and the three perimeter guard towers.

Each hour as required, I would press the "talk" key on the intercom and say, *"Tower check, Tower One."* Tower #1 would then come back by saying something like, *"Tower One, all OK."* or *"Tower One, no problems to report."* This routine was repeated with Towers #2 and #3. But once in a while, one of the tower guards might come back with, *"Tower One, all OK.—AIRBORNE!—All the way!"*

It seemed that there was a lot of friendly hostility between the tower guards from the 82nd Airborne and us non-airborne guys. If a man was non-airborne and didn't have *Jump Wings* on his chest, he was called a *LEGG*. A *"legg" w*as a soldier who used leg-power to get from here to there. So we'd come back over the intercom with something like, *"Hey Airborne, Only two things fall out of the sky around here:—Bird shit and fools!"*

It was the duty of the men manning the cell-block to relieve the three tower guards and walking guard for their meals each day. This took about two hours out of the eight-hour shift. Each guard got a thirty-minute break, during which time he would give his weapon to the relief man until he returned. I did this relief duty on several occasions and it wasn't too bad until winter arrived. While the towers were covered with a roof to keep the rain and snow off the guard, they were also unheated. It was rough duty on cold and windy days and nights. While my heart went out to them on those cold nights, I also realized that they got paid an extra $55.00 per month *Jump Pay* for this extra hazardous duty.

Today, other thoughts come to mind about working in the cell-block. In one of the empty cells down the left side, was a pile of about eight to ten mattresses or more stacked up for lack of a better place to store them. On one or more occasions, my partner and I (on a midnight shift, of course) took turns "cat-napping" here while the other "held the fort down."

But the best thing about working A-block was all the free time I had (especially on midnight shifts) to read books or write letters. At that time, the cost of a *First Class U.S. Postage Stamp* was only five cents. But if the sender preferred his letter to get to its destination a little faster, he could choose to send it via *Air Mail* for only two cents more. In those days, all U.S. mail (with the exception of *Air Mail*) was driven by ground transportation to the addressee. These days, unless I am mistaken, all mail that is sent "out of town" is sent by air.

There was one night shift here that my partner and I decided to raid the mess hall for leftovers to snack on. Believe it or not, the post stockade in my opinion had the very best cook in the entire U.S. Army! Bar none! But while in the mess hall, we discovered a few cases of *C-Rations (Combat Rations)* and brought a few boxes back to A-Block.

C-Rations (referred to by the Army as **Meal, Combat, Individual**) were developed by the Army Quartermaster Corps during World War II, and were intended to be used where field kitchens could not go. While many World War II veterans agreed that the meals included in C-Rations were much preferred over those of **K-Rations**, they had one major disadvantage. The C-Rations were heavier and bulkier, and thus did not fit into the pockets of the *Combat Field Jacket* like the old K-Rations used to.

Available in cases of twelve meals each, a C-Ration meal came in a cardboard box labeled as a *B-1, B-2,* or *B-3 Unit* for *Breakfast, Dinner,* or *Supper.* Each complete meal contained about 1200 calories, thus a daily ration of three meals would provide 3600 Calories. Along with each meal unit, an *Accessory Pack* (sealed in a foil pouch) was included. This pack featured a plastic spoon, salt, pepper, sugar, non-dairy creamer, chewing gum, a packet of instant coffee, toilet paper, moisture proof matches, and a pack of four cigarettes. The smokes were always welcome, but one never knew what brand he'd get. The brands included were usually *Pall Mall, Camel, Chesterfield, Lucky Strike, Winston, Marlboro, Kent, Salem,* or *Kool.* The Instant Coffee packets, hardly known before World War II, changed the way of life for millions of people worldwide.

The **P-38 Can Opener**, developed in 1942, was also included with C-Rations. It was a highly praised, tiny, collapsible light-weight gadget that seemed to have a 1001 uses. Measuring one and a half inches long, it also served as a bottle opener, letter opener, fingernail cleaner, screw driver, toothpick, chisel, and scraper. No one seemed to know where the name actually came from. Some World War II veterans said that it performed with the swiftness of the *American P-38* fighter plane. In the mid-1980s, C-Rations (along with the P-38 Can Opener) finally gave way to the new *M.R.E.s (Meals Ready to Eat).*

"Attention in the compound! Attention in the compound!" Often we'd hear this called out over loudspeakers that were placed high in certain areas around the stockade. This happened several times a day while working the day or afternoon shifts up until "lights out," but never on midnight shifts as I recall. Immediately following this call to attention, we'd then hear announcements, orders, or other instructions directed to either one prisoner in particular, or one guard, or even the entire stockade population and staff. For example, we might then hear, *"Prisoner*

Smith, Daniel J., please report to the Stockade Commander immediately." or *"Prisoner Doe, John T., please report to the Administration Compound. You have a visitor."* When a prisoner was about to be released you might hear *"Prisoner Brown, Robert K., please report to the office with bag and baggage."* Now and then there was even the occasional, *"Attention in the compound! Fire Drill! Fire Drill!"*

Visiting Day was always on Sundays. On this day all prisoners, with the exception of maximum security, were allowed visitors. The only stipulation was that the names of visitors had to be among a list prepared by each prisoner and pre-approved by the Stockade Commander. These visits always took place in one of the buildings in the administration compound while being supervised by a couple of us guards. Most of us guys enjoyed the duty of supervising these visits. After all, many of the inmates had attractive-looking wives, sisters, and girlfriends.

As for my most memorable experience working at the stockade, I'd have to say it was the night **I got caught sleeping on guard duty at Gate #1.** This was on a midnight shift during the cold winter weather in January or February 1967. On nights like this, most of us who guarded Gate #1, usually stayed in the guard shack with the space heater on under the table.

But on this particular night, for whatever reason, I was dog-ass tired. Now occasionally here I would sort of catnap lightly. Not a real *deep* sleep, mind you, but just enough that it allowed me to revive my strength. To do this, I had to rest my feet up on the table while sitting there. Then I'd lean back easy on the metal folding chair, and lay my head lightly against the opposite wall. Now, ninety-nine out of a hundred times, the sound of tires approaching on the gravel outside in the parking lot usually woke me. (I relied on this many times.) Then by the time the occupant of the vehicle neared the guard shack on foot, I'd be standing outside greeting him with a smile and/or a snappy salute, whichever was appropriate.

But not on this night! I did *not* hear the sound of tires approaching on the gravel. Nor did I hear anyone walking up to the guard shack. Nevertheless . . .

I was awakened by the *Duty Officer* knocking lightly on the door of the shack. When I finally came to and snapped to attention, the young 2nd Lieutenant smiled and simply asked me, *"I'm not disturbing your rest, am I Private?"* I was sort of at a loss for words. (Can you imagine *ME* at a loss for words?) The lieutenant then told me that he was going to get someone to relieve me so I could get some sleep. I simply replied, *"Oh, thank you, Sir."* To which he came back with, *"No, you don't understand, Private. Being relieved of duty is supposed to be a great dishonor to you."* After that, I went back to the barracks, got some much-needed sleep, and prepared myself to "face the music" in the morning.

As it turned out, instead of having my head served to him on a platter, all I got the next day was one helluva butt chewing by **Captain Lawrence Seng**, the new Stockade Commander. Knowing it sure as hell could have been much worse, I breathed a long refreshing sigh of relief.

Captain Lawrence E. Seng was the former Battalion S-2 and S-3 for the 503rd MP Battalion until 28-August-1966. Born in May 1937, Lawrence grew up in Jasper, Indiana. After high school, he attended the University of Indiana where he earned a Bachelor's Degree in Business Administration. During that time he received his ROTC training and graduated in 1959. Following graduation, Seng enlisted in the U.S. Army and was assigned to the 101st Airborne Division at Fort Campbell, Kentucky. He went on to serve as the Company Commander for the 545th MP Company which was serving as a Motorized Cavalry unit with the 1st Cavalry Division in Korea. He remained there from July 1964 through June 1965 when he returned to the States. Later he earned a *Green Beret* with the 82nd Airborne Division at Fort Bragg, and married Winifred "Ann" in December 1966, just before being assigned to command the stockade.

While a few of his subordinates and many of the Stockade prisoners thought of Captain Seng as a hard-nosed officer, in reality, he was a damned good leader. Although he led with a firm hand, Captain Lawrence Seng was extremely devoted to his work as an Army officer. There was never any question of the fact that under his command, the Fort Bragg Post Stockade was a smooth running operation.

About 150 yards below Letterman Street just south of the Stockade, stood a large water tower about 100 feet in height. This was behind an area of NCO housing. While driving past there one day Lawrence noticed something that caught his eye. Evidently some disgruntled soldier or an angry Parolee prisoner (he was never certain which) had climbed to the top of the tower and wrote with white paint in tall letters the words, *F—SENG!* But instead of being furious about it, he was actually *proud* to show it off to his new bride, Ann!

Back in our barracks at the 22nd MP Platoon, we had a problem with the guy who was appointed to be our *Mail Clerk*. He wasn't handling the responsibility very well and one day someone found a pile of our mail in the bottom of his footlocker. This pissed off many of us and he got himself into serious trouble for it. Then I heard from another guy that the mail clerk at the stockade gave us the OK to have our incoming mail sent there. A few of us soon took advantage of this. That worked out fine for the remainder of my time with the 22nd MP Platoon. From that day onward (the same as the inmates), our mail from home would be addressed to: *Box*

1000, Fort Bragg, North Carolina 28307. The only exception to this was that unlike the prisoner's mail, our mail would not be opened and censored.

Recently, other thoughts drift into my mind about my days at the stockade. I recall an old sergeant I met there once. Unfortunately I cannot recall his name today. He was a great guy to know and we used to joke around with each other often. I believe that he was in his mid-60s then. When I called him an old man one time, he laughingly replied, *"Ha! I'll dance on your grave, you young sonofabitch!"*

He once told me of some tricks that he had learned during World War II. Once he explained that if I was ever in a big hurry to **shine my brass when** *Brasso* **was not handy, spit and cigarette ashes could be used.** When I finally tried his suggestion, I found that it worked great in a pinch. Live and learn, eh?

Thinking of **brass polish**, I still have my original can of *Brasso* that I purchased in November 1965 at a Fort Knox PX. Who would have thought that the seven-ounce can would last me a lifetime? I also have my original-issue *Low Quarters* (Army Class-A dress shoes) that still fit. And I still have my flat *Garrison Cap* that I was issued in November 1965. It was sometimes called an Overseas Cap. (We had another name for this cap, but it's too nasty to be used here.) Just don't ask me if any of the other items of uniform clothing issue still fit.

There was another time that I recall when I came off an afternoon shift. A couple of us guys were hungry and in no hurry to get back to our barracks. One of the guys had learned that there was a **mess hall over at Pope AFB that was open all night**. This guy, a Specialist-5 whose last name was **Paison** (I cannot recall his first name), happened to have his *P.O.V. (Privately Owned Vehicle)* on post. As I recall, **Specialist Paison** drove a four-door two-tone blue and white American Motors Ambassador. We decided to drive up to Pope and visit the mess hall. We were welcomed by showing our Military Police ID cards and had an early breakfast. It was fantastic. I was convinced that the U.S. Air Force fed its men well. Paison and I became close friends for the short time that he was assigned to the 22nd MP Platoon. On one or two occasions, he allowed me to borrow his car while he was on duty and not using it.

I had a small portable radio that I was able to smuggle with me when working at the stockade. I recall listening to it in the wee hours of the morning at the main gate. What I found out was that late at night when the southern sky was clear, AM radio reception was astonishing. One night I was able to "pick up" **KDKA in Pittsburgh** (the oldest radio station in the world), and also **WLS in Chicago.** But best of all, I was able to pick up my old favorite radio station back home, **WXYZ in**

Detroit, *"1270 on the AM dial."* It was great to hear a familiar *Top-40s* DJ from home again. The voice was none other than *"Lee Allan—On the horn!"*

Fayetteville, North Carolina is located about ten miles south, southeast of Fort Bragg along the western bank of the Cape Fear River. This city was founded in 1873 by uniting the two small settlements of Cross Creek and Campbellton. It was named after the Revolutionary War hero *Marquis de Lafayette*, and today it is North Carolina's sixth largest city.

On buses running between Fort Bragg and Fayetteville we learned that MPs rode free. All we had to do was show our Military Police ID card and take a seat. As for what to do or see in the town, that depended upon whom you were asking. If you had asked me, I'd have told you that there wasn't much that interested me. I noticed a few restaurants, a couple of pawn shops, several Go-Go bars and one USO Club. But that was just my opinion. On the other hand, if you preferred life in "Small Town, USA" then Fayetteville might be just what you were looking for.

I learned about the USO here. Due to the impact of rapid military mobilization on the small towns in America in 1940, the *U.S.O. (United Service Organization)* was born with six organizations. These were the *Young Men's Christian Association (YMCA)*, the *Young Women's Christian Association (YWCA)*, the *National Catholic Community Service*, the *National Jewish Welfare Board*, the *Traveler's Aid Association*, and the *Salvation Army*.

The first government-built USO opened here in Fayetteville in November 1941, serving the military men of Fort Bragg and Pope AFB. Soon afterward, USO centers began popping up all over the country. They became sort of a "home away from home" to soldiers during World War II and beyond, offering a nonmilitary atmosphere. The USO was where a soldier could relax, write letters, or attend occasional dances and other social events.

I couldn't see the need to waste my money in restaurants when I had no particular complaints about the food in the mess halls at Fort Bragg. I only visited a pawn shop here once, and the USO did not interest me at the time. But the Go-Go bars there *did* interest me, not only for the attractive dancing girls, but also for the great music we all seemed to enjoy back then.

On many occasions, I would accompany **Ed Mitchell** and **Anton M. "Tony" Vavrica** of the 503rd on bus trips into Fayetteville. Most times, we'd visit the some of the Go-Go bars and watch these attractive girls dancing. (Topless bars had not yet come into popularity then.) I really wasn't able to drink all night, but I *did* enjoy watching the girls while slowly nursing my 7&7. Like me, Ed and Tony never drank that much either.

Tony Vavrica was a single guy from Bronx, New York. After Basic Training at Fort Jackson, South Carolina, he came through MP School with us at Fort Gordon. During his stay in Dom Rep with the 218th MP Company, he pulled line-duty patrol. He had returned from Dom Rep to Fort Bragg with the 2nd Phase group on 26-August-1966, and was then assigned to the 503rd and Company C. Thereafter, Ed and Tony would often switch schedules with others in the company in order to pull patrol duty together.

After visiting all the Go-Go places in town, the three of us finally agreed upon a place that we liked best. It was called the ***Blue Candle Light Inn*** on Main Street. We met a pretty dancer there named Sharon with beautiful red hair and lovely green eyes. Not only was Sharon the prettiest girl in the inn, there was also a four-foot tall black and white poster of her prominently displayed in the front window. It was clearly observed by everyone coming in off Main Street.

Every night we came there, she would sit at our booth during each break. One evening while she was sitting next to me (Ed and Tony were sitting on the other side of the table), I began running my fingers gently through her hair. I learned some time later that this irritated Tony as after many visits to the place, he had taken a strong liking to Sharon. I therefore decided to back off and let fate take its course. It did. And in only a short time, Tony and Sharon grew to really like each other.

Of all the memories I'd like to forget about Fayetteville was the inevitable bus ride back to Fort Bragg after all the bars had closed. Every time we took a late bus coming back after "closing time," we'd have to straddle the ***River of Barf***. It seemed that on nearly every bus returning to Fort Bragg late at night after all the bars closed, the center isle was always a flowing river of vomit from all the drunken servicemen. Therefore, maneuvering from your seat to the exit without stepping in the "river" was neither easy nor graceful. How does one adequately describe the nauseating smell we had to endure on the ride back? I kept thinking I could never live like this day in and day out.

On another occasion, I rode into town with **Steve Manion,** who was another friend I had made in the 22nd MP Platoon. Steve was also from the Detroit area, but because he was black, no one would serve him in town. That ticked me off and I finally told one bartender, *"If you can't serve my friend, you'll not be serving me either."* We both then returned to Fort Bragg.

As to whether he ever went into Fayetteville after that, I'll never know. He was transferred out of the 22nd MP Platoon shortly after that and I never saw him again. I tried once to look him up after my ETS but was never able to locate him in Detroit. I think about him too now and then.

In time I was able to put in a request for another leave. This time I had a plan to extend it unofficially. I figured out a way to finagle a **ten-day vacation while using up only seven days of leave time!** What I did was schedule a seven-day leave to begin several days *after* a holiday, as I had learned earlier. This was to avoid being "bumped" in favor of a full-fare airline passenger. Then I'd request a *Three-Day Pass* to begin three days *before* the leave was scheduled to commence. The *only* problem that might kill the whole scheme was getting caught on a three-day pass so far from Fort Bragg. You see, according to Army Regulations, on three-day passes, soldiers were not allowed to go any further than a 150-mile radius of their point of departure, which in this case, was Fort Bragg.

One time, I ran into two MPs patrolling on foot at *Washington National Airport* in DC. They had randomly stopped me inside the terminal and asked to see my travel orders. Realizing then that my official leave did not begin for another two days, I produced my three-day pass and handed it to them. As it turned out the MPs in DC didn't catch on. I had pulled it off!

On this leave, I finally came to the conclusion that the U.S. Army dress socks (either issued or bought from the PX) weren't worth a damn. They were good for one wearing *only*, and that was it! This left them so permanently stretched out of shape that I always ended up discarding them. But I had to admit, they were cheap—about 38 cents a pair as I recall. So the price was OK.

Coming back from another leave several months later during the winter, I had arrived back at Fort Bragg one day late. It seemed that an inch and a half of snow on the runway at Fayetteville caused the *Piedmont Airlines* flight to divert to Wilmington, North Carolina, about eighty-five miles southeast of there. Several hours later after another attempt, we were again diverted to Raleigh about sixty miles to the north. But by well after midnight, we were finally able to touch down in Fayetteville.

Up to this time whenever I flew, my AWOL bag was always allowed as "carry-on" baggage, as it would always fit into the "over-head" storage. But this was the first time I was required to check my bag at the counter. As luck would have it, when I finally arrived at Fayetteville, my bag was not so fortunate. It didn't catch up to me until two days later. When our company clerk finally informed me that my bag was at the Fayetteville Airport, I went there to pick it up.

Upon arrival, I approached the ticket counter and asked for directions to *Baggage Pick-up*. Pointing to his left, the ticket agent instructed me to go out that door and turn right. When I got outside and looked to the right, I noticed a sign stating, *BAGGAGE PICK-UP HERE* (with an arrow pointing down and to the right). I found my bag among several others outside, around the corner, and on the pavement under a breezeway. Was this life in the big city, I wondered?

During my months at Fort Bragg, I had also refrained from Church attendance. There was no particular reason for this either, but I *did* feel like I was missing something that I needed. I was certain that one day soon; I'd get back to it again.

Much of my free time was spent visiting **Ed Mitchell** over at the 503rd. It was only a twenty-minute walk to there from the 22nd MP Platoon area, but it was a rough trek during bad weather. Often Ed and I would watch a movie at the **Post Theater across Macomb Street from the 503rd**. This theater was built in 1934. Two of the movies that we saw there still stand out in my mind today. These were: *The Flim Flam Man* starring George C. Scott and Michael Sarrazin, and *In the Heat of the Night* featuring Sidney Poitier and Carroll O'Connor.

Often Ed and I walked over to a hamburger shop a block or two from the 503rd to grab a snack or a soft drink. This place had a jukebox that I often dropped coins in. One song I recall playing often was one that drove Ed Mitchell nuts. It was called, *The Pied Piper* and was recorded in 1966 by a British entertainer named Crispian St Peters.

One day in Fayetteville, Ed and I walked past a pawn shop. Then stopping there momentarily, I noticed a used but shiny guitar hanging in the front window. It was priced at $24.95 including the case. Obviously, I didn't know anything about quality guitars back then, but it sure did look great, and I purchased it. At that time, I wasn't any better playing it than I was in Dom Rep. But I wanted to practice with it anyway. Mind you, at that time I *hated* Country Music with a passion. My real intention was to learn some 1950's and 1960's Rock 'n' Roll with it. But knowing only three chords (C, F, and G7), I was limited in what I could do.

There was another guy in my barracks whose favorite pastime then was to play his phonograph for hours at a time. (I cannot recall his name today either.) Unfortunately, he had only *one* 45rpm record to play on the darned thing. It was a recording by a country singer named Buck Owens, and was called, *Tiger by the Tail*. So this, he played over and over and over again! It drove everybody in the 22nd MP Platoon barracks nuts, and to this day, much as I love Country Music now, I still can't stand listening to Buck Owens.

Whenever I walked back to the 22nd from the 503rd during the dry weather, I always took the shortcut diagonally through an NCO housing area to save time. This was south of Letterman Street and east of Armistead Street. One night while cutting through here past the large round water tower, a German Shepherd dog got loose somehow and began chasing me. During my frantic high-speed run that night I lost my slip-on Penny-Loafers. Up to that moment the animal was swiftly gaining on me. But once I was free of my footgear, I literally *ran like the wind*. I swear, if anyone ever told me then that I could outrun a German Shepherd, I'd have not thought it possible. But it sure did happen to me! Sadly, those were my only pair of civilian shoes. They were brownish oxblood in color and highly shined, and I was sure going to miss them.

Tom Kranch of Lancaster, PA, a friend from the 218th and fellow 22nd MP Platoon member, also had his POV on post. It was a white *1956 Ford Thunderbird* convertible in absolute mint condition. To kill some time one late afternoon, he invited me to go riding down the Atlantic coast with him. It was in the late summer and the weather was sunny and warm so we rode with the top down. He taught me that it was proper etiquette at the time for drivers of sport cars to wave at each other in passing. Anyway, we finally ended up in Myrtle Beach, South Carolina. There wasn't much to do there at that time so we, then headed back to Fort Bragg.

On another occasion, Tom and I drove into Spring Lake to get a snack. He had found a place there that served excellent foot-long hot dogs. It was called *Dot's Drive-in Restaurant* and was located in the town just off post at 250 South Bragg Boulevard.

Formerly called *Clayton Cut,* the town was renamed **Spring Lake** in 1923. Its recent growth began during World War II and was attributed to its close proximity to Fort Bragg. Sitting 276 feet above sea level, the town of Spring Lake encompassed 3.7 square miles.

After his ETS, **Tom Kranch** returned home to Lancaster, Pennsylvania, where he took a Civil Service job with the local *U.S. Postal Service.* Tom was never really satisfied with the position he was offered there and soon left. He then decided to go back to work for the family business at *Kranch Communications.* His father had started in the electronics business in 1936 out of a small garage in Lancaster. Then over the years his father worked on two-way radios and other communication equipment, so the business was well established by the time Tom came to work there.

Tom first met Mary Jane (his wife) at a bowling alley shortly after his ETS while testing out a new ball. He learned later to his surprise that she never really liked bowling or most other sports that he was interested in. In any event, they married on June 26, 1971. Today, Tom still works at *Kranch Communications* and is looking forward to retiring as soon as possible. Tom and his wife, Mary Jane raised three children over the years.

Timothy P. Doyle was another close friend I had in the 22nd MP Platoon. He had come through AIT with most of us at Fort Gordon, and the 218th MP Company in Dom Rep. He was a tall husky guy from New York City. One time Tim and I came into the barracks totally inebriated. As to where we had gone to or what we did that night, I have no recollection today. (Let me point out here for the record that getting drunk was *not* a common occurrence throughout my life. In fact, I can count the number of times in my entire life that alcohol had consumed me on two hands. And *half* of those times were during my days in Olive Drab.) But on this particular night, we staggered into the barracks well after 2400 Hours. Then we continued our two-man party by banging loudly on our wall lockers with our Entrenching Tools. Unfortunately, I cannot recall how the escapade ended. But suffice it to say that we weren't very well received at that hour.

The *U.S. Army M-1943 Entrenching Tool* (*with the M-56 Carrier*) was a single bladed folding Army shovel that doubled as a pick-axe. First introduced in 1943, it was intended to replace the M-1910 that was previously used in World War I.

Tom Marston was another friend from AIT and the 218th MP Company who had also been assigned to the 22nd MP Platoon. But for his entire time with the 22nd, his job was to man the *Post Information Booth* on Randolph Street just inside the Highway 87 entrance to Fort Bragg. He absolutely *loved* the job! In Tom's own words, *"It was terrific duty!"* After his ETS, Tom made his career over the years with the *New York Police Department* (*NYPD*) as a Homicide Detective, and retired in 1996. He and his wife Debbie raised three children.

As for other pastimes besides writing letters, I spent many, many hours reading books that were passed around the barracks. Admittedly, some of them *were* sex novels, but I also enjoyed Science Fiction then, and especially *Mike Hammer* detective novels written by Author *Mickey Spillane*. I'd also have to admit that I read more books during my twenty-four months in Olive Drab than I had all total up to that point in my life. Since then and even today, I love to read as often as I can.

By the end of 1966, the 503rd MP Battalion had logged 51 re-enlistments for the year, and also logged 98.2% participation in the *U.S. Savings Bond Program*.

On 1-January-1967, the strength of the 503rd MP Battalion was listed as 439 Enlisted, 12 Officers, and 3 Warrant Officers.

Strange are some of the things that seep into my memory after all these years! Such as that time on **Sunday, 15-January-1967**, when I pissed off a bunch of guys in the Company C Dayroom at the 503$^{rd.}$ This was the day of the **very first ever, _Super Bowl_ in football**. It was the _Green Bay Packers_ against the _Kansas City Chiefs_ at the Los Angeles Coliseum. The Dayroom was full of guys glued to the TV. (They had a _color_ TV no less at the 503rd!)

I was _never_ really a fan of sports, and always preferred to watch a good movie on TV. So when I made an approach to change the channel, I was threatened to within an inch of my life. What the hell was _I_ supposed to know about important football games? But I _learned_ something valuable that day! There is absolutely _NOTHING_ as vicious as a real _sport fanatic_, when his view of a game has been threatened. In any event, the _Packers_ won by a score of 35 to 10.

There was a large red plastic horn at the 503rd that got famous! (I was not part of this fiasco, but merely learned about it thirty years later at a reunion of the 218th and 503rd guys at my home in East Detroit, Michigan.) It was a plastic horn about 18 inches long, and for the most part, it was always kept in the wall locker of **Gus Gustafson** in the Second Squad area on the second floor of Company C.

Now on certain occasions picked totally at random (but always after _lights-out_), one of the guys would go quietly to the edge of the stairs and blast the damned thing as loud as possible down the stairwell. (And boy, there sure was an echo in that stairwell!) Then the guilty party would run like hell to the open window where a string was dangling down from the third floor and tie the horn to the string. (As you may have guessed, the third floor was in on this caper too.) In short time, this drove **1st Sergeant Amos Terry** absolutely bonkers! He would immediately run up the stairs in an effort to nab the man responsible. But while he was dashing up to the second floor, the horn was being hoisted to the third floor.

Eventually, after many of these annoying and frustrating episodes, Sergeant Terry decided that he had had enough. One afternoon he threw a surprise shakedown inspection. This time he was assisted by all the squad leaders in Company C. He ordered them to do a thorough check of each man's wall locker and footlocker. But just before they got to Gus, he had shoved the horn up the sleeve of his Dress Green jacket.

The squad leader eventually came to Gus's locker and when he pushed the uniforms aside to view the entire space, the horn fell from the sleeve. He quickly shut the wall locker and called out to Sergeant Terry, _"It's not here, Top."_ (_Top_ is a military slang term referring to a First Sergeant. Sometimes the terms _Top Kick_ or _First Shirt_ are used.) Anyway, the inspection continued up to the third floor, but Sergeant Terry never found the horn.

A Sergeant named McKinney was another NCO who was driven nuts by the blasted horn. McKinney was considered as a *Lifer,* which is is, one who makes a career of the Army. He once told John Patterson that most of the Company C guys were, in his opinion, *"the worst soldiers he had ever been around."* McKenney eventually found the horn, but that was another story that John Patterson could fill you in on.

On **Thursday, 2-February-1967, the 503rd MP Battalion hosted the activation of the 11th Military Police Group** at Fort Bragg, and was assigned to oversee its initial growth. Recently promoted LTC (Lieutenant Colonel) Thomas W. Adair, Commander of the 503rd MP Battalion was appointed as Acting C.O. of the 11th MP Group, pending the arrival of personnel to take over permanently.

From **8 through 13-February-1967**, an *Annual General Inspection* by the Inspector General, HQs, XVIII Airborne Corps was held at the 503rd. We referred to this as an *I.G. Inspection.* The 503rd received an *Excellent Rating.*

On **Friday, 10-March-1967,** ten guys from the 100th MP Battalion along with me were **promoted to Specialist-4** with a pay grade of E-4. **2nd Lt. James T. Henry, the 100th MP Battalion Adjutant,** signed this order for the Commander. My monthly pay would now be $164 per month and I felt great about it! So much so that I went to the Main PX off Reilly Street north of Bastogne Drive and bought a new pair of *Paratrooper Jump Boots.* The going price at that time was $18. These boots were highly coveted by anyone preferring to look sharp as a razor.

On **Tuesday, 28-March-1967, my 22nd Birthday** came and went without fanfare again. And also once again, life went onward.

On **Friday, 21-April-1967,** after having just completed all the requirements for my **G.E.D. (General Educational Development)** program, I was finally presented with a *Certificate of Achievement.* The GED tests were administered by the *U.S. Armed Forces Institute* of Madison, Wisconsin and offered through the *Army Education Center* at Fort Bragg. This was considered as a High School Equivalency Achievement. (In time I decided that this would not be enough. So in 1970 as a civilian, I attended night school and finally earned the actual high school diploma that I never received. My father was very proud of me for that, and finally awarded me the $5 he had promised me many years earlier for attaining this high honor.)

On **Thursday, 27-April-1967, 2nd Lt. Ronald V. Varol** arrived at Fort Bragg and was assigned as **the new Commander of the 174th MP Company**

and the 22nd MP Platoon. Lt. Ron Varol was a 23-year-old married man and former college student from Long Island, New York. Enlisted in February 1966 at Fort Hamilton, New York, he took his Basic and AIT at Fort Dix, New Jersey. Following OCS (Officer Candidate School) at Fort Benning, Georgia, Ron came to Fort Gordon for his MP Officer Basic Course. Then upon arrival at Fort Bragg, he and his wife Leonora had one son and lived on post in the officers housing area off Honeycutt Road.

At breakfast the morning after his arrival in the 100th MP Battalion, Ron Varol was disturbed to learn that officers were being served from a menu that was not offered to the enlisted men. He recalled his earlier days as an enlisted man at Fort Dix and the bad meals he had received there. So after discussing the matter with the Battalion Mess Sergeant here, the problem was quickly resolved.

At one time while I was there, the **22nd MP Platoon was being considered for deployment to Vietnam**, but few of us enlisted men at the time knew about this. Lt. Ron Varol was therefore ordered to inspect and take inventory of all equipment assigned to the platoon and prepare it for shipment. The newly assigned equipment at that time included costly cameras, fingerprinting supplies, and other P.O.W. (Prisoner of War) processing items. As it turned out in the end, the 22nd MP Platoon never got the order for shipment to Southeast Asia.

Among some of the other duties given to Lt. Ron Varol at Fort Bragg was that of being assigned as the **Post Game Warden**. Serving in this capacity, he had six E-7s working for and reporting to him. Their responsibility was to feed the local deer population by planting 350 acres of corn. They were also assigned to manage the hunting and trapping of predator animals like foxes, coons and bobcats.

10-May-1967 became *Unit Day* **for the 100th MP Battalion.** This was significant as the date of receipt of the first Unit Crest authorized for the battalion.

Many of us in the 100th MP Battalion chose to pay for a **civilian laundry service** instead of utilizing the Post Quartermaster Laundry at Fort Bragg, with its inevitable broken buttons that we were always responsible to replace. This civilian laundry service was located in Spring Lake. About once a week, a large step-van would arrive in the 100th MP Battalion area to pick up our laundry and return it after it was laundered. The driver of this van also sold used fatigues, field jackets and other uniform items.

Around that time I had about six months left in the Army. I therefore decided to take full advantage of the benefits of the **U.S. Army's Dental Health Care**. At that time I had some cavities that needed filling and an upper front tooth that required some work. So I went to a dental clinic at Fort Bragg and found that to be an experience I would never forget.

In order to fill the cavities in my lower teeth, the area in question needed to be deadened for pain before drilling could commence. When the dentist brought the needle down into my mouth, he just kept pushing downward and downward and downward. *Oh My God!* I sure thought that needle was going to burst out through the bottom of my jaw, and I damn near broke the arms off the dental chair. In the end, I did survive the fillings and the repair of the upper front tooth as well. But for many, many years to come, I never felt comfortable in a dentist's chair. Even today, I still have a serious problem with dentists.

Also in the meantime, the 100th MP Battalion had come up with its own mess hall.

It didn't take long, but on **Friday, 19-May-1967, my bad attitude had come back to haunt me, big time!** Yes, my FTA attitude had reached its pinnacle and was in full swing. This was the day that **I earned my second *Article-15*. But more than that, *this* time I also got busted down in rank.**

We of the 100th MP Battalion were required to fall out that morning at 0800 Hours for *Reveille*. In my mind, with less than six months to go in "this man's army," I felt that this was an unnecessary load of bull crap. But to top that off, we were also expected to run a mile that morning! That was "the straw that broke the camel's back!" I then decided to handle it in a way that I felt was appropriate for the occasion. The resulting Article-15 read:

> *"It has been reported that on or about 0815 Hours, 19-May-1967, at Fort Bragg, North Carolina, you, Specialist-Four (E-4) Thomas E. Oblinger, did, having been issued a Lawful Order by S/Sergeant (E-6) Juan Martinez to wit: to take the Physical Training Test and did on or about 0815 Hours, 19-May-1967 willfully disobey the same."*

This order was signed by Major William C. Robbins, Commanding Officer of the 100th MP Battalion. As a result of this action, I was reduced down to the rank of PFC again, and fined $60 per month for a period of two months.

The real truth of the matter was this: I never really refused the lawful order at all. When Sergeant Martinez blew his whistle, everyone else took off running around the quarter-mile track. However, *I*, on the other hand, defiantly began walking slowly and casually, while lighting up a *Winston*. Needless to say, this was not well received by those in authority.

A few days later, I was so damned disgusted with all of it, that after removing my Specialist-4 insignia, I just didn't feel much like sewing on PFC stripes in their place. I therefore simply taped them on.

When I showed up at the Stockade after that to go to work, I was told by my immediate supervisor, *"Oblinger, if you have a problem with those PFC stripes, I'll be more than happy to have them removed for you entirely."* Well, that was all it took. I got the message, loud and clear, and sewed the stripes on that evening. While I was well aware of my self-damaging and negative attitude, I was *not* exactly sure of what to do about it at the time.

I had another friend back then who I could only describe as a *Cornball!* This was none other than **James J. Simone**, a single guy from Detroit who was also drafted in November 1965 like me. At the time of his induction, Jim weighed in at 217 pounds. He felt that while his Basic Training at Fort Knox had nearly killed him, in reality, it actually got him headed on the right track toward better health. He came through AIT with us at Fort Gordon, and then pulled line-duty patrol and guarded checkpoints in Dom Rep. By the time he came back to the states, he was about sixty-four pounds lighter than he was at the time of his induction.

While assigned to Company C of the 503rd, **Jim Simone** and his partner (another guy named Jim from New York) were out on patrol one afternoon on post. They would often arrange drag races in the woods along the edge of the post with the M-151 MP jeeps. And this particular day was no exception. While racing along, they had come close to the end of a long dirt road. Jim then signaled to the driver of the other vehicle to keep on going. At the end of the road, both jeeps suddenly pulled a wild ***Dukes of Hazard* stunt, and leaped high into the air.** After a heart-stopping moment, they both came down and landed heavily on a main road going through Fort Bragg. This stunt abruptly forced another car off the road and into the ditch to avoid hitting them. The other driver, as it turns out, happened to be a full "bird" Colonel!

Immediately Simone, the resourceful one, said to his partner, *"Follow my lead!"* He jumped out of his jeep, ran over, and opened the door of the other car. Then with a snappy salute, he asked the Colonel to please step out and provide identification. The shaken and bewildered officer asked Jim what the hell was going on. Simone calmly replied, *"Sir, we just received a report of someone impersonating a full Bird Colonel while driving a vehicle stolen from the Motor Pool, and was last seen heading off post in this direction!"*

Not only did the colonel buy it, "hook, line, and sinker," he also thanked the MPs for handling it so well and told them to *"Carry on!"*

Jim breathed a sigh of relief. With five Article-15s already under his belt, he sure as hell didn't need another. The others were for sleeping on duty at the Post Information Center, being caught in the Female Barracks (twice), driving a U.S. Army vehicle off post without official permission, and carrying a weapon while off duty . . . . But that's a fun-loving *Cornball* for you!

On Monday, 12-June-1967, Captain Wallace A. Walker became C.O. of the 100ᵗʰ MP Battalion temporarily in place of Major Robbins who was being assigned to other duties.

On Wednesday, 5-July-1967, at Company C, 503ʳᵈ, Lt. Louis Silverhart left the Army on ETS. Today, Louis Silverhart resides in Pittsburgh, Pennsylvania where he still practices law. In his place, **1ˢᵗ Lt. Peter D. Hoffman** assumed command of Company C.

On Thursday, 6-July-1967, due to his retirement, Sergeant McCallister of the 100ᵗʰ MP Battalion was replaced by Master Sergeant Warren E. Kelly as the new Battalion Sergeant Major.

On Monday, 17-July-1967, Major Frederich R. Ulrich assumed command of the 100ᵗʰ MP Battalion. Major Ulrich was described by his junior officers as a tough guy on the outside, but overall was a good commander once you got to know him.

Due to serious racial tensions in the summer of 1967, riots broke out all over the U.S. in cities like New York, Cleveland, Chicago, Atlanta, Newark, Washington, DC, and Detroit. On the morning of **Sunday, 23-July-1967, Detroit Police** officers raided an illegal Black drinking establishment on 12ᵗʰ Street and in short time, a **full-scale race riot** broke out.

This was the first serious race riot in the city of Detroit since the summer of 1943. In that year, the riot left in its wake some 34 dead, 676 injured, and $2 million in property damage, not to mention over one million lost man-hours of badly needed war production.

Jim Simone was at home on leave in Detroit when this current riot broke out. He received a call from the Company Clerk at Company C of the 503ʳᵈ and was told to report immediately to *Selfridge Air Force Base* north of there in Harrison Township. At this time, the 82ⁿᵈ Airborne Division from Fort Bragg had just arrived there at *Selfridge* to assist.

Jim met with the *Riot Control Unit (Platoon)* of the 82nd Airborne there and was paired up with a partner. The two were then assigned to a Security Check Point in the very heart of downtown Detroit at the corner of Gratiot and Beaubien Avenues.

Jim then noticed the amount of national media attention that had developed due to the riots. The media stated that both the 82nd Airborne from Fort Bragg, North Carolina and the Michigan National Guard were only permitted unloaded M-14 rifles in hopes that this would avoid any further incidents. The *only* loaded weapons permitted, as far as Jim Simone knew, were the M-14 rifles and .45 caliber automatic pistols carried by the MPs of the Michigan National Guard.

Several of the guys at the **503rd MP Battalion** (including **Ed Mitchell**) who were from the Detroit area, were hoping that they'd also be sent to assist the already activated Michigan National Guard. But that never came to pass. The rioting ended two days later on 25-July-1967.

In the wake of the 1967 Detroit riot, there were 7200 arrested, 1189 injured, and 43 were left dead. The city of Detroit was left with 2500 stores looted and burned, and 388 families left homeless. The losses from all the looting and arson totaled somewhere between 40 and 80 million dollars.

While serving at Fort Bragg, **Jim Simone** met a very attractive 16-year-old "Army Brat" named Shirley (five years his junior) and began dating her. By the time of his ETS in November 1967, she was still six months short of her 18th birthday. But Jim was determined that he was not going to leave this pretty treasure behind. He actually extended his ETS for another six months and they were married on her birthday.

After leaving the Army behind in May 1968, Simone returned home to Detroit with his new bride and spent the next twenty-five years working for the *Michigan National Bank*. He began as a teller and in time, worked his way up through Branch Manager, then finally to Regional Vice-President. After his years there, and ten more years at *TCF Bank*, Jim now works for the *Bank of Birmingham*. Today, after forty-plus years, Jim and Shirley have raised two children and are still going strong. They now reside in Lake Orion, Michigan.

At the beginning of August 1967, I made up what many of us called a *Short-Timer's Calendar.* This was a special calendar that many of the guys obtained when having only one hundred days and a wake-up left in the Army. Some of these calendars were quite artistic, with many of them featuring the outline of a naked woman. But mine was quite simple in design. It was just one hundred one-inch squares (10 x 10 inches in size). The squares were numbered down from one hundred, with each square indicating the consecutive dates up to and including my ETS of 2-November-1967. So from the beginning of August, whenever anyone asked me, *"Hey Oblinger, what's new?"* I'd simply reply with, *"___ days and a wake-up!"* (Inserting the appropriate number of days I had left.)

It was around this time in August that **Anton Vavrica** and Sharon (the pretty go-go dancer from Fayetteville) stopped seeing each other for whatever reason that has been long since forgotten. This bothered me at the time and eventually I decided to do something about it if I could. So I borrowed a car from my good friend Specialist-5 Paison, and drove into Fayetteville to see her.

We talked and I persuaded her to come back with me to Fort Bragg. Upon arrival we came inside the lobby at Company C, and I told her to wait there while I went and found Tony. I found him in the Dayroom watching TV and advised him to come out to the lobby and talk to her. He did, and the rest is history! He borrowed a car from another friend at Company C and took her out to dinner. While there, they worked out all their problems and he drove her home later that night.

When **Tony Vavrica's** ETS came in November 1967, Sharon left her home and family behind in Fayetteville, North Carolina, and came with him up to New York. Only five months later they were married, and have been together ever since.

While Ed Mitchell and I were concerned back then that our friends' relationship with this pretty girl wouldn't last, we couldn't have been more wrong. Their love for each other is stronger today than ever before. They've raised three wonderful children and even have three grandchildren today. Over the years Tony Vavrica worked in factories and just recently moved in the year 2000 with Sharon to Poughkeepsie, New York, where he is now semi-retired.

In **mid-August 1967, I met a pretty girl named** *Holly Ann George* while I was at home on another leave. (She would later become my wife.) Holly lived in Harper Woods, only a mile and a half south of my home in East Detroit. We met at a birthday party of a friend of hers up the street. At that time Holly was "going steady" with some guy named Arthur who was away somewhere serving in the U.S. Air Force. So for me, it was "hands off" for the time being. Although Holly George (who was sometimes called, *"George of the Jungle"*) was five and a half years younger than me, I really liked what I saw in her. She was born on December 23, 1950, and was named for Christmas Holly.

On **Friday, 18-August-1967, the 100ᵗʰ MP Battalion had its first annual** *I.G. Inspection.* At first, this was a great concern to Major Ulrich, as he was worried about how the inspection would turn out. But in the end, we "passed with flying colors!"

Also on this same day in the Orderly Room of the Stockade, an entry was made in the *Military Police Desk Blotter (DA Form 19-50)*. This was a daily log of activities that was kept in addition to the daily *Morning Report*. For this date, it reported that *"Colonel Simmons and Lieutenant Colonel Farrell had departed the Post Stockade with no discrepancies noted."*

The *Desk Blotter* also listed the names of prisoners released or confined each day, along with prisoner head counts and silverware counts in the Mess Hall to ensure kitchen flatware and utensils weren't stolen and used for weapons. In addition to this, the *Blotter* also listed security checks by the Guard Commander and reported prisoner escapes, if any.

On Wednesday, 13-September-1967, the men of the 100th MP Battalion were permitted to **re-qualify with the .45 caliber Automatic Pistol**. This time I finished with a score of 384 which is considered as *Expert*. But I knew I had not really earned it. Because we were hurried that morning, we were told to pair up with another MP and mark each other's scores. So in my mind, I still couldn't hit the broad side of a barn with the darned thing.

Wayne Molner, a friend from the Detroit area that I'd met in Basic Training and had known through AIT and Dom Rep, was currently serving with the 174th MP Company of the 100th MP Battalion. He also qualified with the pistol that day and scored as a *Marksman*. But unlike me, Wayne earned his rating the *honest* way. During his time with the 100th MP Battalion, Wayne Molner also served in the 545th MP Platoon, which was officially listed as a *POW Processing Platoon*. This platoon was officially commanded by 2nd Lieutenant Fox along with Sergeant First Class Billy Watson serving as the NCO in Charge.

Wayne's duties here also included being a *School Crossing Guard* from September 1966 through June 1967. For this duty, the crossing guards were taken to and from their posts three times a day by a deuce-and-a-half. Each day, Wayne would be at his post for a total of about two and a half hours. Usually after the morning crossing, he'd head off post to Spring Lake for breakfast. Other times between crossing duties they'd head back to the barracks, pull out a deck of playing cards and play *Hearts*. Occasionally, Wayne would also be called upon to direct rush hour traffic at the main gate to Fort Bragg.

After his ETS, Wayne Molner returned to St Clair Shores, Michigan, where he attended college and married Julie in 1968. He worked for *Chrysler Corporation*, then *Volkswagen of America*, and finally found a position as a Senior Account

Manager in Sales for *Oxford Automotive*. Wayne and Julie Molner raised three children and eventually settled in Clinton Township, Michigan.

"Durwood" Pack, shortly after returning from Dom Rep, was also assigned to the 174th MP Company (100th MP Battalion) pulling School Crossing Guard duty. He served for about six months at a traffic circle in the officers' housing area on post. During that time he was a Specialist-4 serving in the capacity of an *Acting Sergeant* (often referred to as an *Acting Jack*).

One day during this duty, the young son of a General on post had a seizure while crossing the street there. With quick thinking, Durwood summoned medical help using the MP Radio. When the help arrived, the kid was treated and was later OK, but Pack's effort did not go unnoticed by the child's father. In short time, the General wrote a letter to the commander of the 100th MP Battalion, and Durwood was then promoted to Sergeant E-5.

Pack found out that due to a lack of strict supervision in the 174th MP Company, he was able to "go AWOL" for about thirty plus weekends in a row. On those occasions, he'd head for Chapel Hill, North Carolina to visit some friends, or shoot home for the weekend at Winston/Salem.

Then in June 1967, after the school year was over for the summer, Sergeant Durwood Pack and his partner, **Frank Opyt** were assigned to Town Patrol with the local police in Fayetteville. While there one night, they actually arrested a go-go dancer from a place called, *The Pink Pussycat*. Durwood and Frank believed that she was the very first real nude dancer in the state of North Carolina.

Frank J. "Lurch" Opyt was from Chicago, Illinois and was among the tallest men in Military Police Corps at the time. The nickname of *Lurch* was the name of a character played by actor Ted Cassidy in the TV comedy series, *The Addams Family*. Although the U.S. Army officially listed Frank Opyt at six-feet-five inches in height, Durwood and a few of Frank's other friends measured him at six-feet-seven inches, which was actually considered as too tall to be drafted at that time. Everyone who knew him would agree that *Lurch* was an easy going guy and great to get along with.

Doyle "Gabby" Hayes was another guy who pulled School Crossing Guard duty. After having served with us in the 218th MP Company, he returned from Dom Rep with the last group out in September aboard an LST. He was then assigned to Company C of the 503rd before being transferred to the 100th MP Battalion. Among some of the other duties he pulled with the 100th was working in the

Traffic Division, doing Accident Investigation, and pulling Town Patrol duty in Fayetteville with the local police.

Doyle left the Army as a Sergeant E-5 in November 1968 and returned home to Florence, Alabama. He worked for the *Tennessee Valley Authority* for about six months then began a career with the *Reynolds Alloy Company* in Alabama as a Fireman/Guard. During that time, Doyle married Ann in December 1971. Then leaving *Reynolds* after thirty years he took a job with *Wise Alloys, LLC,* also in Alabama and retired there in 2007. Doyle and Ann have raised two children and still live in Florence, Alabama. He is a member of the *Central Volunteer Fire Department* and the *Village Baptist Church.* He is a long-distance runner and loves it, having run in 5-Ks, 10-Ks and three 26.2-mile marathons.

On Saturday, 16-September-1967, Company C, of the 503ʳᵈ MP Battalion won the Fort Bragg Softball Championship.

On Friday, 22-September-1967, at 1830 Hours, an entry was made in the Stockade *Desk Blotter* indicating a total of 169 prisoners present and accounted for. That number included 163 Army, 2 Air Force, 3 Marine Corps, and 1 Navy.

A fire had broken out at the Fort Bragg Post Stockade sometime around the early Fall in 1967. For the record, I have no recollection if this event at all. It must have happened during a time when I was away, possibly at home on leave, as I would have certainly remembered all the excitement. While several others of the 22ⁿᵈ MP Platoon *do* recall this event, I feel obligated to mention it here with as much accuracy as they could recall.

At the time the fire broke out, **Sergeant Brian R. Bryan** was on duty in the stockade office as the *Assistant Guard Commander.* This happened just after the evening meal on an afternoon shift as the prisoners were taking their showers. Reportedly, of the three prisoner barracks buildings, the middle one had caught fire and was considered as completely destroyed. Though no one was ever certain as to how it got started or who started it, it was believed to have begun in a back room where extra mattresses were stored. Thereafter, the prisoners of that building were forced to squeeze into the remaining two barracks.

Brian Bryan had returned from Dom Rep to the 503ʳᵈ with the Third Phase group returning by way of an LST ship. He had transferred to the 22ⁿᵈ MP Platoon with the same group as me on 10-October-1966. Though he was eleven months younger than I was, Brian had risen swiftly to the rank of Sergeant (E-5) due to his positive attitude and strong dedication to duty. At the 22ⁿᵈ MP Platoon barracks,

Sergeant Bryan shared the upstairs cadre room with his close friends, **Sergeant John J. Klich, Jr.** (a single guy from Chicago, Illinois) and **Sergeant Paul W. Hadley** (a single guy from Indiana).

It was my well-known *bad* attitude at that time that clashed one day in October with Sergeant Bryan's positive attitude in the barracks of the 22nd MP Platoon. He had been put in charge of seeing that the 22nd MP Platoon barracks were cleaned for an upcoming inspection. This idea did not sit well with me and I argued with him about it until it got out of hand. It actually resulted in a senseless scuffle that came to fists.

It may have stemmed from the fact that I had been busted back to PFC and probably resented his swift rise to the rank of Buck Sergeant. Fortunately, if the scuffle had not been broken up by others in the barracks, I might have gotten hurt. At that time I was quite slim and still weighed only 128 pounds. Sergeant Bryan was a darn good NCO. And even more than that, he never held any grudges. So in short time all was forgiven, although over the years I felt bad about it and was never able forgot it. These days, he and I are now able to joke about it occasionally on the phone when I mention it to him.

When **Brian Bryan** returned to Ohio after his ETS in November 1967, he resumed his career in Tool and Die. He also resumed his hobby of finishing a 1930 Roadster Pickup Street Rod that he had started before being drafted. To further develop his career, in 1969, Brian took a job at a special machine-building shop in Elida, Ohio. While there, he built a high-speed stamping press for *AMP Incorporated* of Harrisburg, Pennsylvania, a manufacturer of electrical and electronic connectors. In 1973, he learned that the press was being shipped to an *AMP* Plant in Greensboro, North Carolina. Then after marrying Kathy in October of that year, he accepted a position there and moved to Greensboro. Starting as an assembly technician, he worked his way up through the years to become the Plant Manager. During that time he was transferred to Spartanburg, South Carolina, and eventually to Winston/Salem, North Carolina, where they still reside today. He retired in 2004 after thirty-plus years. Since retirement, he has restored a 1929 Model-A Ford and a 1965 Zipper Camper. Today, Brian and Kathy have four children and two grandchildren.

Sergeant Paul W. Hadley was among some of Brian Bryan's closest friends in the 22nd MP Platoon. Paul Hadley was a tall, slender guy from Seymour, Indiana, who married a girl named Ruby from Tennessee. He had come through Basic Training with me in E-13-4 at Fort Knox, AIT at Fort Gordon, the 218th MP Company in Dom Rep, and Company C of the 503rd. Paul Hadley loved to play basketball and was also an ace on a pool table, often winning enough money to pay for gasoline whenever he and Brian went joy riding in Brian's POV.

John Osborne of the **503rd MP Battalion**, with about a month left in the Army, got himself a hot idea. In early October 1967, he did a midnight raid on the Post Theater across the street from the 503rd building. Here he "borrowed" some large letters from the marquis sign out front. Then arranging the letters on a board about one foot wide and two feet long, he came up with a new sign that simply read, *S H O R T !* He then hung the sign out the attic window above the third floor where it remained several days for everyone's amusement. One morning the men of Company C were standing in formation outside. When a platoon leader happened to rock back on his heels and look up, he saw the sign and had a "Wolverine!"

John Osborne got out of the Army a month later in November, returned to Royal Oak, Michigan, and married Marie in 1978. Attending College on the *G.I. Bill*, he earned a degree in Economics and spent the next three years living in the Mountain States (Colorado, Utah, Montana, and Wyoming). Since then, he has spent the remaining years self-employed in Advertising and Publishing. John and Marie have raised three children over the years, and currently reside in Birmingham, Michigan.

Around that time **I was chosen for KP duty** at the 100th MP Battalion. KP was not something I was scheduled for that day. But another guy who *was* scheduled that day was unavailable. So when this happened, the *C.Q. Runner* was told to wake up someone to replace him. As to why the runner picked the second floor in my barracks, I have no idea. But when he got to the top of the stairs, I just happened to be sleeping in the closest bunk from the door on his left.

Damn, I thought! I had *picked* this bunk because it *was* closest to the door, and it finally backfired on me. Oh well . . . Live and learn some more.

By the time I got dressed and made it down to the mess hall, there was no doubt that I was the *last* one to report for duty that day. I was therefore stuck with the job that most guys considered the worst of all jobs on KP. That is the job of **Pots and Pans.**

Most guys by far agreed that the very *best job* on KP duty was what we called **D.R.O. (Dining Room Orderly).** It was a job that was usually handled by two or three guys. On this job after each meal (three times a day), every chair in the mess hall had to be placed up on the tables. Then came the sweeping, mopping, waxing, and buffing of the dining hall floor, followed by putting all the chairs back down. To make matters worse, the job also included "waiting hand-and-foot" on any officers who happened to wander into the Mess Hall any time during the day. Although being a DRO was supposed to be the *cleanest* job in the mess hall, I cannot for the life of me, understand why anyone would volunteer for the job. (Personally, I never cared for kissing all the brass butts and waiting on them while trying to get the floor done.)

The job most guys considered the *second best* was called **Trays.** Two men usually handled this job, which included the washing and stacking of all the mess trays after each meal. In this position, one gets soaking wet but it wasn't really heavy work.

I'll admit, at first when it came to the job of **Pots and Pans,** I felt the same resentment about it as everyone else. But before that day was over, I became thoroughly convinced that it was **the very best job on KP Duty.**

The job description of *Pots and Pans* was really straightforward. All I had to do was wash all the pots and pans. That sure sounds simple enough, doesn't it? Being one of seven kids growing up back home, doing pots and pans was nothing new to me. In no time at all, I came up with a plan that worked great!

I handled this by standing close to the Mess Sergeant all during the meal preparation. Then at the very moment he finished with a pot or a pan, I'd grab it then run to the back sink, which I had already filled with hot water and soap, and drop it in. By the time the cook was finished preparing the meal, my back sink was completely full with soaking cookware.

We (the KPs) were always fed before anyone else was served. So because these items were soaking all during our mealtime, I was more than ready for them afterward. Had they not been soaking, I'd have had a terrible battle trying to scrape and scrub off cooked and baked-on grease and grime. As it was, it took me all of twenty minutes to clean every pot and pan. It meant that for all three meals that day, I worked a grand total of one hour for the entire day. I swear! I could not believe what was happening to me.

I then began to wonder . . . what does one do with all that free time between meals? I took off out the back door and went back to my barracks where I rested, smoked, read books, wrote letters, and generally goofed off till the next meal was about to be prepared. I continued to use the same routine through dinner and supper. In the end, I did far less work in far less time than I would have on any other job in the mess hall. And I couldn't believe how fortunate I was.

On **Thursday, 4-October-1967, the 503rd MPs traveled by bus to Fort Belvoir**, in Virginia, to attend a training drill that was staged there. The actual purpose of this trip was to put on a **Riot Control Demonstration** for the present class members of the *FBI National Academy* located near there and about six hundred other law enforcement officers from across the nation. The Army engineers had built a mock-up city street there for the exercise, which would be made into a training film for future classes. Also present to observe were many U.S. Marshals. During the exercise, men from the 503rd were to be broken up into two groups. Some would serve as MPs in full riot gear, while the others would serve as civilian "hippie" demonstrators.

Ed Mitchell was there, and would always regard this as **his worst experience** of all in the U.S. Army. Ed was one of several guys who were assigned to don civilian clothes and long-haired "hippie" wigs. The weather at the time was sunny, hot and muggy. Sometime during the exercise, Ed pulled his wig off momentarily to wipe some sweat from his brow, and just simply relax for a moment. After what seemed like only minute or so, he was observed by one of the NCOs in authority. The Sergeant told him, *"Well, as long as you have chosen not to participate in this part of the exercise, you might as well join the other group over there."* He was then ordered to get back into his MP flack vest, gas mask and full riot control gear. Ed suddenly realized that the hippies really didn't have it so bad after all.

Gus Gustafson not only donned a wig while he was there that day, but he was also allowed to grow "lamb-chop" style sideburns in advance for the training exercise. **Vern Schwieterman** posed as a hippie that day too, but at least his hair was long enough that he didn't require a wig. Others included in this group were **Jim Simone, Arnold Rhoads, Tony Vavrica,** and **Mike Johnson. John Patterson** was assigned as a sniper for the exercise. It was a job that he found to be a lot of fun.

Following his ETS, **Gus Gustafson** worked as a fire fighter in California with the *L.A. County Fire Department.* After two failed marriages, he finally met Linda, the wife of his dreams, and she is still with him today. He has a daughter that he adopted from his current marriage and one son (who died in 1995) from a previous marriage.

John W. Patterson had taken his Basic Training at Fort Polk, Louisiana and came through MP School with us at Fort Gordon. After pulling MP Patrol for most of his days in Dom Rep, he returned to Fort Bragg and was assigned to Company C of the 503rd, where he continued to pull MP patrol.

Following his ETS in November 1967, Patterson returned to Kaufman, Texas and attended college for a year and a half. For the next twenty-one years, he worked for *Procter & Gamble* until the plant shut down. Thereafter, John became a Production Mechanic for *Colgate Oral Pharmaceuticals* and finally retired in 2006. During that time John had married Debby in August 1988. He has one child from a previous marriage and Debby has two. They currently reside in Dallas, Texas.

On Thursday, 19-October-1967, fifteen guys from the 22nd MP Platoon of the 100th MP Battalion (including myself) were awarded the **Good Conduct Medal** for *"exemplary behavior, efficiency and fidelity for the period indicated."* I wondered at the time how in the heck this happened after my earning an Article-15 twice! Oh well! This was the Army! The medal gave us another piece of colorful *"fruit salad"* with which to decorate our Dress Green uniforms.

Now and then we at the 100th MP battalion were called out on early mornings for Reveille formation. I noticed that while the majority of us wore fatigue uniforms and several others wore their Dress Greens, I also became aware of the fact that a few of the guys standing in the ranks were dressed in their civilian clothes. Later on, when I asked someone what that was all about, it was explained to me that during Reveille formations, it was required that each person falling in would wear his *"duty uniform"* for the day.

Then I learned that these few guys dressed in "civies" were assigned to what I later believed was the most prestigious job as an MP. That is, the job of **AWOL Apprehension.** On this job, the duty uniform for the day might be old and faded cut-off shorts, a torn and dirty T-shirt, and sandals. They simply dressed in anything that was not considered military attire while they hunted down and apprehended AWOLs. Once their subject was apprehended, the Dress Green uniforms were required while escorting them back to Fort Bragg. Even to this day, I thought they had the very *best* job in the entire Military Police Corps.

Mike Johnson was one of the men assigned to *AWOL Apprehension.* About ten months after his return to the U.S. from the 218th MP Company, he went home on leave and got married. Soon after that, his wife joined him in North Carolina and they lived off post. Around that time he was transferred from Company C of the 503rd to the 100th MP Battalion where he served in the 22nd MP Platoon.

Mike's MP partner at that time was a guy named Dennis Bugg from Detroit, Michigan. They drove all around the state of North Carolina tracking down and apprehending AWOLs. Once as they approached a little town on one of their trips, they passed a large road sign that read, *"WELCOME TO MOUNT GILEAD, NORTH CAROLINA—THIS IS KLAN COUNTRY"* *What a shocker,* Mike thought.

Three months after his ETS in October 1968, Mike Johnson joined the *Seattle Police Department* as a member of their *Mounted Patrol* and stayed with them for fourteen years. From there he transferred to their *Motorcycle Unit* and remained there until his retirement in 1997. Over the years, he always enjoyed running in

10-K events and marathons. Since then he has been running his own Town Car service, mostly driving people to and from the airport. Having raised one daughter, Mike and Marilou Johnson still live in Seattle, Washington.

But Mike Johnson and his partner weren't the only MPs that came upon road signs depicting racial hatred in the south. **Tom Kranch** also found a huge billboard while driving out in the country somewhere north of Spring Lake. It was red, white, and yellow in color, proudly boasting, *"JOIN & SUPPORT UNITED KLANS OF AMERICA, Inc.—HERE YESTERDAY—TODAY & FOREVER."* Feeling certain that no one back home would believe him if he told them of this, Tom took a moment to photograph the billboard. All the while he silently wondered, how much longer would racial hatred continue to go on in the world?

On one late midnight shift at the stockade in mid-October, I was on duty at Gate #1. Looking out the window while sitting there on this cool evening, low in the southwestern night sky I saw a large orange **October Moon**. With less than a month to go in Olive Drab, seeing that moon made me as homesick as I could be. But I realized that I had made it this far OK, and I was sure looking forward to going back home for good very soon.

The men over in the 503rd were issued brand new bunks and mattresses around this time. But unlike the old bunks that we referred to as "steel racks" with hard and lumpy two-inch-thick mattresses that the Army used for over thirty years, these new ones were of twin-bed size with **mattresses eight inches thick!** Absolutely fantastic, I thought! When I visited Ed Mitchell later, I tried one out and could not believe how comfortable these were. I found comfort that was absolutely indescribable! I remember wondering back then how many guys would actually "re-up" (re-enlist) for this!

Around **20-October-1967, I was officially relieved of all assignments** and no longer listed on duty rosters. I was then given what was called an *Installation Clearance Record (DA Form 137)*. From 20-October until my ETS date in early November, I would be reporting to a number of places on post in order to be "cleared" of any and all obligations that might exist on my behalf. At each of these places, my *DA Form 137* was to be initialed by the appropriate person.

These places included:

Army Education Center, Classified Documents, Courts and Boards, Dental Clinic, 82nd Airborne NCO Mess, Field Military 201 File, Financial Records, Medical Treatment Facility,

Postal Officer, Post Quartermaster, Quarters Assignment, Unit Supply, Company Mail Room, Reenlistment NCO, Orderly Room, and **Battalion S-4.**

I knew that I was going to have to turn in some of my uniforms before my final outprocessing was completed. Then I recalled being warned by others before me that, attempting to turn in uniforms that had been tailored was unacceptable to the U.S. Army. And I was told further that others paid no regard to this, and were forced to stay around another day or so longer in order to purchase these items for official turn-in. I wasn't going to take any chances in this area. So knowing this, I had to find someone who was willing to do some swapping with me.

The next morning after breakfast, I took a walk over to an area on post that housed new recruits. As I approached the back of an old wooden mess hall, I noticed a couple of guys smoking and sitting on the steps at the back door. Upon seeing me, they suddenly jumped up and snapped to Attention. It took me a moment or two to figure out why.

These new recruits were dressed in their brand-new, un-starched, dark-green, Olive Drab fatigues. No doubt they noticed me in my lightly starched, somewhat faded, pressed, and tailored fatigues. Seeing me from that distance, they probably thought I was someone of rank and/or authority. It occurred to me then just how sharp guys looked in tailored uniforms . . . at least to new recruits!

Anyway, I said to them, *"At ease, men!"* Then I introduced myself and explained to them why I was there. One of the guys looked to be about my size, and eagerly offered to help me out later after he had finished KP duty. We met later that evening and I traded him some of my faded and altered uniform items (with pant legs tailored down to fourteen inches at the cuff) for his un-tailored newly issued ones. He seemed to be more than thrilled with the swap.

As I recall, I had to turn in two of the four sets of fatigues that I had been issued, along with two of the four sets of khakis, and one of the two sets of Dress Greens. The end result was that I had no problem at all with the Post Quartermaster on turn-in day.

In most cases at that time, clearing post took only two or three days. Once I had cleared post, the remainder of the time I had left was for all intents and purposes, mine to do with as I pleased. I therefore took every advantage of the time I had left to put some cash in my pocket. To do this, I put the word out that I was willing to **pull anyone's scheduled KP for $20 a day**. In October 1967, twenty bucks was considered decent money for a day's work on KP.

But this time of course, I had a plan! As long as I was the last to arrive at the Mess Hall for KP, I was sure to be "stuck" with the lousy job of *Pots and Pans!* Therefore, I was in no particular hurry to break my neck getting there. I simply took my sweet old time getting out of my bunk, had a smoke or two while getting dressed, and then wandered leisurely down to the Mess Hall.

On one of those days while pulling KP for someone and working *Pots and Pans*, I came across a large cast aluminum meat tray that I could not scrub clean. These trays were about 24 x 24 x 6 inches in size. Even after having soaked it for hours, and giving it my very best effort, it was still no use. So after what seemed like an eternity of scrubbing without success, I finally decided . . . "*Horse Manure!*" I wrapped the damned pan in paper and, along with the other trash, tossed it into the Dumpster out back . . . . Problem solved!

In the end as I recall, I believe I pulled KP about four times during the last days in October 1967, earning myself an extra $80 to go home with, and I sure felt good about it.

On Sunday, 22-October-1967, the 503rd MP Battalion was placed on Full Alert. At this time, **Dennis Wood** of Company B (formerly of the 218th MP Company) and his wife Jean lived just off Highway 87 about two miles south of Fort Bragg. At about 0400 Hours in the morning, Dennis got a call from the 503rd and was told that the entire battalion had been alerted for movement. He was then ordered to report to Fort Bragg immediately. With only ten days left before his ETS, Dennis instructed Jean to pack up everything right away and move back to Michigan with their five-an-a-half-month-old child. He then jumped in his car and drove out to Fort Bragg.

Upon arrival at the 503rd, he was ordered to draw a jeep from the Motor Pool, get it fully loaded with riot control gear and equipment, and prepare to move out at once. Their destination was to be unknown for the time being.

At daybreak, the 503rd MP Battalion began heading out of Fort Bragg moving northeast along Interstate 95. The convoy of mostly M-151 jeeps and a few two-and-a-half-ton trucks, moved up into the state of Virginia a few hours later, then continued northeast. Still, no destination was given. After moving 317 miles in over seven hours of hard driving, a sign up ahead indicated that they were pulling into *Fort Belvoir, Virginia* about twenty-one miles south of Washington, DC.

It was just after dark when the convoy arrived and came to a stop. They were then placed in a vacant barracks building and, thinking that they'd be there for the night, they all climbed into bunks for a good night's sleep.

About an hour later they were yanked out of their slumber and told to *"mount up"* again. Back on the road, the convoy continued heading north toward **Washington, DC.** As they neared their final destination, the convoy moved down a long ramp into an underground tunnel network near the **Pentagon.** Here they joined up with other Army units totaling over 5,000 troops in all.

Once there, they were ordered to immediately prepare for crowd control. Flack vests were passed out to the men along with "steel pots" (helmets) and helmet liners. M-14 rifles were also to be used, but only with shielded bayonets.

On Monday, 23-October-1967, at about 0830 Hours in the morning, the order came. The large door of the underground garage opened, and the men were moved at *Double Time* up the ramp and out the door holding their rifles at *High Port.* When Dennis saw what lay ahead, his heart nearly dropped to the pavement.

The size of the crowd around the Pentagon was unbelievable. There were more than 100,000 anti-war demonstrators about to storm the building. This was the first national demonstration against not only the *Vietnam War,* but also the *Selective Service System.* The intention of the protesters there was to promote *Stop-the-Draft Week.*

The men of the 503rd formed into ranks and moved out in a skirmish line at double-arm intervals. They then formed a large circle around the Pentagon, along with 236 U.S. Marshals who were standing "at the ready" with three-foot-long nightsticks. While many of the demonstrators burned their draft cards there, others placed flowers into the barrels of the M-14 rifles pointed in their direction and taunted the MPs. As soon as the men were in position, they were ordered to stand at *Parade Rest.*

Unfortunately, at that very same moment, the crowd began charging toward the skirmish line. Dennis firmly believed that seeing the MPs in combat and riot gear, probably riled the defiant crowd. Then as luck would have it, the man leading the charge was headed strait for Dennis. He had no time to think. It was going to be either Dennis or the rushing mad man. Abruptly Dennis brought his rifle up with a *Left-Perry* and laid a short *Butt Stroke* to the center of the man's forehead. This stopped the forward motion of the man as blood shot out of his head. Then U.S. Marshals jumped the man with their batons. Later on, Dennis Wood received an *"Atta Boy!"* from the U.S. Marshals.

I wonder how many of us would have done the same in that situation. I'd like to believe that most of us would. Over the years, this scene was relived many times in the mind of Dennis Wood, but he never had regrets about it. He knew that he did what had to be done.

Ed Mitchell of Company C, 503rd, was also on the scene during all of this. But unlike the guys of Company B, the MPs of C Company were well informed as to where they were going upon leaving Fort Bragg.

During the breaks between assignments on the perimeter, Ed Mitchell recalls sleeping in the basement of the Pentagon.

Over the rest of that weekend, whenever skirmishes broke out around the Pentagon, the forward motion of demonstrators was halted in actions that resembled battles of the *Civil War.* Fortunately in the sector where Ed stood guard on the perimeter, there was no forward offensive movement from the crowd.

Mike Johnson, also of Company C, was there too. He recalls standing in front of the steps of the Pentagon for hours while some girls among the demonstrators placed flowers in the barrel of his M-14 Rifle. He simply ignored them as best he could. In all, by the time it was over, a total of 680 persons were arrested.

Tony Vavrica stayed behind at Fort Bragg with ten to fifteen others from Company C to "hold down the fort" at the 503rd. During that time he had to take his meals at the 82nd Airborne Division Mess Hall.

While many of the guys from the 503rd remained at the Pentagon in Washington, air-conditioned buses soon arrived to pick up those guys whose ETS dates were coming up in early November.

At the time of his ETS in November 1967, **Dennis Wood** returned to St Clair Shores, Michigan where he joined his wife Jean and their six-month-old child. Through the years Dennis and Jean moved several more times, living in Mount Clemens, Shelby Township, Sterling Heights, Macomb Township, and back again to Shelby Township, Michigan, where they still reside today. During all this time, Dennis made a career as a Pipefitter while he and Jean raised five children.

On Monday, 30-October-1967, After having finished "clearing post" a week earlier, I took my *DA Form 137* to be finally signed by my platoon leader, Lt. **Ron Varol**. My orders were now cut. I was to report on this day to the *USAGTP (U.S. Army Garrison Transfer Point)* over near the 503rd MP Battalion. After one full year and twenty days, my duties with the 22nd MP Platoon of the 100th MP Battalion were finally over.

Around 1330 Hours on that sunny afternoon, I was able to hitch a ride in a jeep with another MP. When the jeep arrived, I tossed both my duffel bag and AWOL bag into the back seat, then jumped in on top of them. We then drove out of the 100th MP Battalion area and headed southwest over to Macomb Street. I don't recall looking back.

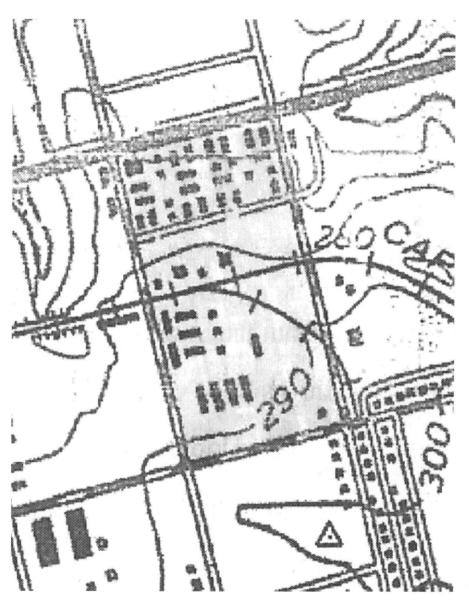

100th MP Battalion area & Post Stockade from a 1957 map

Fort Bragg Post Stockade

Sitting on 9 acres about 280 feet above sea level at the **northeast corner of Armistead and Letterman Streets**, this was about a 3-minute walk just south of the 22nd MP Platoon Barracks. The property on which the stockade sat was divided into two "compounds." The front (Administration) compound, occupying the southern half of the property, housed the Orderly Room, Supply Room and 2 other buildings. A single 10-foot chain link fence surrounded this compound, topped off by concertina wire. Beyond Gate #2, a double chain link fence enclosed the inner (Prisoner) compound. These were also 10 feet high, with 10 feet of space between them and filled with several strands of concertina wire. This inner compound included 3 prisoner's barracks buildings, the maximum-security cell block and mess hall.

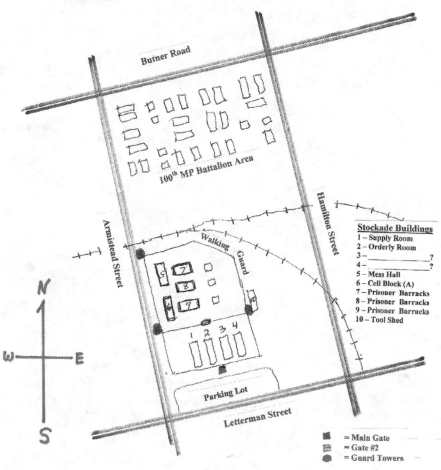

Stockade Buildings
1 – Supply Room
2 – Orderly Room
3 – _____?
4 – _____?
5 – Mess Hall
6 – Cell Block (A)
7 – Prisoner Barracks
8 – Prisoner Barracks
9 – Prisoner Barracks
10 – Tool Shed

■ = Main Gate
▨ = Gate #2
● = Guard Towers

100th MP Battalion area & Post Stockade (Diagram by Tom O.)

100th MP Battalion Officers

100th MP Battalion HQ Personnel

Major William C. Robbins &
First Sergeant Joseph A. McCallister, 100th MP Battalion

2nd Lt Ronald V. Varol, C.O. of 22nd MP Platoon

Lt Ron Varol

Lt Ron Varol receives Army Commendation Medal

Capt. Wallace A. Walker, C.O. of Fort Bragg Stockade, 1966

Capt. Lawrence E. Seng, C.O. of Fort Bragg Stockade, 1967

2nd Lt James T. Henry, Adjutant, 100th MP Bn

Mark Horvath & Ed Novak, HQs, 100th MP Battalion

School Crossing Guards from 100th MP Battalion

Sgt Doyle W. Hayes

Doyle Hayes—Graduate of Vascar Training Course

Sgt Paul W. Hadley in Stockade parking lot at Fort Bragg

Brian Bryan & John Klich, 100th MP Battalion

Sgt Brian Bryan at 100th MP Battalion

Sgt John J. Klich, Jr.

Outside of 22nd MP Platoon Barracks—
Sgt Ken Hoss (L) and Sgt Hatch (R)

Brian Bryan at 22nd MP Barracks

Brian Bryan near 100th MP Battalion

John Klich & Paul Hadley

Brian Bryan, Mike Moots, Paul Hadley

New Matresses arrived at 503rd

Franklin & Gustafson in Riot Control Training at Fort Belvoir, October 4, 1967

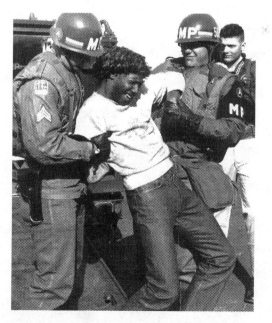

Franklin & Gustafson at Fort Belvoir, October, 4, '67

A sad but thruthful part of our past. A Road sign in rural North Carolina in 1966-67

503rd arrived at the Pentagon in DC, October 23, 1967

503rd getting set up at the Pentagon

503rd holding the line at the Pentagon

P-38 C-Ration Can Opener

Chapter 7

Homeward Bound

MONDAY, *30-October-1967*—(1400 Hours) U.S. Army Garrison Transfer Point.

After leaving the 100th MP Battalion, I arrived and reported as ordered to the *USAGTP (U.S. Army Garrison Transfer Point)* on Macomb Street for *Rations, Quarters and Processing* from the U.S. Army. This was located up the street to the east of the 503rd MP Battalion building. It was a bright and sunny day as I recall and by mid-afternoon, the temperature had reached its high of 73 degrees. I found myself thinking that back at home this would have been considered as quite warm for late October or early November.

Moving up to the second floor, I quickly found an empty bunk and stowed my gear. This was near a window overlooking the northwest side of the building. After settling in there, I decided to walk down the street to visit Ed Mitchell over at C Company for a few hours. By the time "lights out" rolled around that night at 2130 Hours (9:30 PM), I was back in my bunk at *USAGTP* and sound asleep. It had been a long and stressful day.

The next morning, **Tuesday, 31-October-1967**, I awoke and realized that there wasn't really much to do here at USAGTP. I therefore decided to stay in bed for a little while longer and try to catch up on a little more "sack time." In no time at all, I was fast asleep again. As it turned out, except for a couple of needed latrine breaks, I had actually stayed in bed and slept on through the entire day. It was well after dark when I finally awoke and realized that for the first time in my life, I had just slept for a full twenty-four hours! That has never happened before, and it has never happened to me again since then.

On **Wednesday, 1-November-1967**, while processing the last of my Personnel Records and paper work, I got one final pleasant surprise! I found out that I still had twelve days of accrued leave time coming to me that I didn't know I had. Up until that point, I was pretty certain that had I used up every last day of leave I had coming in my two years of service. It was explained to me at that time, that the days I had spent between duty stations after Basic and AIT were *not* considered as *Leave* time by the U.S. Army, but instead were considered simply as *Delay Enroute* time. And now this was the first that I had ever really heard of it.

Then as required by Army regulation, I was given the expected short sales pitch about re-enlisting. This also included an explanation about all the benefits that the Army could offer me. All I had to do was devote three more years of my life to continued service in Olive Drab. Tempting as it was, I of course decided to pass on this fine and generous offer of serving three more years protecting and defending this great nation of ours. (Now, thinking back with 20/20 hindsight, I wonder if I should have given more thought to the idea.) But I was just a kid then with a lousy attitude.

Anyway, with the last of my records signed, dated, and filed, I was given a copy of it all and told that tomorrow (Thursday) I would be a civilian again. With all the excitement of my last day in Olive Drab on my mind, I slept miserably that night.

THURSDAY, 2-November-1967—E.T.S. at last!

I was up early on the morning of Thursday, 2-November-1967. After breakfast, in eager anticipation of the day's events, I got on with my final outprocessing from the U.S. Army. There was only one last item in my military records to be processed. This was commonly known to us all as the **DD Form 214.** This was officially referred to as the ***Armed Forces of the United States Report of Transfer or Discharge.*** As soon as the form was completed, it was finally signed by **2nd Lt. Ralph E. Reznik,** the Assistant Adjutant of the U.S. Army Garrison Troop Command.

As of about noon, I was a civilian at last! But more than that, I was also a U.S. Army *Veteran*, and was therefore qualified to join the *VFW* and the *American Legion.* (It wasn't until 1988 when I began researching my father's World War II experience that I finally joined both.)

But now, instead of immediately heading for home, I decided to stay around just one more day. The next day was **Ed Mitchell's ETS**, and I thought I'd stick around and ride back home to Detroit with him. This got me a lot of ribbing from not only Ed, but also a lot of the other guys in Company C of the 503rd. After all these months of my bad FTA attitude and all my constant complaining about the U.S. Army, I was actually going to stay around one more day? To this day, Ed has never let me live it down.

But at least I got to experience what it was like sleeping one night in one of the 503rd's new bunks! . . . On one of their new eight-inch thick mattresses, no less! What an unbelievable night to remember!

FRIDAY, 3-November-1967—Homeward Bound. Finally!

After his final outprocessing, Ed and I left Fort Bragg under a bright and sunny sky that afternoon. We took a bus from the 503rd to the Fayetteville Airport, even though our *Piedmont Airlines* flight wasn't scheduled to leave out of there until later that night.

The flight from Fayetteville, North Carolina to Washington, DC was uneventful as usual. Then when we arrived at *Washington National Airport*, we still had the usual layover before boarding a flight out to Detroit in the early morning.

During this time, while walking about the terminal looking for a snack counter, I met an attractive girl with long dark hair who was also waiting for a flight out in the morning. I bought us both a coffee and brought one back for Ed. After introducing the two, I told Ed that she and I were going to stroll around the terminal for a while. Ed told me to go ahead while he tries to snooze on one of the benches here. What an understanding guy Ed was!

She and I began walking together slowly while discussing our lives and experiences. Unfortunately, I learned that her flight in the morning was heading in a different direction than mine. After a short time she pulled a cigarette from her purse and I immediately pulled out my *Zippo*. Then I lit hers while reaching for a cigarette of my own. Once hers was lit, she stepped back, looked me square in the eye and proclaimed, *"I now owe you an hour of pure passion."*

This caught me off guard and I thought to myself, this only happens in the movies, doesn't it? So I asked her if she would please explain. And she did. She explained to me that when a gentleman lights a lady's cigarette, she was then obligated to him for *an hour of passion.*

At first, I was a bit dumbfounded at the prospect of this. But I sure enjoyed the mere thought of taking her up on it. She was, after all, quite a "knock-out" to look at. It was then that we suddenly realized that we were both going our separate ways in less than an hour. We both knew that we had very few choices and too little time.

In the end, it never came to pass. It might have made a great passionate love novel, but the timing was all wrong. After kissing goodbye, we went our separate ways. But now and then over the years, I have a pleasant moment or two remembering her.

SATURDAY, 4-November-1967—Home at last!

Ed Mitchell was met by his parents at Detroit's "Metro" Airport, and I was met by my father and sister, Mary. After introductions all around, Ed and I went our separate ways, but we stayed in touch now and then over the coming years.

After his ETS, **Ed Mitchell** went to work as a skilled draftsman for the *Modern Engineering Company* in Berkeley, Michigan, about a forty-five minute drive from his home in Detroit. He finally retired from there in 2004, and today lives in Livonia. Over the years, Ed never seemed to find the right "girl of his dreams," and is therefore still single today.

Chapter 8

Life After Olive Drab

We left Metro Airport by mid morning, and the temperature outside had already reached its high of 51 degrees for the day. Right away, I began to feel regret for the FTA attitude I'd harbored for the past two years. While I firmly believed I'd never wear a military uniform again, I also felt proud of the fact that I had served my country, and I knew that Dad was proud of me for having done so. Two weeks later, I returned to work at the *Detroit Plastic Molding Company* in Roseville at $1.90 an hour. While there, I did stock handling work on and near the shipping dock. In time, with a few pay raises, I was making $2.45 an hour.

A few days after I got home from the Army, I also paid a visit to my **Aunt Catherine** in St Clair Shores. I needed to return to her the small plastic case with the statues of *Jesus* and *Mary* that I had carried with me for two years. By now, the plastic case was quite worn, but just the same, she was still happy to see me safe and sound. She told me that she had prayed for me everyday while I was away, and I never forgot that, even to this day. When she died many years later, I felt a sense of deep loss. I miss her, and still think of Aunt Catherine now and then.

After dating several girls for a few months I began to feel sort of empty, like something was missing in my life. Then I thought about **Holly Ann George** again. I had learned from a friend of hers that, while she still had an attachment to that guy in the Air Force, he had given her the OK to date other guys while he was away. I wondered what kind of an idiot would allow his girl to do that while he served in uniform. But, I decided not to look a gift horse in the mouth. I therefore took full advantage of this and started dating Holly on a regular basis. I really liked being with Holly. She had a warm and welcome smile that attracted me. She was tall and slim, and I thought she had great looking legs. She still does today.

In 1968, I was fired from the *Detroit Plastic Molding Company* due to a dispute with my Foreman. In short time though, I landed in a job with the *Chrysler Corporation* at their *Dodge Truck Assembly* Plant in Warren, Michigan. I started there at $3.26 an hour on their *Dashboard Assembly Line*. Then a year later in 1969, I moved on from there to work for the *American Can Company* on Seven Mile Road in Detroit at $4.10 an hour. While there, I operated a machine that put lids on twelve-ounce cans for beer and pop.

During that time Holly and I continued dating, but as time went by, I noticed that she mentioned "Mr. Air Force" less and less often. I asked her about this one day, and she said that she hadn't heard from him in a long time. I knew something wasn't right about that. I was certain that while being in the Air Force, he had *more* than enough free time to write to her. So I decided right then to make my move the next time the moment seemed right.

So the very next night when I dropped her off at home after a date, we stood at her back door looking at each other. We then kissed goodnight, but just before she stepped inside, I told her that if he didn't want her, I'd be more than happy to claim her. Her instant reply to me was simply, *"Forget it!"*

Well, that was direct and to the point, and I was certainly stunned for a moment or two. Then sadly I decided to do just that. I would try to forget her. So I did. I turned and walked down the driveway, got back in my burgundy-colored 1968 Mustang and went home.

I stopped calling Holly altogether. And for a few weeks or so, I tried to put the matter out of my mind and just forget about it. But in order to do this, I turned my efforts to dating others again, and chalked it all up to her young age. After all, she was over five and a half years younger than me. I felt that at the tender age of eighteen, she still wasn't ready for a serious and mature relationship, and I wasn't going to push the issue.

After a period of time Holly began calling my house, but I wouldn't talk to her. Then one night my mother answered the phone when she called. Mom gave me the phone and with a stern look, told me not to keep the girl wondering where she stood. So I took the phone and told Holly that I was simply too old for "going steady" and that I was seeking a serious and permanent relationship. But Holly still insisted that she wanted me to come over. So I made it clear to her that if I came over to see her, it would have to be for keeps. She eagerly agreed with this, and I was at her door in Harper Woods ten minutes later.

By this time I had decided that, in spite of the fact that I had already obtained my G.E.D. while still in Olive Drab, I still wanted a High School Diploma. So I enrolled in night school while still working during the day.

As it turned out, Holly and I both finished High School together in June 1970. Dad was so proud of me for having finally received my diploma. He felt that way about all of his children mostly because of the fact that he never made it beyond the eighth grade in school. But that was due to hard times in the 1930s.

Holly and I continued dating for a couple more years before finally setting a wedding date for mid-March, 1971. However, *American Can Company* went out on strike four weeks before the wedding, leaving me out in the cold. I then learned of an opening in the life insurance business with the *Western & Southern Life Insurance Company* and began training as a new Sales Representative there on Monday, March 8, 1971.

Holly and I got married twelve days later on Saturday, March 20, 1971, and surprisingly, I was given the entire week off work with pay. Standing up for me at the wedding was my life long close friend **Bob Eddy** as my Best Man. Bob and I had grown up together as next-door neighbors. Also standing with me were my older brother **Ray**, and **Ed Mitchell** from my Army days. I stayed with *Western & Southern Life* until 1974, winning a few sales contests and awards along the way.

Somewhere along here I applied for a job with the *Detroit Police Department*. I had already tried the *East Detroit Police*, but was told that they had no openings. The Detroit Police, however, turned me down due to what they called, "psychological" reasons. While I had passed their physical and written exams "with flying colors," they just didn't like my attitude toward long-haired Hippie draft dodgers. Just as well, I thought . . . . I really couldn't picture myself delivering a baby in the back of a patrol car.

I joined the *Army National Guard* for one year along with my friend Bob Eddy, and during that time soon regained my rank of *Specialist-4*. (Bob was a combat veteran of the *11th Armored Cavalry Regiment* in Vietnam.) In 1974, I enrolled at the *Control Data Institute* full time, and took their five-month course in *Computer Repair Technology*. Then after graduation, I began seeking employment in that line of work.

When I found that it was taking me longer than I had hoped to find work in the computer repair field, I took a job with the *Prudential Insurance Company* as a *Special Agent* in August 1975. My intent was to sell insurance while I kept seeking an opening in the computer field. But insurance sales with Prudential went far better than I expected, so much so, that I stayed there eight and a half years.

After all, *Prudential* was the largest life insurance company in the world, and I found that I didn't have to sell the name of the company. Have you ever met anyone that hasn't heard of getting "a piece of the rock?" While working at Prudential, I became a graduate of *L. U. T.C. (Life Underwriters Training Council)*. Though I also took courses in *Estate Planning* and *Business Insurance,* I also dabbled for a while in sales of *Group Life and Health Insurance.* But through it all, I always preferred what was called "kitchen-table" selling. That is, selling mostly family life insurance needs. For several of those years I stayed within Prudential's top 20% in sales, earning several more awards, including their *Regional Business Conference* a few times, and the *Century Club Award* once.

In 1982, with a changing economy and my sales in life insurance slumping, I moved on to accept a position as an agent for the *Allstate Insurance Company.* Working for *Allstate,* I found myself standing behind a booth in a *Sears* store at the *Macomb Mall* in Roseville, Michigan. With *Allstate,* about 85% of my sales walked up to me for a change. But due to a serious personality conflict with my District Sales Manager, I left Allstate after only one and a half years.

I was devastated. But more than that, I felt totally lost. I wasn't sure *where* to go from there. So I began searching for that "certain place" in the working world that was meant for me. This kept me jumping from one so-called "career" to another, while sometimes taking temporary minimum-paying jobs and struggling just to make ends meet. I tried sales of furniture, used cars, new cars, and even cemetery property. I even retried insurance sales again with smaller debit-type companies, but I still felt like a fish out of water.

Between many of these "short careers" I found that I still had to pay the bills. So I pumped gasoline, drove a taxicab, worked in a fast-oil-and-lube place, managed a car wash, and even managed an *Earl Scheib* auto paint shop for about one and a half weeks. I was still lost, but I never gave up hope that I would find my special place in the workforce someday soon.

In May 1979, a couple of my close friends sponsored me for a *Cursillo* weekend. This was a three-day Catholic "get-away" weekend, intended to re-awaken one's desire to get back in touch with God. It worked. Although Holly and I grew closer in our walk with God, I was still lost in my search for fulfillment in the work place.

During the off periods between these so called "careers," I went to work with a friend of mine named **Ralph Abad.** Ralph was self-employed in the building trades. Working with Ralph, I learned how to do carpentry, drywall, plumbing, electrical, tile, roofing, and vinyl siding. And I found that I really loved this kind of work. But the pay was unsteady. This was due to the fact that I got paid only when Ralph got paid for the jobs we did.

I joined the *Air Force Reserve* at *Selfridge Air National Guard Base* northeast of me. I didn't really want to get back into a uniform, but when I was told that my E-4 status in pay grade in the Air Force would make me a Buck Sergeant, I was hooked! I was now an NCO!

While there, I qualified as an *Expert* with the M-16 Rifle. However, this time I qualified with it the *honest* way. But in less than a year, I got disenchanted with the Air Force Reserve, as there were way too many NCOs telling the few lower-ranking Airmen what to do. So I decided to leave there and side-stepped back over into the *Army National Guard*. This was at the *Light Guard Armory* on East Eight Mile Road in Detroit. In less than a year, I got fed up with that too. It seemed that too many in the outfit there were always late for the Reveille formation every month, and nothing was ever done about it. It also seemed that very few of the guys in the outfit were really serious about serving. So, I decided then to leave military service for good.

Somewhere along the way, I bought a *Gibson* Guitar. Although I was still only able to strum three chords on it, I practiced with it anyway until I improved enough to try it professionally. Then together with a close friend of mine named **Dan Morris**, who played mostly a combination of lead and rhythm guitar, we formed a country music band that we called the *Silver Saddle*.

I did the lead singing and loved every minute of it. At first, Dan and I specialized in doing older country music standards that audiences hadn't heard in years. Many of them were songs my father used to sing when I was a young kid. And it went over great! In time I added another chord (*A minor*) to my *C, F, and G-7*. Then with four chords, I was able to do a few of the old familiar tunes from the 1950s and 1960s. In 1978, I bought a *Martin D-35* guitar that I still have today. While doing our music, occasionally my dad and mom would come to our appearances and I could tell they were proud to be there.

Dad died in December of 1985, and Mom died a year and a half later in June of 1987. Then in August 1988, I began twelve long years of research to learn what my father experienced in World War II. Over the years, Dad never talked about his days in World War II, except to say that the guys he served with called him *"Old Man."* He was thirty years old when he arrived in Europe in August 1944. He told how he once used the butt of his weapon to break up the ice around his feet in the bottom of a foxhole during the *Battle of the Bulge*. The more I learned about his days in World War II, the more painful it became. It was then that I finally realized why he could never discuss his war experiences in depth with his family.

Our daughter Anna Marie was born on Tuesday, August 15, 1989. She was our one and only child after many, many years of trying,—sometimes twice a day!

During my twelve years of World War II research, I was able to locate and/or account for, all but three of the forty-four men who served in my father's platoon. At that time, twenty-two of them were still "kickin," and I have personally met more than half of those. The effort has turned into a book that I had just recently published in 2007. It is called, ***Old Man from the Repple Depple*** (published through *Xlibris Publishing* of New York), and is now available through most booksellers.

Once the book was published, I found I had a lot of free time on my hands. So I turned to reading. Down in the basement, I had several dozen books that I had accumulated over the years but never took the time to read. They were mostly old classics written by famous authors in history. It took me about a year and a half, but I was finally able to read them all. I discovered by all this reading that I had missed out on a lot of wondrous adventures over my lifetime. I also read many of the top best sellers by well-known authors of today. And best of all, I've also read the *Bible* cover-to-cover several times. There are not many Roman Catholics who can say that.

In the meantime, I got older and continued smoking, even after numerous efforts to quit, and two collapsed lungs within a ten-year period. Then finally, unable to physically continue with the heavy labor sometimes required in the building trades, I took a maintenance position for *Motel-6* in Warren, Michigan. My new manager, who was thrilled with my dedication and what I had accomplished in three short months, tried unsuccessfully to get me a raise in pay. Then, being frustrated with higher management, *he* finally left Motel-6. After that, two more managers were hired, got discouraged, and left, as it seemed that they were paid little for all their responsibility. After a year and a half, I finally left too.

I tried doing maintenance work for a few apartment complexes, but when management learned that I had a hard time tossing fifty-pound bags of rock salt around during the winter, it cost me my last two jobs. Finally at the age of sixty-two in March 2007, I decided to take early Social Security Retirement.

Then in March 2008, it occurred to me that in a tall file cabinet I had downstairs in the basement, I had stored many notes, photos, and recollections of my own days in Olive Drab. So I gathered them up, brought them upstairs, sat down at my computer, and began typing and researching. And you know the rest.

During the last twenty-six years since I left the insurance business, I had worked for so many employers, that it would be too difficult to list them all. But even still, I never found that perfect career. I now believe that the journey itself was what I was really meant to live and experience. And today I have very few real regrets.

Over the years, Holly and I struggled through many problems in our relationship, not the least of which was my taking her for granted for so long. And this nearly cost me my family. But in time I came to realize that she was truly a special gift to me from God. We still struggle now and then, but we're still together, growing stronger and weathering the storms.

God sure has been good to me.

Holly Ann George (my future wife), April, 1968

Holly Ann George & my new Ford Mustang, April, 1968

Holly Ann George, Harper Woods High School, Memorial Day Parade, June, 1968

Holly Ann George, 1970 January

Tom & Holly Oblinger, Fall of 1971

Tom O (front center) & the Silver Saddle Band

Tom O & Daughter Anna Marie, February of 1990

2007-08

Anna Marie Oblinger, 2008

Tom & Holly Oblinger, 2006

In the years that followed . . .

The 218th MP Company—

On 18-August-1966, while still in the Dominican Republic, the 218th MP Company was again redesignated as Company C, of the 503rd MP Battalion, and returned to the continental U.S. in three phases. Upon arrival at Fort Bragg, North Carolina, the 218th was then restructured there with all new personnel from the 118th MP Company (of the 100th MP Battalion). Along with a few volunteers from the "Dom Rep" veterans, the new 218th then began training for combat readiness and overseas movement.

On 28-December-1966, the 218th MP Company sailed from Oakland, California, aboard the U.S. Navy Destroyer Escort Ship *USS Darby (DE 218)*. On 18-January-1967, after twenty-one days at sea, they docked at *Cam Ranh Bay* in the Republic of South Vietnam. Cam Ranh Bay was a deep-water bay on an inlet of the South China Sea. This was on the southeastern coast about 180 miles northeast of Saigon.

In Vietnam, the 218th served under the 97th MP Battalion of the 18th MP Brigade. After moving southwest, they performed security patrols for the supply port at *Vung Tau Bay*. This bay received the Saigon River on the northeast Mekong Delta about 75 miles south of Saigon. The 218th remained there for the next fifteen months, until being inactivated on 17-April-1972.

On 21-October-1977, the 218th was reactivated again in Germany, and assigned to serve under the 385th MP Battalion. Then in 1982, while still in Germany, the 218th was finally reunited with its World War II parent, the 793rd MP Battalion. Today, the 218th MP Company is still serving under the 793rd and spread throughout Bavaria in southeast Germany. Also serving under the 793rd MP Battalion today are the 212th, 615th and 630th MP Companies.

The 503rd MP Battalion—

In September 1969, the 503rd MP Battalion was called upon to provide disaster relief following the extensive destruction of *Hurricane Camille* in Mississippi. At that time, fifty MPs were selected from the 503rd to assist men of the 100th MP Battalion, which had already been deployed to the disaster area a month earlier. Personnel and equipment were then transferred by air from Pope AFB to Camp Shelby, Mississippi, in this effort.

Over the next few years, the 503rd was called upon several times to conduct surprise shakedown inspections at the Fort Bragg Post Stockade. These inspections usually produced several items of contraband to be confiscated. On 1-November-1970, the 503rd Military Police Battalion (including Companies A, B, and C) were inactivated at Fort Bragg, North Carolina.

Then beginning in 1983 and the years that followed, the 503rd Military Police Battalion was called upon again to serve in expeditions in Grenada, Panama, Haiti, and Southwest Asia. By the mid-1990s, the 503rd had become *Airborne*. Serving under the 503rd at that time in place of companies A, B, and C, were the 21st, 65th, and the 108th MP Companies. They went on to serve in the defense of Saudi Arabia, and the participated in the liberation and defense of Kuwait in Operations *Desert Shield* and *Desert Storm*.

Following the terrorist attacks on the U.S. on September 11, 2001, the 503rd was immediately deployed to Washington, DC, to protect the Pentagon once again. In 2002, they were sent to Iraq to participate in *Operation Iraqi Freedom*, and were still there in December 2005. As of today, the old 503rd MP Battalion building at the northeast corner of Macomb and Reilly Streets, is occupied by the Fort Bragg Education Center.

The 22nd MP Platoon (100th MP Battalion)—

On 5-May-1969, the 22nd MP Platoon was officially inactivated at Fort Bragg, North Carolina, per *General Order #37, Headquarters, Third United States Army*.

Three months later, in August 1969, the 100th MP Battalion was tasked by the XVIII Airborne Corps to support Disaster Relief Operations following *Hurricane Camille* in Gulfport, Mississippi. Later, during periods when the 503rd MP Battalion was called upon for duty away from the post, the 100th MP Battalion would step in to provide Military Police support missions for the entire installation at Fort Bragg. **(No other information is available.)**

A recent computer image from a satellite photo provided by *Virtual Earth* online, shows that the land formerly occupied by the buildings of the 100th MP Battalion (south of Butner Road, between Armistead and Hamilton Streets) is now occupied by two newer buildings and a parking lot for fifty or more school buses. These buildings include the offices of the *Fort Bragg Emergency Services*, and an all-new *Law Enforcement Center* building.

The Fort Bragg POST STOCKADE (from the limited info I found available)—

By mid-1968, the Post Stockade had become overcrowded with many AWOLs and political organizers, many of whom were American servicemen, strongly protesting the war in Vietnam. On 23-July-1968, seven prisoners climbed over a fence in the Stockade to defend a black prisoner from being beaten by his white *"Lifer"* guard. (The term *Lifer* refers to a career soldier.) In short time, several dozen other prisoners followed suit and by the day's end, 238 prisoners in all had taken control of the stockade and held it for three days.

One year later in May 1969, one prisoner died as a result of being burned in an accidental fire at the stockade. The overcrowding continued and by the end of the Vietnam War, the era of massive G.I. resistance was over.

The draft had ended in 1973, and the U.S. military was then converted to an all-volunteer fighting organization. In the years since then, the all-volunteer Army resulted in fewer AWOLs, thus the need for a post stockade gradually decreased with time. Though the requirement for Draft Registration was suspended in 1975, President Jimmy Carter resumed it in 1980, in response to the Soviet invasion of Afghanistan. Draft Registration still continues today.

In 1977, with only eleven prisoners left, Fort Bragg turned over the Post Stockade to Colonel Charlie A. Beckwith to use as a base for his new *Delta Force*, which was the Army's elite counterterrorist unit. Prisoners were thereafter taken "downtown" to the civilian jail in Fayetteville. In 1987, the *Delta Force* finally moved out of the stockade to a new $75 million complex.

In the opinion of Henry Cuningham, Military Editor of the *Fayetteville Observer* newspaper, *"In recent years, the stockade went through many tenants; including MPs who did actually use the old jail cells for returning AWOLs."*

As of today, an image from a satellite photo shows that the land formerly occupied by the old Post Stockade, is now vacant land that had been converted into two baseball diamonds.

* * *

Major Daniel G. Scheuermann—retired from the U.S. Army as a Major and eventually resided in Council Bluffs, Iowa. He was a member of his local *VFW Post*

#737. Daniel died on June 9, 1994 at the age of 71 and was survived by his wife Myrtle, son Gary, and two grandchildren. Myrtle died nine and a half years later on January 8, 2003. (**No other information available.**)

Captain Dennis T. Ellis—after the U.S. pulled out of the Dominican Republic, was sent to Fort McPherson, Georgia, near Atlanta, where he served until leaving the Army with the rank of Major in 1973. Then in 2001, Dennis retired after 28 years with the U.S. Postal Service. He and Ursula raised two daughters and currently reside in Columbia, South Carolina.

1ˢᵗ Lieutenant Terrance M. Fiore—after being released from the 218ᵗʰ MP Company in the Dominican Republic, returned to Fort Bragg, North Carolina, and awaited his ETS several weeks later in mid-July 1966. Terrance then returned home to New York, attended Graduate School, and married in 1967. Starting out in banking, he became a Financial Planning Analyst for the *Colombia Broadcasting System*, then later for *Time-Life*. At *Time-Life* he served as a Vice-President of Finance while stationed in Mexico City until 1982. He then moved over to their Marketing Department in 1986. In the meantime, he was divorced when his wife declined to move back to New York with him upon his transfer there. But in 1991, Terrance married again. His new wife, Margaret, prefers to be called by her middle name, Blair. In 1997, Terrance began teaching Advertising and Marketing at the *Fashion Institute of Technology* in New York City. Today, he is still there on a semi-retired basis enjoying tennis, theater, and some acting in a community theater.

    Among the proudest memories Terrance Fiore has of his days in Olive Drab, was his service with the 503ʳᵈ MP Battalion during their deployment to Selma, Alabama, in May 1965, while helping the advancement of social justice in the world. He is also very proud of his days with the 218ᵗʰ MP Company, and the contribution they made to peace in our hemisphere.

1ˢᵗ Sergeant Amos Terry—after his ETS in July 1969, took up residence in Fayetteville, North Carolina where he still resides to this day. At first, Amos went to school and studied Real Estate. Then instead of pursuing that as a career, he went to work for the *Orkin Exterminating Company* in 1969, and became a Sales Manager, eventually leaving there in 1975.

    That same year, Amos became self-employed in the building and home improvement business. He ran two complete operations called *Custom Builders & Home Improvement, Inc.* and *Custom Seamless Gutters, Inc.* and finally retired in December 1995.

    Through the years, he was married three times. His last wife died of Cancer in 1996. Amos had four children in all and is still single today. He owns a condominium on the island of Freeport in the Bahamas, and four homes in Fayetteville. Still in great health today, Amos Terry has always been a non-smoker and is proud of it!

2nd Lieutenant Ronald V. Varol (**Leader of 22nd MP Platoon**)—was assigned in early-1968 to the S-4 section of the 11th MP Group at Fort Bragg. After receiving an Army Commendation medal for his duties at Fort Bragg, Ron was Honorably Discharged in May 1969. He then returned to college and received a degree in Economics. In 1970, Ron joined *IBM* in New York and stayed with them for the next 38 years. During that time, he moved to North Carolina in 1979 working in management. He spent two years with IBM in London, England, then returned to the U.S. in 1993 and retired in 2008. Today, Ron and Leonora reside in Cary, North Carolina and have raised two children.

Captain Lawrence E. Seng (**Commander of the Fort Bragg Post Stockade**)—had spent nine years on active duty with the U.S. Army. This was followed by thirteen years in the Army Reserves, and the Ohio National Guard, eventually rising to the rank of Major. Following his military career, Lawrence and Ann Seng settled in Toledo, Ohio, where he became a manager for the *Dana Corporation*. In 1973, he became a Stock Broker for the firm of *Prescott, Ball & Turben*, then went on to work for *Paine-Webber*, and later *Smith-Barney* in Toledo until his death on February 18, 2009. He loved the brokerage business, and found that his greatest joy was in helping people. Over the years, Lawrence and Ann raised four children.

My Special Thanks

Most of the facts, dates, details, and information used in this story came from the following sources:

U.S. Military History Institute, Carlisle, PA
U.S. Army Center of Military History, Fort McNair, DC
National Personnel Records Center, St. Louis, MO
National Archives and Records Administration, College Park, MD
National Climatic Weather Service Data Center, Asheville, NC

. . . and also from . . .

Donna Tabor, Command Historian, *XVIII Airborne Corps and Fort Bragg,* Fort Bragg, NC
Michelle Luther, Dir. of News Research, *Fayetteville Observer Newspaper,* Fayetteville, NC
Patricia Campbell, Secretary, *Fayetteville Regional Airport,* Fayetteville, NC

Books and other publications used in this story:

*Power Pack, (U.S. Intervention in the Dominican Republic, 1965-1966)
Leavenworth Papers #15—by Dr. Lawrence A. Yates

*United States Army Unilateral and Coalition Operations in the Dominican Republic Intervention
A CMH Study—by Major Lawrence M. Greenberg

*Inter-American Peace Force—
by Public Affairs Office, Santo Domingo, Dominican Republic, 1966

Dominican Crisis, 1965-1966—by Frank Walsh

*And from the actual daily *Morning Reports* of the *218th MP Company*—obtained from the *National Personnel Records Center* in St. Louis, MO.

But the most valuable contribution to this story came from the actual veterans of:

> The *218th Military Police Company*
> The *503rd Military Police Battalion, Company C*
> The *22nd Military Police Platoon (100th MP Battalion)*.

I also owe a note of sincere gratitude to our friend and comrade, *Ronald W. Cook,* the unofficial *"Keeper of the Records"* from whom I was able to obtain copies of the *After Action Reports* of the 218th MP Company, for the period of time we were all there.

These are the men that I served with between November 1965 and November 1967. Their "stories" not only helped to make my story possible, but they also helped to add color and a lot of humor to my portrayal of life in *Olive Drab*.

They are a great bunch of guys, and I am honored to have served with them.

Thomas E. Oblinger